Virginia Woolf:
The Common Ground

Virginia Woolf:
The Common Ground
Essays by Gillian Beer

GILLIAN BEER

EDINBURGH
UNIVERSITY PRESS

© Gillian Beer, 1996

Edinburgh University Press,
22 George Square, Edinburgh

Typeset in Monotype Horley Old Style
by Koinonia Ltd, Manchester and
printed and bound in Great Britain

A CIP record for this book is available from the British Library

ISBN 0 7486 0814 1

The right of Gillian Beer to be identified as author of this work has been
asserted in accordance with the Copyright, Designs and Patent Act (1988)

The publisher acknowledges The Society of Authors
as the literary representative of the Estate of Virginia Woolf

Contents

Preface

The essays gathered here all seek to explore the range of Woolf's pleasure in thinking and being. Some of them emphasise fresh intellectual contexts for her writing, some register her place in communal experience. As I have engaged with Woolf's writing over the years, I have circled on certain works that have yielded more and more for me. Attentive readers of this collection may notice points of overlap between the essays. Fugitive ideas in one essay become central to another, sentences occur again, shifted into a new context. I have not expunged these repetitions but have arranged the book's sequence in terms of Woolf's chronology, not that of the essays' composition. Dates of first publication are given as footnote sources to each chapter and I am grateful to the original publishers for permission to reprint the essays here and to the Hogarth Press for quotations.

Teaching Woolf's novels is always an exhilarating experience: people illuminate the works, often with fizz and brio, sometimes with silence, mourning, resistance. I am grateful to the members of seminars and, indeed, to the texts which so persistently yield experience in a group. Woolf brings friendships too: for me, Rachel Bowlby, Jane Marcus, Suzanne Raitt, and Alex Zwerdling are among those whom I first met by her agency.

And I regret greatly that in the nature of written books I cannot gather here one of the most revealing experiences of Woolf's work that I have shared in: a complete reading aloud of the 'play-poem' *The Waves* that lasted, like the novel, from early morning to late evening and that opened further, through the six unlike voices of the speaking characters, the humour, lucidity, and passion of the work.

Introduction

In May 1940 Virginia Woolf gave a talk at the Workers' Educational Association in Brighton: it became her late essay 'The Leaning Tower'. The title invokes and throws away allusion to the cultural wealth of Italy; it fastens instead on the uneasy balance of left-wing middle-class male writers of the 1930s (particularly MacNeice and Spender) imprisoned in their public school education, perched in privilege at the top of a tower from which they cannot descend. The tower slopes, it dizzies, it denies them a secure footing on common ground. 'Directly we feel that a tower leans we become acutely conscious that we are upon a tower.'[1] Everyone is invited by that 'we' to recognise the vertigo, but Woolf and her first audience seem exempted from the criticism: they by class, she by gender. Together, they are excluded from the peculiar rituals of a classical education and from the assumption that knowledge is private, as well as sacred, ground.

She imagines Aeschylus, Shakespeare, Virgil, and Dante speaking direct to readers unskilled in the niceties – eager, greedy readers. She advises, with them: 'It never does to be a nice feeder: each of us has an appetite that must find for itself the food that nourishes it.'

> They [the writers] do not mind if we get our accents wrong, or have to read with a crib in front of us. Of course – are we not commoners, outsiders? – we shall trample many flowers and bruise much ancient grass. But let us bear in mind a piece of advice that an eminent Victorian who was also an eminent pedestrian once gave to walkers: 'When you see a board up with "Trespassers will be prosecuted", trespass at once.'
> Let us trespass at once. Literature is no one's private ground; literature is common ground. It is not cut up into nations; there

1

are no wars there. Let us trespass freely and fearlessly and find our own way for ourselves.[2]

The spirited invitation is both heartfelt and paradoxical. She does not know Greek, has never been to university, may not walk on Trinity's lawn, or enter the Wren Library. Not being part of England's aristocracy she can claim a part in 'the other class, the immense class to which almost all of us must belong' which has been left by England 'to pick up what we can in village schools; in factories; in workshops; behind counters; and at home'. She claims the freedom of the outsider, the community of the mass, the 'we' of common life. Yet she invokes 'an eminent Victorian' for permission to walk and to trespass – Leslie Stephen, her father. The parent she has so long fled from becomes the companion who broaches the private and makes the land available to everyone. Implicitly, private ground is especially precious: the thrill of entering depends on the privilege it ruptures. 'Trespassing' acknowledges possession. Woolf cannot quite shake free of the allure of privilege nor leave behind the paternal. Her work needs them and resists them – *needs to resist*.

This backward glance is not surprising; what is remarkable is how her access to quite new territory goes alongside her solidarity with all those alive beside her in the streets, and over time. 'I am talking of the common life which is the real life and not the little separate lives which we live as individuals.'[3] Instead of concentrating only on the chosen relationships of love and friendship, which fiction usually privileges, her work declares the fundamental kinship that goes beyond even family romance: living in the same time, sometimes in the same place – whether or not you ever meet.

She valued the ordinary. While she was writing *Mrs Dalloway*, she copied out from Wordsworth a 'Good quotation for one of my books':

> The matter that detains us now may seem,
> To many, neither dignified enough
> Nor arduous, yet will not be scorned by them,
> Who, looking inward, have observed the ties
> That bind the perishable hours of life
> Each to the other, & the curious props
> By which the world of memory and thought
> Exists & is sustained.[4]

Her last work, in progress while she was writing *Between the Acts*, concerned 'Anon' the nameless multiple author of that accumulation of works essential to the experience of a people, a figure rather like that of the storyteller in Walter Benjamin's essay of that name, written only a couple of years before hers.[5]

In 'The Leaning Tower' common land and literature become equal expressions of freedom. England in the midst of war at last acknowledges its people; its free public libraries express that attempt at recognition, she argues: 'This book was not bought; it was not hired. It was borrowed from a public library. England lent it to a common reader.'[6] For Woolf the common reader and the common ground are at once earth-bound and sacred, as near as she ever gets to the language of faith or of patriotism. Yet of course she is often skittish and imperious, conscious of her own strangeness, troubled by her shudder of snobbishness. Her diaries and letters, more than her novels and essays, reveal that aspect of her. Like the novels and essays they also reveal her eagerness.

When Woolf is placed in the midst of the concerns of her contemporaries at large, rather than sequestered within Bloomsbury, the speed and omnivorousness of her appetite for understanding becomes apparent. She tastes and devours, nibbles, licks, drinks, savours, sniffs: her relation to her daily surroundings, to the streets and conversations of London, to the books she reviews, the parties she records, to political events, and to philosophy, science, Dante, Montaigne are all equally appetitive. *To the Lighthouse* draws the whole disparate group at the Ramsays' holiday house together at table – the table which may or may not endure when you are not there, according to the philosophers who haunt the novel. *The Waves* clusters upon meals, with their gatherings and partings, and ends with Bernard's great thought-soliloquy brooding late at night in a restaurant, the food and wine ebbing into his old body and his unaged consciousness.

To be driven as she was by impetuous pleasure in language and observation might imply haste and imprecision but her art teases out as well as kneads in. She is fastidious, never quite replete. She also has the power to seize the unlike together in a grasp so strong it makes the reader know pain. No one but Woolf would have thought of placing the constriction of Electra and Jane Austen side by side and thus communicated for those who, like her, do not know Greek 'the dangerous art where one slip means death'.[7]

Woolf did not set thinking apart from ordinary experience: she managed to avoid 'changing the natural stumbling trip of speech into the solemn and stately mark of pens'.[8] The intimacy that she sought with her reader she knew was best found through a common meeting place: 'And it is of the highest importance that this common meeting place should be reached easily, almost instinctively, in the dark, with one's eyes shut.'[9] She picked up lightly the thoroughgoing arguments of historians, physicists, astronomers, philosophers, politicians, and the stray talk of passers-by. That lightness is not superficial. Rather, it 'lets the light through'. Her glance has a wide arc. In the first essay here I look at the ways she responded to Darwin and to other versions of prehistory; in 'Hume, Stephen, and Elegy in *To the Lighthouse*' I raise to the surface the implicit allusions to her father's favourite philosopher and argue that questions about what's there when you are not there are necessary to mourning and survival as well as to British empiricism; in *The Waves*, then-current work in physics and astronomy communicated by Eddington and Jeans helps to produce a language for a world 'insubstantised' and thus all the more 'real'. Yet, as I also show, in *The Waves* Woolf sought to explore women's bodies across the whole spectrum of sex and to cross Catullus and Shelley with the impulses of the moment. In *Between the Acts*, newspapers, current events, village pageant, the violence of the imminent and present war, and of an actual rape, combine with the remote past before England was named or split off from the Continent. The essays here that draw on this work demonstrate how repetition and nursery doggerel give comfort against the dread that things may not repeat, that England and Europe are ending. And from *Mrs Dalloway* through to the end of her writing career the figure of the aeroplane accrues meaning that draws on fantasy, Freud, feminism, and the experience of living near Gatwick aerodrome in the 1930s – first a place for light aircraft then a military airfield. My final essay, 'The Island and the Aeroplane: The Case of Virginia Woolf', asks what happened to 'our island story' with the coming of the aeroplane and pinpoints Woolf's tonic responses to that question.

Woolf is never consolatory, always aware – like the Greeks she admires – of 'a sadness at the back of life which they do not attempt to mitigate'.[10] But for her that sadness is spiked with humour, a humour drawn from the haphazard bunching of impressions and events. Her writing poises extraordinarily disparate intellectual, emotional and cultural elements, as I hope these essays demonstrate. She draws on, and resists, 'the populous undifferentiated chaos of life which surged behind the outlines of my friends and the willow tree' as Bernard puts it in *The Waves*.[11] The act of setting alongside, refusing to order in a line or a hierarchy, becomes her expression of the common life, with literature its 'common ground'. 'It is thus', she ends 'The Leaning

INTRODUCTION

Tower', 'that English literature will survive this war and cross the gulf – if commoners and outsiders like ourselves make that country our own country, if we teach ourselves how to read and write, how to preserve and how to create.' In literature, at least, something of what she hoped has come to pass, both in the efflorescence of writing in English across the world and in the passion with which readers respond now to her own writing.

Notes

1. Virginia Woolf, 'The Leaning Tower', *A Woman's Essays*, vol. 1, ed. Rachel Bowlby (London, 1992), p. 168.
2. Ibid., p. 178.
3. *A Room of One's Own* (London, 1929), p. 171.
4. Brenda Silver, *Virginia Woolf's Reading Notebooks* (Princeton, 1983), p. 30.
5. See Brenda Silver, ed., '"Anon" and "The Reader": Virginia Woolf's Last Essays', *Twentieth Century Literature*, XXV (1979), pp. 356–435.
6. 'The Leaning Tower', p. 177.
7. Ibid., p. 96.
8. 'Montaigne', *A Woman's Essays*, p. 57.
9. 'Mr. Bennett and Mrs. Brown', *A Woman's Essays*, p. 81.
10. 'On Not Knowing Greek', *A Woman's Essays*, p. 106.
11. *The Waves*, ed. Gillian Beer (Oxford, 1992), p. 208.

1

Virginia Woolf and Prehistory

I

The primeval and the prehistoric have powerfully fascinated many twentieth-century writers, notably Conrad and Eliot. The idea of origins and the idea of development are problematically connected in that of prehistory. And in the twentieth century the unconscious has often been presented in the guise of the primeval. These associations have been engendered by the most powerful new metaphor of the past 150 years. The development of the individual organism has always been a rich resource for metaphor; but evolutionary theory and, in particular, Darwin's writing suggested that species also developed and changed. The analogy between ontogeny (individual development) and phylogeny (species development) has proved to be the most productive, dangerous, and compelling of creative thoughts for our culture, manifesting itself not only in biology, but also in psychology, race theory, humanism, and in the homage of our assumptions about the developmental pattern of history.

What were the particular difficulties raised for Virginia Woolf by the idea of prehistory, and what particular new meanings did she make from it?

The problem of what is truly 'natural and eternal' and what is susceptible to change is one difficulty that expresses itself in Virginia Woolf's work. Social and historical factors claim for themselves 'natural' and 'eternal' authority; social determinism claims to be biological determinism. A wry footnote to *Three Guineas* shows Virginia Woolf tussling with the problems of the imputed permanent characteristics of man and woman and the possibility of change:

First published in: Eric Warner (ed.), *Virginia Woolf: A Centenary Perspective* (London: Macmillan, 1984), pp. 99–123.

The nature of manhood and the nature of womanhood are frequently defined by both Italian and German dictators. Both repeatedly insist that it is the nature of man and indeed the essence of manhood to fight. ... Both repeatedly insist that it is the nature of womanhood to heal the wounds of the fighter. Nevertheless a very strong movement is on foot towards emancipating man from the old 'natural and eternal law' that man is essentially a fighter. ... Professor Huxley, however, warns us that 'any considerable alteration of the hereditary constitution is an affair of millennia, not of decades'. On the other hand, as science also assures us that our life on earth is 'an affair of millennia, not of decades', some alteration in the hereditary constitution may be worth attempting.[1]

So the nature/nurture question is one associated issue, here alleviated by the immense span of time that science promises to humankind in which to attempt 'alteration in the hereditary constitution'.

But there are other ways, more diffused, expressed more as form, less as argument, in which the primeval and problems of development move through her writing. How does she rewrite that major figure in her own upbringing, her own 'development', Charles Darwin?

Before going further we need to consider her attitudes to 'history' and to discriminate some meanings of prehistory. Is prehistory and the primeval in her work simply part of her strong interest in history? In the last entry recorded in *A Writer's Diary* Virginia Woolf writes:

No: I need no introspection. I mark Henry James' sentence: observe perpetually. Observe the oncome of age. Observe greed. Observe my own despondency ... Suppose I bought a ticket at the Museum; biked in daily and read history. Suppose I selected one dominant figure in every age and wrote round and about. Occupation is essential.[2]

She didn't do it, of course. Instead she drowned. History here for Virginia Woolf is a lifeline to pluck her out of the deep waters of introspection.

'History', almost in a textbook sense, is a recurrent theme in her work. *Orlando* jubilantly fantasizes the possibility of the self surviving history, looking different, gendered differently, but not much changed from century to century. *A Room of One's Own* creates a counter-history in the image of Shakespeare's sister, and *Night and Day* and *The Years* follow those long contours of family saga which allow the writer to record changes in how it felt to be alive. History in her

7

writing is a matter of textures (horse-hair or velvet), changing light (flam-beaux or gas-light), not of events or 'dominant figures of the age'. In 'A sketch of the past' she writes of the problems of memoir or biography:

> Consider what immense forces society brings to play upon each of us, how that society changes from decade to decade; and also from class to class; well, if we cannot analyse these invisible pres-ences, we know very little of the subject of the memoir; and again how futile life-writing becomes. I see myself as a fish in a stream; deflected; held in place; but cannot describe the stream.[3]

Such analysis, such discriminations, are the business of the historian. But *her* representations of history have something of the picture-book in them, figures held in superb but picturesque moments – a series of tableaux, a pageant. And that, of course, is the image she turns to in her last novel, *Between the Acts*.

> From behind the bushes issued Queen Elizabeth – Eliza Clark, licensed to sell tobacco. Could she be Mrs Clark of the village shop? She was splendidly made up. Her head, pearl-hung, rose from a vast ruff. Shiny satins draped her. Sixpenny brooches glared like cats' eyes and tigers' eyes; pearls looked down; her cape was made in cloth of silver – in fact swabs used to scour saucepans. She looked the age in person. ... *For a moment she stood there, eminent, dominant, on the soap box with the blue and sailing clouds behind her.*[4]

History is stationary, inhabited by replaceable figures whose individu-ality is less than their community with other lives lived already 'with the blue and sailing clouds behind'. This paradox is at the heart of her representation of history: with all her acute sense of the shifts in material and intellectual circumstances, she figures human being as unchanging, standing in for each other across the centuries. This sense of the inertness of the human condition means that history for her is playful, a spume of language. In *Between the Acts* it seems to Isa that the three great words are Love, Hate, Peace. And nothing else matters. The strangeness of the past is all on the surface. At base, it is familiar.

Playfully and with great intensity, such problems create the fabric of thought and association in *Between the Acts*. Mrs Lynn Jones wonders what happened to the home of her youth.

> Change had to come, she said to herself, or there'd have been yards and yards of Papa's beard, of Mama's knitting. ... What

she meant was, change had to come, unless things were perfect; in which case she supposed they resisted Time. Heaven was changeless.

'Were they like that?' Isa asked abruptly. She looked at Mrs Swithin as if she had been a dinosaur or a very diminutive mammoth. Extinct she must be, since she had lived in the reign of Queen Victoria....

'The Victorians,' Mrs Swithin mused. 'I don't believe' ... 'that there ever were such people. Only you and me and William dressed differently.'

'You don't believe in history,' said William.

The stage remained empty. The cows moved in the field. The shadows were deeper under the trees.[5]

Virginia Woolf's first and last novels, *The Voyage Out* (1915) and *Between the Acts* (1941), are the two works which engage most directly with ideas of the primeval. In *The Voyage Out* it is necessary to travel to remote countries to discover it. The primitive is still figured as outside self. But in *The Waves*, and even more in *Between The Acts*, the prehistoric is seen not simply as part of a remote past, but as contiguous, continuous, a part of ordinary present-day life.

In recent years 'prehistory' has become a useful technical term for describing those conditions of production and of reception which determine the relationship between text and reader. (What do we know about the conditions of production and how does this knowledge define our reading?) The term 'prehistory' is also sometimes used to describe the means by which a work of fiction creates its own past, suggesting a continuity between an unrecorded previous existence for the characters and the language of the text that makes them be. That is, it can be used as a way of claiming a non-linguistic, prior presence for people whom we simultaneously know to be purely the verbal products of a particular act of writing. But there is a further sense of the term which seems particularly apt to Virginia Woolf's work: prehistory implies a pre-narrative domain which will not buckle to plot. Just as Freud said that the unconscious knows no narrative, so prehistory tells no story. It is time without narrative, its only story a conclusion. That story is extinction. Once there were primeval forests, massive land creatures, sea-beasts crawling in the swamp. Now they are gone.

In their place is mankind and its recorded history of war, politics, empire, its unrecorded history of generations obscured by profound oblivion. Virginia Woolf was always distrustful of narrative, finding herself unable to make up plot or accept its resolutions.[6] She was fascinated by recurrence, perpetuity, and both by the difficulty of forgetting and by the fragmentary vestiges which are remembered.

In an early draft of *The Waves* she writes:

> I am not concerned with the single life but with lives together. I am trying to find in the folds of the past such fragments as time preserves ... there was a napkin, a flowerpot and a book. I am telling the story of the world from the beginning, and in a small room, whose windows are open.[7]

The single self in the small room with windows open to the outer world attempts to make again from fragments the continuity of time. She seeks to 'explicate', that is, to 'unfold', the folds of time, to renew the lapsed materiality of the past.

'The story of the world from the beginning' has been, in the past hundred years or so, seen predominantly as a story of development and succession. In *Civilization and its Discontents* Freud accepts an evolutionist basis for psychoanalysis but distinguishes between organic and mental evolution:

> As a rule the intermediate links [in organic evolution] have died out and are known to us only through reconstruction. In the realm of the mind, on the other hand, what is primitive is so commonly preserved alongside of the transformed version which has arisen from it that it is unnecessary to give instances as evidence.[8]

That is very much the position of Conrad in *Heart of Darkness*. Virginia Woolf, however, emphasizes the extent to which the 'primitive is ... preserved alongside of the transformed version' in the material as well as the mental world. She tempers the triumphalist narrative of development and meditates instead upon ways in which the prehistoric permeates the present day. Sometimes this becomes an opposing comedy to the Tennysonian insistence that we let 'the ape and tiger die' and move beyond the animal:

> There is the old brute, too, the savage, the hairy man who dabbles his fingers in ropes of entrails; and gobbles and belches; whose speech is guttural, visceral – well, he is here. He squats in me. Tonight he has been feasted on quails, salad, and sweetbread. He now holds a glass of fine old brandy in his paw. He brindles, purrs and shoots warm thrills all down my spine as I

sip. It is true, he washes his hands before dinner, but they are still hairy. He buttons on trousers and waistcoats, but they contain the same organs. ... That man, the hairy, the ape-like, has contributed his part to my life.

That passage from Bernard's final soliloquy in *The Waves* is succeeded by the morphological ecstasy of

I could worship my hand even, with its fan of bones laced by blue mysterious veins and its astonishing look of aptness, suppleness and ability to curl softly or suddenly crush – its infinite sensibility.[9]

The example of the hand was one that Darwin used in *The Origin of Species* to track the identity of structures across species and to establish continuity with our uncouth progenitors, hard to acknowledge as kin.

The ready, inter-metaphorical movement to and fro between the development of the individual and the development of the species makes for new relations and anxieties. It informs the thinking of the past hundred years. Though we take it for granted, Virginia Woolf, like Freud, belonged to a generation in which its novelty of meaning was still perceptible. It is the idea which allows Freud, in 'The Wolf-Man', for example, to speak of 'the pre-historic period of childhood', and which earlier had led T. H. Huxley to explain the lack of experimental evidence for the evolutionary process thus: 'the human race can no more be expected to testify to its own origins than a child can be tendered as witness to its own birth'.[10] Both quotations emphasize oblivion, the impossibility of recording. Darwinian theory required that we accept forgetfulness and the vanishing of matter, and yet insisted at the same time on descent from a remote and changed precursor. Origins can never be fully regained or rediscovered. Origins are always antecedent to language and consciousness. That same emphasis upon lost and unreclaimable origins, upon antecedent oblivion, is found in Freud's working of Darwinian theory. But there is also, in Freud and in Woolf, a counter-insistence on perpetuity and on the survival of what precedes consciousness, precedes history.

In *Moses and Monotheism* (which Virginia Woolf was reading as she worked on *Pointz Hall*, the first title for *Between the Acts*) Freud writes:

assume that in the history of the human species something happened similar to the events in the life of the individual. That is to say mankind as a whole also passed through conflicts of a sexual-aggressive nature, which left permanent traces but which were for the most part warded off and forgotten; later, after a long period of latency, they came to life again. ... Since it can no longer be doubted after the discovery of evolution that mankind had a pre-history and since this history is unknown (that is to say, forgotten), such a conclusion has almost the significance of an axiom ... the effective and forgotten traumata relate, here as well as there, to life in the human family.[11]

The gossips in *Between the Acts* muse crudely on these connections:

No, I thought it much too scrappy. Take the idiot. Did she mean, so to speak, something hidden, the unconscious as they call it? But why always drag in sex. ... It's true, there's a sense in which we all, I admit, are savages still. Those women with red nails.[12]

The coinage of evolutionary ideas and of Freudianism is here brought to the surface and daringly trivialized. I say 'daringly' because she thus draws attention to and simultaneously deflects us from the depth of these issues in her own creativity.

Oddly little attention has been given to the possible reading relationships between Woolf and Freud, as opposed to Freudian plumbings of Woolf's neuroses. The Hogarth Press published translations of Freud from 1921 on. Virginia Woolf was reading him in the 1930s. Once, in Freud's old age, they met, and he handed her a narcissus. Frank Sulloway, in *Freud: Biologist of the Mind*, makes the point that what distinguished Freud from earlier psychologists was his adoption of an evolutionist as opposed to a psychologistic description of the mind. Prehistory is anterior to knowledge. It lies beneath the polarizations and emplotments of knowledge. It lies, as it were, *beneath* history in that same spatial-geological metaphor that Freud used to describe the relationship of consciousness and the unconscious which lies beneath. The unconscious is both prior in time and beneath in space. It is not known, but equally not gone, nor voided. It escapes registration.

One of the features of Virginia Woolf's style is her fascination with taking language out towards obliterativeness, towards things she feels cannot be described, like the clouds near the beginning of *Between the Acts* and the sky whose blue cannot be symbolized:

Was it their own law, or no law, they obeyed? Some were wisps of white hair merely. One, high up, very distant, had hardened to golden alabaster; was made of immortal marble. Beyond that was blue, pure blue, black blue; blue that had never filtered down;

that had escaped registration. It never fell as sun, shadow, or rain upon the world, but disregarded the little coloured ball of earth entirely. No flower felt it; no field; no garden.[13]

The blue 'had escaped registration'. The escape from registration was an ideal, a necessarily unachievable ideal, of her writing. Virginia Woolf is fascinated by the persistence of prehistory as well as its impenetrable distance. The sky, the clouds, changing, unchangeful, are outside history, there from the beginning of time.

These objects of meditation (absence of origins, survival of the primeval, the impacting of race in individuals) haunt Woolf and help to explain certain of the shapes her narratives take, and certain of the exemplary renunciations she makes. Her scepticism about developmental narratives and about irreversible transformations are part of her debate with her Victorian progenitors, her Victorian *self*. Leslie Stephen attributed his loss of faith quite directly to reading *The Origin of Species*. Virginia Woolf, in her career as a writer, assays the forms for experience offered by evolutionary theory. One insistence of evolutionary theory was on changed forms which could not be reversed. Perhaps, in the light of the dominant forms for understanding experience developed by her father's generation, her resistance to the idea of transformation has particular meaning.

It is certainly striking how little transformation means in her work. Certainly there are *oscillations* to and fro between metaphor and the material world. There are momentary illuminations, mistaken identities. But transformations, in her writing, can always be reversed. Indeed, I wonder whether her much discussed frigidity is a necessary renunciation of climax and of the obliterativeness of climax. It is a way of keeping everything persistingly elated, never completed. In our reading experience of Virginia Woolf, one of the most striking attributes of her style is the sensuous arousal it creates in the reader even while it constantly evades moments of completion. She eschews the authoritarian inevitability of sequence implied in plot. Instead, her writing offers constant shifts between discourses from moment to moment. She has abraded some of the conventional notions of 'development' apparently authenticated by evolutionary story, and in doing so she is responding with great subtlety to the other implications of Darwin's myths.[14]

Let me turn now to *The Voyage Out*, the first of her novels, since this bears traces not only of a struggle with Victorian narrative but of Woolf's own reading of Darwin's writing. *The Voyage Out* still uses the form of the *Bildungsroman*. The particular shape that she uses here is that of the voyage which is to be also a voyage of self-discovery. In *Bildungsroman*, typically, the hero learns by means of his growing-up experiences both to know his self and to accept its limitations, to conform to the demand made on the ego by society. A typical form for romantic narrative is that of the circular voyage – away from home until at the furthest point of distance the meaning of home is understood and the return can be accomplished. That narrative was brought into question by other early twentieth-century writers as well as Virginia Woolf; by Conrad, in *Heart of Darkness*, where the voyage upriver and into the forest takes you back into the primeval, into the primal self whose core of darkness is indescribable and can never be taken into narrative. Certainly, as Conrad expresses it, it can be explicated only through negations: unfathomable, immeasurable. These are the form through which he measures the density of the forest and the activity of the primitive self. Like Freud, Conrad condenses unconscious and prehistoric.[15] We see another reading of the voyage, later, in *A Passage to India*, where Forster shows the voyage out into empire and beyond it, the discovery that the *extent* of India reaches beyond the power of human language to record or British imperial power to suppress. For Virginia Woolf, *The Voyage Out* had a particular meaning.

The book has a closely realistic surface. Rachel Vinrace goes out on her voyage of pleasure and discovery to South America. The narrative implies self-development and promises an according with society's expectations. But in this we are disappointed. Development is thwarted. Rachel dies. There is no voyage back. The book offers an enquiry typical of women's plot: can the heroine survive her own growth? Initiation into society for women involves initiation into descent. They will become vessels of descent, not borne aloft by the boat that carries them, but themselves bearing and carrying: child-bearing. At the moment of entry into sexual life, Virginia Woolf's heroine falls ill and dies. Rachel's voyage to South America is extended into a special voyage of exploration upriver into the primeval forests. It is on this voyage that Rachel and Terence declare their love, and on this voyage also that she contracts the fever from which she dies.

In these passages describing the forest Virginia Woolf draws directly on another book about a voyage: *The Voyage of the Beagle*, Darwin's account of his early travels around the globe which provided him with the experience and evidences from which emerged his theory of evolution by means of natural selection. Some of the passages of

14

description of the South American forest in Darwin seem to provide 'local colour' for Virginia Woolf – though I shall argue that they provide more than that. His incandescent, sometimes eerie, descriptions chime in closely with hers.

> In vain we tried to gain the hill, The forest was so impenetrable that no-one who had not beheld it could imagine so entangled a mass of dying and dead trunks. I am sure that often for more than ten minutes together our feet never touched the ground and we were frequently ten or fifteen feet above it, so that the seamen as a joke called out the soundings. At other times we crept one after another on our hands and knees under the rotten trunks. In the lower part of the mountain noble trees with winter's bark and the laurel-like sassafras with fragrant leaves, and others the names of which I do not know were matted together by a trailing bamboo or cane. Here we were more like fishes struggling in a net than any other creature.[16]

That is Darwin. This is *The Voyage Out*:

> As they moved on the country grew wilder and wilder. The trees and the undergrowth seemed to be strangling each other near the ground in a multitudinous wrestle; while here and there a splendid tree towered high above the swarm, shaking its thin green umbrellas lightly in the upper air....
>
> As they passed into the depths of the forest the light grew dimmer, and the noises of the ordinary world were replaced by those creaking and sighing sounds which suggest to the traveller in a forest that he is walking at the bottom of the sea. The path narrowed and turned; it was hedged in by dense creepers which knotted tree to tree, and burst here and there into star-shaped crimson blossoms.... The atmosphere was close and the air came at them in languid puffs of scent.[17]

Darwin similarly emphasized the mingling of life and death in the atmosphere of the forests:

> The day was beautiful and the number of trees which were in full flower perfumed the air and yet even this could hardly dissipate the gloomy dampness of the forest. Moreover the many dead trunks, that stand like skeletons never fail to give these primeval woods a character of solemnity absent in countries long civilised. Death instead of life seemed the predominant spirit.[18]

The return to primary forms may reveal a squandering of life rather than its renewal. Virginia Woolf's writing seems to be quite alert to its own intertextuality here, to be conjuring another prehistory. Darwin's book records the period in his life when, setting sail as an orthodox Christian, he had, by the time he returned to England, begun to conceive the theories which were to change our ways of perceiving experience. *The Voyage of the Beagle* is the pre-text to *The Origin of Species*, its prehistory.

In *The Voyage Out* the scene immediately after that in the forest is full of Darwinian echoes and Darwinian references. An immense amount of sexual force has been generated which spills about among the other characters. People crudely use some of the more specious extensions of evolutionism. Mrs Flushing laughs at the idea of disinterestedness and love. 'Savin' yourself' is all that matters.

> 'One reads a lot about love – that's why poetry's so dull. But what happens in real life, eh? It ain't love!' she cried.
> ...'Tell them about the bath, Alice.'
> 'In the stable-yard,' said Mrs Flushing. 'Covered with ice in winter. We had to get in; if we didn't we were whipped. The strong ones lived – the others died. What you call the survival of the fittest – a most excellent plan, I dare say, if you've thirteen children!'[19]

The intellectual Hirst is beset by the silence: 'These trees get on one's nerves – it's all so crazy. God's undoubtedly mad. What sane person could have conceived a wilderness like this, and peopled it with apes and alligators?' In the following chapter Rachel and Terence come upon the remote tribe of 'soft instinctive people' where mother 'drew apart her shawl and uncovered her breast to the lips of her baby', watching them the while; Helen, also watching them, 'standing by herself in the sunny space among the native women, was exposed to presentiments of disaster'.

> The cries of the senseless beast rang in her ears high and low in the air, as they ran from tree-trunk to tree-top. How small the little figures looked wandering through the trees! She became acutely conscious of the little limbs, the thin veins, the delicate flesh of men and women, which breaks so easily and lets the life escape compared with these great trees and deep waters.[20]

The sense of unchanging life and of the sheer chanciness of survival is more important there than descent. And the abrupt cutting-off of her heroine's life is her challenge to developmental narrative.

II

Darwin's early writing elated Virginia Woolf, I think. The young Darwin, like the young Rachel, is discovering the world and in some of the same regions. But he, active, independent, completes the circular journey. She, surrounded by protectors, hemmed in by reserve, has the journey curtailed by death. Virginia Woolf's resistance to transformation does not deny death, but in this book death is received as silence and diminution, not transformation. The individual life is muffled. The flesh easily lets life escape 'compared with these great trees and deep waters'.

Evolutionary theory had made a new myth of the past. Instead of the garden, the swamp. Instead of fixed and perfect species, forms in flux. It also renewed the peculiar power of the sea as the first place of life. Most myth systems had given the sea a primary place in the formation of life; now scientific theory historicized this concept. The sea resists transformation. Yet the sea is never old; it is constantly renewing itself. That, I think, was important for Virginia Woolf, and became increasingly so. Her fascination with the sea and with the primeval and prehistoric may be related to her search for a way out of sexual difference, or, equally, for a continuity with lost origins. Her mother died when she was 12. Because of this loss, and her own gender, the mother in her work is conceived as origin, the father as intervention. In an early version of *The Waves* she wrote of the waves as 'sinking and falling, many mothers, and again, many mothers, and behind them many more, endlessly sinking and falling'.[21] Mothers – matrices: re-formation, not transformation; the acceptance of oblivion: these are connections crucial to Virginia Woolf's writing. The search for lost origins had been powerful throughout the nineteenth century. Darwin himself may have had an unrecognized personal incentive in his impulse to work back towards ultimate origins, and to repopulate the past of the world by means of natural history. His own mother died when he was 8 and he was troubled by the scantiness of his memories of her.

What I want to argue is that the need to discover origins, the vehement backward plumbing of history, the insistence on causality and judgement, was *allayed* for Virginia Woolf by her awareness of the survival of prehistory. The continued presence of sea, clouds, leaves, stones, the animal form of man, the unchanged perceptual intensity of the senses, all sustain her awareness of the simultaneity of the prehistoric in our present moment. This absolves her from the causal forms she associates with nineteenth-century narratives.

17

She is drawn most to what is perpetually changing: and I give equal force here to both elements, perpetual and changing. A passage strikingly related to her imagination of the waves of the sea is to be found in Ruskin's *Modern Painters*, where he writes:

> Most people think of waves as rising and falling. But if they look at the sea carefully, they will perceive that the waves do not rise and fall. They change. Change both place and form, but they do not fall; one wave goes on, and on, and still on; now lower, now higher, now tossing its mane like a horse, now building itself together like a wall, now shaking, now steady, but still the same wave till at last it seems struck by something, and changes, one knows not how, becomes another wave.[22]

For Ruskin, waves change, but are not transformed. They become other waves. This absence of transformation, the acceptance of sustained obliteration and continuity, becomes of great moment in Woolf's later writing.

Writing for her can less and less claim infinity of recall. By the time she reaches her last work she is content with gaps and contradictions. In *Between the Acts*, the characters themselves are vestiges of creation; the language is fraught with citation, pastiche, and allusion. 'Orts, scraps, and fragments are we.' Yet the phrase itself, through its recurrence in the text, is a binding chant, linking unlike together in kinship and difference. Merely to look at the work on the page signals difference when we come to *Between the Acts*. Whereas in the submarine world of *The Waves*, 'that mystical eyeless book', as she calls it, we are 'deflected, held in place' by the way in which the language of the book covers every space, the writing occupies the page, in *Between the Acts* white spaces abound, unprinted, unrestored.

Between the Acts is set in June 1939, just before the coming of the war. In it, she deliberately substitutes 'we' for 'I'. She was writing it from 1938 onwards. She was writing it through the coming of the war. In a contemporaneous work, 'Little Gidding', Eliot wrote that 'History is now and England'. In *Between the Acts* history is the past. The *present* is *prehistory* in a double sense. Whenever the action of the historical pageant falters it is saved by the unwilled resurgence of the primeval: the shower of rain, the idiot, the cows bellowing for their lost calves. At the same time, the book describes a moment which may be the last of this culture. The planes swoop overhead. June 1939 is the prehistory to a coming war which, the book makes clear without hysteria, may mark the end of this society:

'It all looks very black.'
'No one wants it – save those damned Germans.'
There was a pause.
'I'd cut down those trees. ...'
'How they get their roses to grow!'
'They say there's been a garden here for five hundred years. ...'[23]

In the intense comedy of *Between the Acts*, with its shifty lexical play, its apocalyptic imminence, its easy vacillation between the domestic and the monstrous, we reach her most unsettling meditation on the meanings of prehistory. Since Darwin, humankind could no longer take for granted its own centrality or its own permanence.

It is from the period of composition of this work that Virginia Woolf's one direct reference to Darwin in her diaries occurs. We know from references in *To the Lighthouse* that she used him naturally as an example of the apex of human achievement. ('We can't all be Titians and we can't all be Darwins.') In October 1940 the Woolfs' house in Tavistock Square was bombed. She and Leonard Woolf went up to London to salvage some of their possessions.

> A wind blowing through. I began to hunt out diaries. What could we salvage in this little car? Darwin and the silver, and some glass and china.[24]

The diaries, Darwin, some silver, glass and china. It is an intriguing list and a revealing one. Later she records: 'I forgot the Voyage of the Beagle'. I have already shown, I hope, that the problems bequeathed by Darwin's narratives troubled Virginia Woolf creatively in ways that led her to subtle appraisals and meditations on his work. There is no need to assert the prevalence of evolutionary ideas during Virginia Woolf's lifetime and we know that Darwin's writings had had direct effects upon her early family circumstances. We all live within post-Darwinian assumptions now, and hence, paradoxically, we are not alert to the extent to which imaginatively we take for granted shapes for experience suggested by his theories and their extensions. We need therefore to measure the level of awareness at which Virginia Woolf was engaging with Darwin and the implications of his work. We need to do this in order to clarify the particular difficulties he posed for her as a writer and to perceive the new forms that her rewriting of these difficulties created. In the diary passage we have external evidence that she valued his books. And in *Between the Acts* we have her fullest exploration of the new relations of experience to prehistory that had been fuelled by Darwin's theories. Those theories were indefatigably extended by the two succeeding generations in terms of development, race theory, the unconscious.

> 'Once there was no sea,' said Mrs Swithin. 'No sea at all between us and the continent. I was reading that in a book this morning. There were rhododendrons in the Strand; and mammoths in Piccadilly.'
> 'When we were savages,' said Isa.
> Then she remembered; her dentist had told her that savages could perform very skilful operations on the brain. Savages had false teeth, he said.[25]

Much of the wit of the book depends upon its turning aside any notion of development as implying improvement. And, because so much of it takes the form of thought, past and present lie level, culled as needed by the individual's associations. The novel is a spatial landscape, not a linear sequence. The pastiches of the pageant set periods of the past alongside each other and beside the present. Most of the people in the book say 'Adsum' for their ancestors. Bart's dog is still a wild dog. Bart himself appears a monster, with his rolled newspaper for snout, to his small grandson. The child is convinced, the grandfather is comically offended. The single disturbingly graphic scene of traditional 'action' brings to the surface of the text the matter of prehistory: children, savages, the coming war, the devouring chain of life are all expressed in the awkward scene where Giles acts, running counter to the indications of book and title, 'Between the Acts':

> He kicked – a flinty yellow stone, a sharp stone, edged as if cut by a savage for an arrow. A barbaric stone; a pre-historic. Stone-kicking was a child's game. He remembered the rules.[26]

He stamps on toad and snake: 'It was birth the wrong way round – a monstrous inversion. ... The mass crushed and slithered. The white canvas on his tennis shoes was bloodstained and sticky. But it was action. Actions relieved him.' The four-square allegorization of violence, of the oncoming war and greed, is forcefully set apart from the method of most of the book in a way which apes its own subject-matter. It is vividly heraldic. In contrast, there is the narrative's sly habit of pointing, and thus making enigmatic, simple statements by the intervention of 'he said' or 'she said'. The word 'origin' is a favourite for such play:

Lucy rapping her fingers on the table said: 'What's the origin –
the origin – of that?'
'Superstition,' he said.

'What's the origin,' said a voice, 'of the expression "with a flea in
his ear"?'[27]

In this work interruption is as important as association. Spaces on the
page give room to the unrecorded areas between the acts of language.
And characters and narrative discourse alike persistently break in upon
thought as well as speech. In the same mode, the prehistoric breaks in
upon the present as well as surviving within it. At the end of the book
'the great carp himself, which came to the surface so very seldom' is
momentarily visible as a flash of silver. At the end of the vicar's speech
'Every sound in nature was painfully audible; the swish of the trees;
the gulp of a cow; even the skim of the swallows over the grass could
be heard.' Characters break in on each other's vivid reveries. The book
is permeated with Lucy Swithin's reading of H. G. Wells.[28] Virginia
Woolf here amalgamates his *The Outline of History* with his *Short
History of the World* and writes her own version rather than quoting
Wells directly. Old Mrs Swithin, so pious, repetitive, and faithful, has
an imaginative life swarming with sensual images of power and birth.
During the book's twenty-four hours, she inhabits the repeated present
of the day of pageant, and the primeval worlds of her book's description. The two sometimes flow together, are sometimes disjunct, are
each other's unacted part. Wakened early by the birds,

> she had stretched for her favourite reading – an Outline of His-
> tory – and had spent the hours between three and five thinking of
> rhododendron forests in Piccadilly; when the entire continent, not
> then, she understood, divided by a channel, was all one; popu-
> lated, she understood, by elephant-bodied, seal-necked, heaving,
> surging, slowly writhing, and, she supposed, barking monsters;
> the iguanodon, the mammoth, and the mastodon; from who pre-
> sumably, she thought, jerking the window open, we descend.

That last thought is taken into narrative discourse to describe 'the
great lady in the bath chair' later: 'so indigenous was she that even her
body, crippled by arthritis, resembled an uncouth, nocturnal creature,
now nearly extinct'. This passage continues:

> It took her five seconds in actual time, in mind time ever so much
> longer, to separate Grace herself, with blue china on a tray, from

the leather-covered grunting monster who was about, as the door opened, to demolish a whole tree in the green steaming undergrowth of the primeval forest.[29]

Two pages later the small boy grubbing in the ground, his perceptions unchanged from primitive man, is terrified by 'a terrible peaked eyeless monster moving on legs, brandishing arms'. It is known by us as his grandfather joking, with a newspaper. Lightly, through comic juxtaposition and pastiche, she concurs with Wells's more sonorous description of 'our ancestors' who are also us. Wells writes:

> His ancestors, like the ancestors of all the kindred mammals, must have been creatures so rare, so obscure, and so remote that they have left scarcely a trace amidst the abundant vestiges of the monsters that wallowed rejoicing in the steamy air and lush vegetation of the Mesozoic lagoons, or crawled or hopped or fluttered over the great river plains of that time.[30]

No wonder Cleopatra is Mrs Swithin's marvellously unexpected 'unacted part' – Queen of the Nile – in which all first life seethed and grew. 'You've made me feel I could have played ... Cleopatra!' As Wells wrote:

> wallowing amphibia and primitive reptiles were the very highest creatures that life had so far produced. Whatever land lay away from the water or high above the water was still altogether barren and lifeless. But steadfastly, generation by generation, life was creeping away from the shallow sea-water of its beginning.[31]

Wells's romantic language infuses that of Mrs Swithin and invigorates the book with its sensual movement: 'Amid this luxuriant primitive vegetation crawled and glided and flew the first insects.' Diverse scopes of the past are interlaced: hot images of empire thread the work, particularly in Bart's memories of his youth in India. The word 'savages' keeps recurring, tempered, made sceptical, reinvoked. The untamed dog who either cringes or bites, the fish stirring the pond, the membranes of plants, all suggest the primeval pouring through the present.

The swallows lace Africa and Europe, connecting England's present with its prehistory:

> 'They come every year,' said Mrs Swithin. ... 'From Africa.' As they had come, she supposed, when the Barn was a swamp.

> Before there was a channel, when the earth, upon which the Windsor chair was planted, was a riot of rhododendrons, and humming

birds quivered at the mouth of scarlet trumpets, as she had read that morning in her *Outline of History*, they had come.[32]

That is one aspect of the continuance of prehistory; the elegant survival of swallows reassures and sustains a consonance between different time modes in the work. There are other, less beautiful continuities, presented as cliché, as covert allusion, as gossip. Immediately after the description of the swallows we have Mrs Manresa in 'the little game of the woman following the man', connected through Cobbet's observation: 'He had known human nature in the East. It was the same in the West. Plants remained – the carnation, the zinnia, and the geranium.' William Dodge, in the next paragraphs, masturbates as Giles approaches:

> 'The idiot?' William answered Mrs Parker for her. 'He's in the tradition.'
>
> 'But surely,' said Mrs Parker, and told Giles how creepy the idiot – 'We have one in our village' – had made her feel. 'Surely, Mr Oliver, we're more civilized?'
>
> '*We?*' said Giles, '*We?*' He looked, once, at William. He knew not his name; but what his left hand was doing.[33]

Giles has blood on his boots. Isa obsessively recalls the scene of rape she read about in the newspaper. The 'sister swallow' is linked, through myth, with the raped woman, and the rape is trivially re-enacted in Giles's insistence in this same passage on the double standard: 'It made no difference; his infidelity – but hers did.' The sexual drive of individuals, though masked by diverse cultural signs, remains fiercely unchanged. 'Vénus toute entière à sa proie attachée.' Racine's metaphor, almost cannibalistic in its intensity, is part of the immoveable repertoire of Isa's thought – Isa, whose *acts* in this book consist merely of receiving a cup of tea from the hand of the gentleman farmer.

It is as though, compacted yet spacious, the matter of the past is more fully *there* the more remote it is. The captious pastiche of the pageant's language presents snatches of English history as a series of linguistic gestures and tropes. But the remote past of prehistory crowds the everyday present in its untransformed actuality. It is as though she concurs with Freud's observation that individual and masses 'retain an impression of the past in unconscious memory traces' and 'there probably exists in the mental life of the individual not only what he has experienced himself, but also what he brought with him at birth, fragments of phylogenetic origin, an archaic heritage'.[34]

The parallel between ontogeny and phylogeny in Freud's argument here, which Virginia Woolf read as she worked on the novel, strengthens her own imagery of individual and mass. 'Drawn from our island history. England I am', begins the pageant. Why are prehistory, 'unconscious memory traces', and 'our island history' of such importance in the work?

The allusions to all levels of the past function as 'beot', in *Beowulf*'s term. Repetition, encrustation, recurrence, continuity – all are under threat.[35] Plot in this book is the coming of war, the impending obliteration, which makes the ordinary at last *visible* in all its richness. When Miss La Trobe, at the end of the pageant, holds up the mirrors to the audience, they cannot see anything but shallow images of themselves. But we, as outer audience, replenish the emptiness they experience, even while we share it. 'Orts, scraps, and fragments are we.' The entire life (historically bound, and synchronically present) which has been figured in the work is under threat, and momentarily sacred.

Miss La Trobe imagines the scene for her next play:

> It was growing dark. Since there were no clouds to trouble the sky the blue was bluer, the green greener. There was no longer a view – no Folly, no spire of Bolney Minster. It was land merely, no land in particular. She put down her case and stood looking at the land. Then something rose to the surface.
>
> 'I should group them', she murmured, 'here.' It would be midnight; there would be two figures, half concealed by a rock. The curtain would rise.[36]

The landscape of sky and land, from which all particular relics of England have been obliterated, could as well be at the beginning of the world as now. The two figures are anonymous, progenitors perhaps, only perhaps. She is 'singing of what was before Time was'. At the end, the book itself repeats Miss La Trobe's project. It takes us back before the beginning of history but it takes us there through reading endoubled:

> 'England', she was reading, 'was then a swamp. Thick forests covered the land. On the top of their matted branches birds sang. ...' [Bartholomew] looked leafless, spectral, and his chair monumental. As a dog shudders its skin, his skin shuddered. ... 'Prehistoric man,' she read, 'half-human, half-ape, roused himself from his semi-crouching position and raised great stones.'

The old people retire to bed. Giles and Isa are left alone. 'The Record of the Rocks ... begins in the midst of the game', writes H. G. Wells. 'The curtain rises on a drama in the sea that has already begun, and has been going on for some time.'[37]

Giles and Isa, in the final paragraphs, are linked with other species, and with other texts preoccupied with the force of the primeval.

> From that embrace another life might be born. But first they must fight, as the dog fox fights with the vixen, in *the heart of darkness*, in the fields of night. ... It was the night before roads were made, or houses. It was the night that dwellers in caves had watched from some high place among rocks.
>
>   Then the curtain rose. They spoke.[38]

With the image of the rising curtain and of the bared landscape of night Virginia Woolf simultaneously enregisters the artfulness of history, the perpetuity of the material world. Language, like fishes, rises to the surface. 'Then something rose to the surface', we are told of Miss La Trobe. 'Ourselves', thinks Mrs Swithin as she looks at the fish. But the Dover sole is eaten for lunch. The deftness of the book is in its refusal ever quite to become elegy or threnody. It hopes for survival and gives space to the disruption of comedy. Simultaneity and conglomeration are, it seems, comic as well as comforting:

> So one thing led to another; and the conglomeration of things pressed you flat; held you fast, like a fish in water. So he came for the week-end, and changed.
>
>   'How d'you do?' he said all round; nodded to the unknown guest; took against him; and ate his fillet of sole.[39]

Nothing in this work is renounced. But equally nothing is claimed for ever. Levels of discourse persistingly shift, accept their own inadequacy. Not for nothing is Mrs Swithin, who holds history and prehistory together, nicknamed 'Old Flimsy'.

In an almost exactly contemporaneous work, composed equally under the impact of the coming of war, Eliot was writing:

> The river is within us, the sea is all about us;
> The sea is the land's edge also, the granite
> Into which it reaches, the beaches where it tosses
> Its hints of earlier and other creation:
> The starfish, the horseshoe crab, the whale's backbone;
> The pools where it offers to our curiosity
> The more delicate algae and the sea anemone.

In 'Dry Salvages', of which a draft was finished on 4 January 1941, Eliot repudiates 'superficial notions of evolution / Which becomes, in the popular mind, a means of disowning the past'. He continues, in a passage which chimes in with those I have cited from Freud as well as Woolf, responding as they all are to Darwin's writing:

> the past experience revived in the meaning
> Is not the experience of one life only
> But of many generations, not forgetting
> Something that is probably quite ineffable:
> The backward look behind the assurance
> Of recorded history, the backward half-look
> Over the shoulder, towards the primitive terror.[40]

At first, that passage sounds very close to *Between the Acts*, but what is important is that for her that 'backward half-look over the shoulder' does not result in terror. She looks 'behind the assurance of recorded history' *for* assurance.

Prehistory can be described only in the mirror of history, since language and history are inextricable, Yet, outside language and analysis, origins are all about us. She is no longer thrusting back to the past; she has renounced the search for origins. At one level, that is a political act which disengages her from the racial madness of the time. The medium of her work is largely choric, gossip, emerging from 'mass observation'.

> 'No, I don't go by politicians. I've a friend who's been to Russia. he says. ... And my daughter, just back from Rome, she says the common people, in the cafés, hate Dictators. ... Well, different people say different things.'...
> 'And what about the Jews? The refugees ... the Jews. ... People like ourselves, beginning life again. ... But it's always been the same. ...'[41]

In her earlier work, when attention is called to it, the present moment has been empty, as at the conclusion of *Orlando*. Here the present moment lightly engages all the past. She refuses that metaphor which assumes that prehistory is deeper, grander, more sonorous, than the present moment, and instead disperses it throughout the now of *Between the Acts*. The book holds the knowledge that cultures and histories are obliterated, that things may not endure. The immediate history of England is interrupted and threatened by the insistent murmur of aeroplanes moving overhead in preparation for war. Is man 'essentially a fighter'? Does the primeval validate war?[42] Clouds, sky, swallows, pike, sea, earth, appetites, and perceptions figure the simultaneity of prehistory and the present, and yet also sustain the idea of a future. The engorged appetite of empire, the fallacy of 'development' based on notions of dominion or of race, are given the lie by the text's insistence on the untransformed nature of human experience – lightly dressed in diverse languages – absurdly knit together by rhymes. Here she registers for once the fullness of the present, not as moment only. The urgency of the connection between militarism and masculine education which Virginia Woolf asserted in *Three Guineas* is here articulated as part of a text which goes beyond it to emphasize the alternative insights offered by Darwin into kinship between past and present forms, the long pathways of descent, the lateral ties between humankind and other animals, the constancy of the primeval. For us living in an age where we can foresee the possibility of a post-nuclear world inhabited at most by sea, grass, scorpions, and sky, the salutary comedy of *Between the Acts* realizes its fullest intensity.

Notes

1. Virginia Woolf, *Three Guineas* (1938; repr. London: Hogarth Press, 1943), pp. 326–7. For Julian Huxley's views, see, for example, his presidential address to the zoology section of the British Association in 1936 on 'Natural selection and evolutionary progress'.
2. Virginia Woolf, *A Writer's Diary*, ed. Leonard Woolf (London: Hogarth Press, 1953), p. 365.
3. Virginia Woolf, 'A sketch of the past', *Moments of Being*, ed. J. Schulkind (Brighton: Sussex University Press, 1976), p. 80.
4. Virginia Woolf, *Between the Acts* (London: Hogarth Press, 1941), pp. 101–2.
5. Ibid., p. 203.
6. For a related discussion of Virginia Woolf's evasion of plot, see my article 'Beyond Determinism: George Eliot and Virginia Woolf', *Women Writing and Writing About Women*, ed. M. Jacobus (London: Croom Helm, 1979).
7. Virginia Woolf, *The Waves: The Two Holograph Drafts*, ed. J. Graham (London: Hogarth Press, 1976), I, p. 42.
8. Sigmund Freud, *Civilization and its Discontents* (London: Hogarth Press, 1930; rev. edn 1963), p. 5.
9. Woolf, *The Waves* (1931; repr. London: Hogarth Press, 1946), pp. 205, 206.
10. T. H. Huxley, 'Lectures on Evolution', *Science and Hebrew Tradition* (London: Macmillan, 1893), p. 73.
11. Sigmund Freud, *Moses and Monotheism* (London: Hogarth Press, 1939), pp. 129–30.
12. Woolf, *Between the Acts*, pp. 232–3.
13. Ibid., p. 30.
14. For an analysis of Darwin's narrative language and of his myths, see my study, *Darwin's Plots* (London: Routledge & Kegan Paul, 1983).
15. For discussion of Conrad's reading of evolutionary theory, see Ian Watt, *Conrad in the Nineteenth Century* (London: Chatto & Windus, 1979).
16. Charles Darwin, *The Voyage of the Beagle* (London: J. M. Dent, n.d.), p. 308.
17. Virginia Woolf, *The Voyage Out* (1915; repr. London: Hogarth Press, 1929), pp. 327, 331.
18. Darwin, *The Voyage of the Beagle*, p. 321.
19. Woolf, *The Voyage Out*, pp. 335–6.
20. Ibid., pp. 349–50.
21. Woolf, *The Waves: Holograph Drafts*, I, p. 64.

22. John Ruskin, *Modern Painters*, vol. III (1856; repr. New York: John Wiley, 1881), part IV, chs 12, 6, 11, p. 161.

23. Woolf, *Between the Acts*, p. 177.

24. Virginia Woolf, diary entry dated 10 October 1940, *The Diary of Virginia Woolf*, ed. Anne Olivier Bell and Andrew McNeillie (London: Hogarth Press, 1982), vol. V. In *Between the Acts* itself, Darwin is named at the end of Isa's reading list, p. 26.

25. Woolf, *Between the Acts*, p. 38.

26. Ibid., p. 118.

27. Ibid., pp. 33, 145.

28. H. G. Wells, *The Outline of History: Being a Plain History of Life and Mankind*, rev. edn (London: Cassell, 1920). The quotations are all from ch. 3, on 'Natural Selection'.

29. Woolf, *Between the Acts*, pp. 13–14.

30. Wells, *The Outline of History*, p. 24.

31. Ibid., p. 14.

32. Woolf, *Between the Acts*, pp. 123, 130.

33. Ibid., pp. 132–3.

34. Freud, *Moses and Monotheism*, pp. 151, 157.

35. Roger Poole, in *The Unknown Virginia Woolf* (Cambridge: Cambridge University Press, 1978), convincingly establishes connections between *Three Guineas* and *Between the Acts*.

36. Woolf, *Between the Acts*, pp. 245–6.

37. Ibid., p. 255; Wells, *The Outline of History*, p. 11.

38. Woolf, *Between the Acts*, p. 256; my italics.

39. Ibid., p. 59. Compare the quotation from 'A Sketch of the Past' on p. 3.

40. T. S. Eliot, 'Dry Salvages', *Four Quartets, Collected Poems, 1909–1962* (London: Faber & Faber, 1974), pp. 205, 208–9.

41. Woolf, *Between the Acts*, pp. 144–5.

42. Compare Woolf's comments on militarism and evolution quoted at the beginning of this essay.

2

Hume, Stephen, and Elegy
in *To the Lighthouse*

When my perceptions are remov'd for any time, as by sound sleep; so long am I insensible of *myself*, and may truly be said not to exist. And were all my perceptions remov'd by death, and cou'd I neither think, nor feel, nor see, nor love, nor hate after the dissolution of my body, I shou'd be entirely annihilated, nor do I conceive what is farther requisite to make me a perfect non-entity.

(David Hume, *A Treatise on Human Nature*)[1]

Father's birthday. He would have been 96, 96, yes, today; and could have been 96, like other people one has known; but mercifully was not. His life would have entirely ended mine. What would have happened? No writing, no books; – inconceivable. I used to think of him and mother daily; but writing The Lighthouse, laid them in my mind. And now he comes back sometimes, but differently.

(Virginia Woolf, *Diary*, 28 November 1928)[2]

Several of Virginia Woolf's books compose themselves about an absence: Jacob's absence from his room, Mrs Ramsay's in the second half of *To the Lighthouse*, and in *The Waves* Percival's in India and in death. Absence gives predominance to memory and to imagination. Absence may blur the distinction between those who are dead and those who are away. In one sense, everything is absent in fiction, since nothing can be physically there. Fiction blurs the distinction

First published in: *Essays in Criticism*, 34 (1984), pp. 33–55.

between recall and reading. It creates a form of immediate memory for the reader.

Writing about Hume, the eighteenth-century philosopher he most admired, Leslie Stephen glosses his position thus:

> The whole history of philosophical thought is but a history of attempts to separate the object and the subject, and each new attempt implies that the previous line of separation was erroneously drawn or partly 'fictitious'. (p. 48)[3]

In *To the Lighthouse* the fictitiousness of the separation between object and subject, the question of where to draw the line, is passionately explored, not only by the painter, Lily Briscoe, but by the entire narrative process. It is through Lily that the philosophical and artistic problem is most directly expressed and the connection between Mr Ramsay and Hume first mooted. Near the beginning of the book, Lily asks Andrew what his father's books are about.

> 'Subject and object and the nature of reality,' Andrew had said. And when she said Heavens, she had no notion what that meant. 'Think of a kitchen table then', he told her, 'when you're not there.' (p. 40)[4]

In the book's last paragraph, remembering Mrs Ramsay, looking at the empty steps, Lily at last solves the problem of the masses in her picture to her own satisfaction:

> She looked at the steps; they were empty; she looked at her canvas; it was blurred. With a sudden intensity, as if she saw it clear for a second, she drew a line there, in the centre. (p. 320)

The separation of the object and the subject, and the drawing of a line less erroneously, less 'fictitious', than in previous attempts, defines the nature of elegy in this work. Virginia Woolf attempts to honour her obligations to family history and yet freely to dispose that history. In the course of doing so, she brings into question our reliance on symbols to confer value.

Virginia Woolf's other books imply aesthetic theories and draw upon the ideas of contemporary philosophers, particularly Bertrand Russell's warning against assuming that language mirrors the structure of the world: 'Against such errors', he writes in *The Analysis of Mind* (1921), 'the only safeguard is to be able, once in a way, to discard words for a moment and contemplate facts more directly through images.'[5] That is an ideal and a difficulty which moves through Virginia Woolf's practice as a writer. Only in *To the Lighthouse*, however, is the power of philosophical thinking and its limitations openly a theme of the book. That has to do with the work's special nature as elegy. In 1925, when she was beginning *To the Lighthouse* Virginia Woolf wrote in her diary:

> I will invent a new name for my books to supplant 'novel'. A new
> ———— by Virginia Woolf. But what? Elegy?

In elegy there is a repetition of mourning and an allaying of mourning. Elegy lets go of the past, formally transferring it into language, laying ghosts by confining them to a text and giving them its freedom. Surviving and relinquishing are both crucial to the composition of *To the Lighthouse*. Learning how to let go may be as deep a difficulty in writing and concluding a novel as it is in other experience.

The problem of achieving and of letting go is shared by mothers and artists. Mrs Ramsay lets go through death. After her death the book continues to explore what lasts (how far indeed has she let go or will others let her go?). The novel questions the means by which we try to hold meaning and make it communicable.

> Meanwhile the mystic, the visionary, walked the beach, stirred a puddle, looked at a stone, and asked themselves 'What am I?' 'What is this?' and suddenly an answer was vouchsafed them (what it was they could not say). (pp. 203–4)

All Virginia Woolf's novels brood on death, and death, indeed, is essential to their organization as well as their meaning. Death was her special knowledge: her mother, her sister Stella, and her brother Thoby had all died prematurely. But death was also the special knowledge of her entire generation, through the obliterative experience of the First World War. The long succession of family and generation, so typically the material of the nineteenth-century *roman fleuve*, such as Thackeray's *Pendennis* and *The Virginians*, or Zola's Rougon-Macquart series, becomes the site of disruption. The continuity of the family can with greatest intensity express the problems of invasion and even extinction.

Lawrence originally imagined *The Rainbow* and *Women in Love* as one long novel to be called *The Sisters*. But when the two books eventually appeared the first was a rich genealogical sedimentation, the second was thinned, lateral, preoccupied with a single generation. The parents in *Women in Love* are enfeebled and dying; the major relationships explored in the work are chosen, not inherited. In *To the Light-house* Virginia Woolf still tried to hold within a single work what Lawrence had eventually had to separate: the experience of family life and culture, before and after the First World War. She held them together by separating them. 'Time passes', like Lily's line, both joins and parts. It is one formal expression of the profound question: 'What endures?' 'Will you fade? Will you perish?', 'The very stone one kicks with one's boots will outlast Shakespeare'. 'Distant views seem to outlast by a million years (Lily thought) the gazer and to be commun-ing already with a sky which beholds an earth entirely at rest.'

> 'Ah, but how long do you think it'll last?' said somebody. It was as if she had antennae trembling out of her, which, intercepting certain sentences, forced them upon her attention. This was one of them. She scented danger for her husband. A question like that would lead, almost certainly, to something being said which reminded him of his own failure. How long would he be read – he would think at once. (p. 166)

This passage brings home the other anxiety about survival which haunts the book: how long will writing last? Mr Ramsay's ambition to be remembered as a great philosopher registers some of Woolf's ambi-tions and longings as an artist too. They are expressed in another mode by Lily, who must complete her picture and complete it truly, but who foresees its fate: 'It will be hung in the attics, she thought; it would be destroyed. But what did that matter? she asked herself, taking up her brush again' (p. 320). So the topics of the British empiricists, Locke, Hume, Berkeley – the survival of the object without a perceiver, the nature of identity and non-entity, the scepticism about substance – lie beneath the activity of the narrative. They bear on the question of how we live in our bodies and how we live in the minds of others. Hume writes of mankind in general that 'they are nothing but a bundle or collection of different perceptions, which succeed each other with an inconceivable rapidity, and are in a perpetual flux and movement' (p. 534). The emphasis on perception and on 'flux and movement' is repeated in Virginia Woolf's writing. But, as I have already suggested, there was a more immediate reason for Hume's insistent and some-times comic presence in *To the Lighthouse*.

When Hume is named in *To the Lighthouse* he is strongly identified with Mr Ramsay's thoughts. He is first mentioned at the end of Mr Ramsay's long meditation on the need for ordinary men and on their relation to great men (exemplified in the twin figures of Shakespeare and the 'liftman in the Tube'). The section ends with Mr Ramsay's self-defeated questioning of his own powers. Yet, he thinks:

> he was for the most part happy; he had his wife; he had his children; he had promised in six weeks' time to talk 'some non-sense' to the young men of Cardiff about Locke, Hume, Berkeley, and the causes of the French Revolution. (p. 73)

His meditation had begun with the question: 'If Shakespeare had never existed ... would the world have differed much from what it is today?' (p. 70). The apposition of empiricism and revolution ('Locke, Hume, Berkeley, and the causes of the French Revolution') suggests a possible partial answer to that question, but it is self-deprecatingly framed as 'some nonsense'. The issue remains unresolved.

Hume's name next appears interrupting, and yet almost a part of, the current of thought generated by Mrs Ramsay in section 11 as she thinks about 'losing personality', eternity, the lighthouse, and finds herself repeating phrases: 'Children don't forget.... It will end.... It will come.... We are in the hands of the Lord.'

> The insincerity slipping in among the truths roused her, annoyed her. She returned to her knitting again. How could any Lord have made this world? she asked.... There was no treachery too base for the world to commit; she knew that. No happiness lasted; she knew that. She knitted with firm composure, slightly pursing her lips and, without being aware of it, so stiffened and composed the lines of her face in a habit of sternness that when her husband passed, though he was chuckling at the thought that Hume, the philosopher, grown enormously fat, had stuck in a bog, he could not help noting, as he passed, the sternness at the heart of her beauty. (p. 102)

Hume, philosopher of mind, has grown so absurdly substantial that he sinks into the bog. That physical episode becomes meta-memory for Mr Ramsay, who *sees* it, not having been there. The full story is reserved for section 13, when at the end:

> the spell was broken. Mr Ramsay felt free now to laugh out loud at Hume, who had stuck in a bog and an old woman rescued him on condition he said the Lord's Prayer, and chuckling to himself he strolled off to his study. (p. 116)

Hume, the sceptical philosopher, is obliged to repeat the words of faith. We remember Mrs Ramsay's involuntary 'We are in the hands of the Lord'. Communal faith usurps the individual will. At the end of this episode (section 13) Mr Ramsay feels comfortable: Hume has been worsted. The giant towering above his own endeavours as a philosopher proves to be a gross man subsiding. For a moment he can be held to scale, contained in anecdote. But Mr Ramsay is himself measured by his will to worst. The narrative engages with the difficulties that Hume's work raises. And by this means, as we shall see, Virginia Woolf movingly allows to her father, Leslie Stephen, within her own work, a power of survival, recomposition, rediscovery even.

Hume's presence in the work allows her to bring sharply into focus the question of what is 'when you're not there', a topic traditional to elegy but here given greater acuity. In 1927 Bertrand Russell wrote in *The Analysis of Matter*:

> I believe that matter is less material, and mind less mental, than is commonly supposed, and that, when this is realized, the difficulties raised by Berkeley largely disappear. Some of the difficulties raised by Hume, it is true, have not yet been disposed of.[6]

Hume's persistence, the fact that his difficulties cannot be disposed of, makes him a necessary part of the book's exploration of substance and absence, of writing as survival.

We know that Virginia Woolf read Hume, perhaps not for the first time, in September 1920. But his importance in *To the Lighthouse* is connected with his special value for Leslie Stephen. In the process of transformation from Leslie Stephen to Mr Ramsay, Virginia Woolf notably raises the level of creativity and attainment at which the father-figure is working, placing him in the rearward and yet within reach of major philosophers. Whereas Leslie Stephen was a doughty thinker, high popularizer, and man of letters, Mr Ramsay is a possibly major, though self-debilitated, philosopher. This raising and enlarging sustains the scale of the father in relation to the writer and at the same time allows a process of identification between writer and father in their artistic obsessions. Virginia Woolf did not acknowledge having read much of Leslie Stephen's work. But when we turn to Stephen's *History of English Thought in the Eighteenth Century* the congruities between the themes of that work and *To the Lighthouse* are remarkable enough, and Stephen's actual exposition of Hume and the directions in which he seeks to move beyond him are closely related to the concerns of *To the Lighthouse*. The first of these is reputation and survival.

The first sentence of Stephen's book simultaneously places Hume at a pinnacle of achievement and presents the problem of literary reputation.

> Between the years of 1739 and 1752 David Hume published
> philosophical speculations destined, by the admission of friends
> and foes, to form a turning-point in the history of thought. His
> first book fell dead-born from the press; few of its successors had
> a much better fate. (p. 1)

The first section of the Introduction is entitled 'The influence of great
thinkers' and it grapples with the question of how far the thinker
thinks alone or as an expression of communal concerns. How does
thought affect society? Stephen argues:

> The soul of the nation was stirred by impulses of which Hume
> was but one, though by far the ablest, interpreter; or, to speak in
> less mystical phrase, we must admit that thousands of inferior
> thinkers were dealing with the same problems which occupied
> Hume, and though with far less acuteness or logical consistency,
> arriving at similar conclusions. (p. 2)

Thinking is not exclusively the province of great thinkers, nor – more
strikingly – are their conclusions different from those of others.

In *To the Lighthouse* Mr Bankes suggests:

> We can't all be Titians and we can't all be Darwins, he said; at the
> same time he doubted whether you could have your Darwin and
> your Titian if it weren't for humble people like ourselves. (p. 114)

The relationship between 'humble people like ourselves' – or not quite
like ourselves – and great art, great ideas, great events, haunts and
troubles *To the Lighthouse*. It is part of the work's deepest questioning
of what will survive. The question includes the questioning of the
concept of 'great men', of indomitable achievement, of a world centred
on human will, and extends to human memory and the material world.

> Does the progress of civilization depend upon great men? Is the
> lot of the average human being better now that in the time of the
> pharaohs? Is the lot of the average human being, however, he
> asked himself, the criterion by which we judge the measure of
> civilization? Possibly not. Possibly the greatest good requires the
> existence of a slave class. The liftman in the Tube is an eternal
> necessity. The thought was distasteful to him. (p. 70)

Stephen, pursuing the relationship between 'great men' and the mass
of thinking, writes:

> Society may thus be radically altered by the influence of opinions

which have apparently little bearing upon social questions. It would not be extravagant to say that Mr Darwin's observations upon the breeds of pigeons have had a reaction upon the structure of society. (p. 12)

Abstract thought and social action seem at times in *To the Lighthouse* to be polarized between Mr and Mrs Ramsay, but most of the thinking in the book is sustained by the activity of laying alongside and intermelding the separate thought processes within individuals in such a way that the reader perceives the connections which the characters themselves cannot. The interpenetration of consciousnesses in language on the page allows us to think through problems of substance and absence unreservedly.

In his analysis of Hume's thought Stephen gives particular emphasis to the idea of fictionality. Stephen writes: 'The belief that anything exists outside our mind when not actually perceived, is a "fiction". ... Association is in the mental what gravitation is in the natural world.' (Lily's floating table is anchored by association, not gravitation, we remember.)

> We can only explain mental processes of any kind by resolving them into such cases of association. Thus reality is to be found only in the ever-varying stream of feelings, bound together by custom, regarded by a 'fiction' or set of fictions as implying some permanent set of external or internal relations.... Chance, instead of order, must, it would seem, be the ultimate objective fact, as custom instead of reason, is the ultimate subjective fact. (p. 44)

There are obvious connections with *To the Lighthouse* in such an emphasis on reality as an 'ever-varying stream of feelings'. 'Life', he writes in his discussion of Hume, 'is not entirely occupied in satisfying our material wants, and co-operating or struggling with our fellows. We dream as well as act. We must provide some channel for the emotions generated by contemplation of the world and of ourselves' (p. 11)

Stephen, with Hume, affirms chance and custom rather than order and reason as the basis of perception. Nevertheless, such affinities with Virginia Woolf's writing appear at a very general level and need not imply any particularly intense recall of Stephen's work or conversation. If such consonance were all, I would feel justified only in calling attention to similarity, rather than implying a process of rereading, replacing. However, the actual examples that Stephen selects are so crucial in the topography of *To the Lighthouse* as to suggest that Virginia Woolf's writing is meditating on problems raised in the father's text.

In the novel there is an extraordinary sense of the substantiality of people. The children are always pelting here and there; words like 'plummeting', 'darting', 'full tilt', express the *impact* of the body. We are, in the moment, in our bodies, and that makes the moment both the most substantial and the most ephemeral of all experiences. We are never for more than a moment in the same place, the same time, in our bodies. That gap between body and time fascinates her in *To the Lighthouse*; and so does the question of substantiality, and its nature. Hume remarks:

> A substance is entirely different from a perception. We have, therefore no idea of substance. (p. 518)

> That table, which just now appears to me, is only a perception and all its qualities are qualities of a perception. (p. 523)

In *To the Lighthouse* we read:

> 'Think of a kitchen table then', he told her, 'when you're not there.'
> So she always saw, when she thought of Mr Ramsay's work, a scrubbed kitchen table. It lodged now in the fork of a pear tree, for they had reached the orchard. And with a painful effort of concentration, she focused her mind, not upon the silver-bossed bark of the tree, or upon its fish-shaped leaves, but upon a phantom kitchen table, one of those scrubbed board tables, grained and knotted, whose virtue seems to have been laid bare by years of muscular integrity, which stuck there, its four legs in the air. (pp. 40–1)

For the reader, pear-tree and table are poised equally as fictive images. The oddness of their conjunction makes us especially aware of them as images in the mind, though Lily's hefty imaginative work concentrates on the individuality of the table as perceived object (scrubbed, grained, and knotted) even more than on the tree (silver-bossed bark, fish-shaped leaves). By her imaginative effort she lurches the table *beyond* table, into some moralized and comically anthropomorphic form. 'Virtue' is shifted from being a question of essence, or of meaning, to one of moral endurance. Lily sees the table *upside-down* so that it becomes humanoid, its legs in the air, bare and muscular, a table of integrity, naked but not violated.

This inversion of the generalized image expresses through comedy the artist's urge towards the particular and the substantial. And yet the major process of Lily's picture throughout the book is *away* from representationalism towards abstraction, as though only pattern finally can satisfy and survive. At the book's end the line in the centre of her picture is distanced almost as far as it is possible to go from the particularity of the tree with which she began. It is almost entirely free of reference. But it was generated out of the referential. The narrative does not itself show any sustained parallel movement away from the referential towards the purely lexical, but it does move away from the burdened authority of symbolic objects. That movement of creativity seems to bear on the function of Virginia Woolf's parents in the work of art she composes, and on the means by which we all seek to make things last.

Table, house, tree, and stone: those four objects, and particularly the first two, are crucial to the narrative and the play of associations in *To the Lighthouse*. Discussing the problem of the relationship between idea and language Stephen remarks in his essay on Hume:

> Looking, in the first place, at the external world, nothing seems simpler than the idea corresponding to the name of an individual object, man, or tree, or stone.

But he adds:

> The man and the tree change visibly at every moment; if the stone does not change so rapidly, we discover that its qualities are at every instant dependent upon certain conditions which vary, however slowly. All things, as the old sceptics said, are in ceaseless flux; and yet, to find truth, we must find something permanent. (pp. 26–7)

Man, tree, stone: much of the emotion and thought of *To the Lighthouse* moves through those objects, surrounded by the 'ceaseless flux' of the sea. Mr Ramsay meditates on enduring fame and its vicissitudes;

> The very stone one kicks with one's boots will outlast Shakespeare. His own little light would shine, not very brightly, for a year or two, and would then be merged in some bigger light, and that in a bigger light still. (He looked into the darkness, into the intricacy of the twigs.) (p. 59)

Hume sees the attempt to escape from the self into a wider world to free ourselves of our own perceptual constraints as inevitably doomed, and Stephen quotes a famous lyrical passage from Hume to illustrate this:

> Let us fix our attention out of ourselves as much as possible. Let us chase our imaginations to the heavens, or to the utmost limits

of the universe; we never can really advance a step beyond ourselves, nor can conceive any kind of existence but those perceptions which have appeared in that narrow compass. This is the
universe of the Imagination, nor have we any idea but what is
there produced. (p. 46)

Stephen at this point abruptly turns the argument and opens a new
paragraph thus: 'Yet it is a plain fact of consciousness that we think of
a table or a house as somehow existing independently of our perception of it' (p. 46)

'A table ... a house' begin to suggest more fully the way in which
technical daring and emotional homage combine in *To the Lighthouse*,
particularly in 'Time Passes'. The empty house, flooded with darkness, has been relinquished by its human inhabitants: 'there was
scarcely anything left of body or mind by which one could say "This is
he" or "This is she".' No perceiver is there to see the house. The
darkness of forgetfulness, death, absence, enters the house. 'Certain
airs' ask of the wallpaper, 'would it hang much longer, when would it
fall? ... How long would they endure?' At the end of the third section,
'Mrs Ramsay having died rather suddenly the night before', the airs
advance in anthropomorphic order, 'advance guards of great armies',
to meet 'only hangings that flapped, wood that creaked, the bare legs
of tables' (p. 200).

The material world is here sustained by writing, but it is a kind of
writing which deliberately obliterates any suggestion of a single
perceiver. Language draws attention to its own anthropomorphism, its
habit of remaking objects in the image of human perception, the
impossibility in Hume's words of 'conceiving any kind of existence but
those perceptions which have appeared in that narrow compass'.

Near the book's conclusion, in the section which comes close to ghost
story, Mrs Ramsay appears to Lily as Lily strives to resolve her picture.

> One must keep on looking without for a second relaxing the
> intensity of emotion, the determination not to be put off, not to
> be bamboozled. One must hold the scene – so – in a vice and let
> nothing come in and spoil it. One wanted, she thought, dipping
> her brush deliberately, to be on a level with ordinary experience,
> to feel simply that's a chair, that's a table, and yet at the same
> time, It's a miracle, it's an ecstacy. (pp. 309–10)

The precision and obduracy of artistic feeling rejects any raising, or
symbolizing, though it floods the ordinary with ecstasy. Lily's old

experience of longing, 'to want and want and not to have', itself at last becomes

> part of ordinary experience, was on a level with the chair, with the table. Mrs Ramsay – it was part of her perfect goodness to Lily – sat there quite simply, in the chair, flicked her needles to and fro, knitted her reddish-brown stocking, cast her shadow on the step. There she sat. (p. 310)

Physical (she casts a shadow as no ghost can do), revenant, actual, unhaloed, and unalloyed by symbol, she 'simply' knits her reddish-brown stocking. Absence and substance momentarily resolve.

Earlier in the work Lily had intensely, though fleetingly, seen Mr and Mrs Ramsay as 'symbolical', 'the symbols of marriage, husband and wife'. The moment of transcendence sinks down again and concludes with the anecdote I earlier quoted:

> Still for one moment, there was a sense of things having been blown apart, of space, or irresponsibility as the ball soared high, and they followed it and lost it and saw the one star and the draped branches. ... Then, darting backwards over the vast space (for it seemed as if solidity had vanished altogether), Prue ran full tilt into them and caught the ball brilliantly high up in her left hand, and her mother said 'Haven't they come back yet?' whereupon the spell was broken. Mr Ramsay felt free now to laugh out loud at Hume, who had stuck in a bog and an old woman rescued him on condition he said the Lord's Prayer, and chuckling to himself he strolled off to his study. (pp. 115–16)

The repertoire of associations is richly at work here: the tree, so freely moved in the course of the book between substance, metaphor, thought, art, until at last it becomes line without reference. (Is Lily's final line tree or lighthouse? By then it no longer matters.) Here the tree figures as space; looking up they saw 'the one star and the draped branches'. In Hume's phrase, they 'chase their imaginations to the heavens' until solidity has vanished, but immediately Prue runs 'full tilt into them'. There is an extraordinary joyousness in that substantiality; the warmth and prowess of the body is regained, and regained as comedy. Mr Ramsay immediately turns to his enjoyment of Hume stuck in the bog and the moment can dissolve as they all take their separate ways. Living, here, means letting things be, holding them a moment, 'a brilliant catch', then letting them go. The 'symbolical' is valuable only if it is not freighted with permanence.

In this novel Virginia Woolf most acutely polarizes the sexes. Never again in her later novels was the binarism of male/female, husband/ wife, father/mother allowed predominance. Instead, in works like *The Waves* and *Between the Acts*, she creates a spectrum of gender, a fan of possibilities. In *To the Lighthouse*, however, the formalization of difference is crucial to the activity of the novel. It is her homage to symbol, to generation, and to parenthood, but it represents also the 'writing out' of the symbolic weight of parenthood. It is tempting, in considering difference, and the polarization of sex roles, to see Lily Briscoe as some sort of Hegelian third term, representing the artistic resolution of sexual fracture and contradiction. But geometric patterning offers a false stability of reading, a judging optimism, which serves to protect the reader against the evanescence studied in the work. That emphasis on evanescence requires a reappraisal of the authority of symbol.

To the Lighthouse, is a post-symbolist novel. By this I mean that symbolism is both used and persistently brought into question. The act of symbolizing is one of the major means by which in language we seek to make things hold, to make them survive. But, above all, it is the means by which we make *things* serve the human. Symbol gives primacy to the human because it places the human at the centre, if not of concern, yet of signifying. Symbol depends for its nature on the signifying act. By its means concepts and objects are loaded with human reference.

Though *To the Lighthouse* is weighted with the fullness of human concerns, there is a constant unrest about the search after a permanence which places humanity at the centre. This search manifests itself in many ways: as continuity, through generation; as achieved art object; as storytelling; as memory; as symbol.

Language can never be anything but anthropocentric. In this book Virginia Woolf struggles not only with the deaths of her father and her mother but with the death of that confidence in human centrality which was already being abraded in her father's generation by evolutionary theory. When Stephen attempts to move beyond Hume he does it by means of evolutionist arguments, emphasizing the progressive, the developmental in the theory. The 'race' is Stephen's new element (and it is an element that Virginia Woolf turns to, much later, in *Between the Acts*). Stephen writes:

> Hume's analysis seems to recognise no difference between the mind of man and a polyp, between the intellectual and the merely sensitive animal ... the doctrine that belief in the external world

is a 'fiction' is apparently self-destructive. If all reason is fiction, fiction is reason. (p. 49)

Modern thinkers of Hume's school meet the difficulty by distinguishing between the *a priori* element in the individual mind and in the mind of the race. Each man brings with him certain inherited faculties, if not inherited knowledge; but the faculties have been themselves built up out of the experience of the race. (p. 56)

Stephen moves away from individualism to a confidence in communal development. *To the Lighthouse* brings into question all such attempts to propose a stable accord between inner and outer, past and present, to seal the contradiction of subject and object through symbol.

Did Nature supplement what man advanced? Did she complete what he began? With equal complacence she saw his misery, condoned his meanness, and acquiesced in his torture. That dream, then, of sharing, completing, finding in solitude on the beach an answer, was but a reflection in a mirror. (pp. 207–8)

The signalled anthropomorphism in passages like this ('she saw ... condoned ... acquiesced') edges into sight our assumption of equivalence between inner and outer. In the passage describing the house left without people to observe it Virginia Woolf uses a neoclassical personification which strikes oddly, and which is intermelded with animal imagery. 'It is a plain fact of consciousness that we think of a table or house as somehow existing independently of our perception of it', writes Stephen. Here, Virginia Woolf faces the problem of how we describe a house when it exists 'independently of our perception of it'. The answer in 'Time Passes' is to see the object through time, and to use a discourse which points to human absence, sometimes with playful comfort, as in the following passage, sometimes in mourning or ironic abruptness, as in those passages cut off within square brackets '[A shell exploded. Twenty or thirty young men were blown up in France, among them Andrew Ramsay, whose death, mercifully was instantaneous.]'

Loveliness and stillness clasped hands in the bedroom, and among the shrouded jugs and sheeted chairs even the prying of the wind and the soft nose of the clammy sea airs, rubbing, snuffling, iterating, and reiterating their questions – 'Will you fade? Will you perish?' – scarcely disturbed the peace, the indifference, the air of pure integrity, as if the question they asked scarcely needed that they should answer: we remain.

The transposed, ludic quality of this passage is part of the decaying humanism of the concept 'house' – an object constructed for human use and so now, without function, present only as lexical play. Beyond the ordinary house is the *lighthouse*, the furthest reach and limit of human concerns, an attempt to create a margin of safety before the sea's power becomes supreme.

The sound of the waves is heard throughout the book, sometimes louder, sometimes softer, but always there to remind us of the expanse of the world beyond the human, in the face of which all attempts at signifying and stabilizing are both valiant and absurd. House and table are human objects, made to serve. Can the world of objects be made to sustain our need for signification, continuity, or permanence? These questions, brought to the fore by Hume's scepticism, and struggled with anew in the light of evolutionary theory by Stephen's generation, grind, like the dislimning sea, through *To the Lighthouse*.

The formlessness of the sea and the formed completeness of objects challenge equally the authority of the human subject. 'Subject and object and the nature of reality' turns out not to be a vapid philosophical trope but the book's grounded enquiry, an enquiry which thrives through her father's concerns.

In generation and in language equally (the making of children and of text) there is an attempt to ward off evanescence. In the course of her novel Virginia Woolf brings these desires within the surveillance of the reader. The tendency of the human to allow predominance to the human, to concur with our sense of our own centrality, is measured. Loading events and objects with symbolic weight comes to be seen as self-gratulation. So, as the work proceeds, she emphasizes momentariness and lightness. She empties and thins. The fullness of part I is replaced by the plainness of part III. The work is filled with a sense of how ephemeral is human memory: bodies gone and minds with them. All substance is transitory.

In May 1925, as she was beginning *To the Lighthouse*, she wrote in her diary:

> This is going to be fairly short: to have father's character done complete in it; and mother's; and St Ives and childhood; and all the usual things I try to put in – life, death etc. But the centre is father's character, sitting in a boat, reciting We perish, each alone, while he crushes a dying mackerel – However I must refrain. (III, pp. 18–19)

In the completed work Mrs Ramsay becomes characteristically the centre. The start of part I, 'The Window', as opposed to part III, 'The Lighthouse' imitates the self-doubting complexity of Mrs Ramsay's sensibility, a fullness which is resolved later into others' simpler and more ideal memories of her. Certainly much of the emotional and artistic resourcefulness of the work goes into the making again, the repossession, of what the writer too soon had ceased to know: of Vita Sackville-West Virginia Woolf said in December 1925 that she 'lavishes on me the maternal protection which, for some reason, is what I have always most wished from everyone'. But the resourcefulness is also in composing what she could never have known: the meditative consciousness of the mother.

The sexual reserve of the writing is considerable. We never know the first names of Mr or Mrs Ramsay. We do not accompany them to the greenhouses. The distance and decorum do not encourage the same knowingness in the reader as does our pleased recognition that the letter of the alphabet of philosophical knowledge that Mr Ramsay cannot quite reach is that which begins his own name. Yet the Ramsays, the text assertively makes clear, are there when we are not. Their withdrawal emphasizes substantiality and sexuality.

All signification relies on memory. In the language of the middle section of 'Time Passes' there is a wilful element, a reclaiming, a making demands, by which the distributor of the language seeks to ward off the immersing sea, the elements, the air, the non-linguistic world of human absence. The assertiveness, stylism, the hyperbole of linguistic desire, have parallels with that haunting figure, Grimm's fisherman's wife, whose story Mrs Ramsay reads to James. And the grossness of the wife's demands has links also with the eagerness of the human to dominate the non-human.

> She read on: 'Ah, wife,' said the man, 'why should we be king? I do not want to be king.' 'Well, said the wife, 'if you won't be king I will; go to the Flounder, for I will be king.' ... and when he came to the sea, it was quite dark grey, and the water heaved up from below and smelt putrid. Then he went and stood by it and said,
> > 'Flounder, flounder, in the sea,
> > Come, I pray thee, here to me.'

The last pages of the work void that final claim of the human on the world of process. They pare away symbol. The lighthouse itself when approached proves to be 'a stark tower on a bare rock'. The obsessional symbol-making urge of Mr Ramsay, which is associated with his desire to clutch and hold on to experience, begins to ebb. In the fiction, despite his children's fears, he does *not* say, 'But I beneath a rougher sea' or 'we perished, each alone', though in her diary she projected the scene with him 'sitting in a boat, reciting We perish, each alone, while he crushes a dying mackerel' (*Diary*, III, p. 19). Throughout the book Mr Ramsay has raucously, anxiously, raised his voice against oblivion, terrified by death, and by that longer obliteration in which writing also is lost. But when they reach the place on their journey to the lighthouse where the boat sank in the war (and in 'Time Passes')

> to their surprise all he said was 'Ah' as if he thought to himself, But why make a fuss about that? Naturally men are drowned in a storm, but it is a perfectly straightforward affair, and the depths of the sea (he sprinkled the crumbs from his sandwich paper over them) are only water after all. (p. 316)

It is a poignant and comic moment. At the moment when highest mystification is expected we are offered a complete demystification. His small gesture, in parenthesis, which recalls and then lets go of the parallel of dust to dust, ashes to ashes, is simply the sprinkling of crumbs on the sea, for the fishes.

That episode is immediately succeeded by another in which symbolism and the mystifying properties of human language and human gesture are relinquished. Lily, thinking their journey, imagines their arrival; '"He has landed," she said aloud. "It is finished."' The last words on the cross are half conjured. Mr Ramsay's journey and agony are momentarily, and uneasily, accorded a scale commensurate with his desires, though one on which, as readers, we are not obliged to dwell. The reference is fleetingly there. But it is immediately succeeded, and submerged, by Lily's finishing of her picture. The last words of the book are:

> With a sudden intensity, as if she saw it clear for a second, she drew a line there, in the centre. It was done; it was finished. Yes, she thought, laying down her brush in extreme fatigue. I have had my vision.

The change of tense, 'It was done; it was finished', obliterates the earlier allusion. The scale of reference becomes immediate, and exact. The step is empty. The picture is finished.

The extraordinary serenity of the book, even while it includes desolation and harassment, depends upon its acceptance of attenuation.

Loss, completion, ending, absence, are acknowledged. Evanescence is of the nature of experience, and, although language can for a time make things survive, the work calmly rides out the anxieties of authorship. Though rhyme claims to outlive marble monuments, the pebble survives longer than Shakespeare. But people and language have lived. She renounces the grand, the symbolical, the enduring. The moment is the moment of being alive in body and mind. In her diary in June 1927 she wrote: 'Now one stable moment vanquishes chaos. But this I said in The Lighthouse. We have now sold, I think, 2555 copies' (*Diary*, III, p. 141).

Lacan argues that symbol and the act of symbolization represent the father. In freeing characters and text from the appetite for symbol Virginia Woolf may be seen as moving language and persons beyond subjection to patriarchy. And in doing so she transformed and absolved her own father through the act of writing. He comes back, but differently:

> I used to think of him and mother daily; but writing The Light-house, laid them in my mind. And now he comes back sometimes, but differently.... He comes back now more as a contemporary. I must read him some day. I wonder if I can feel again, I hear his voice, I know this by heart? (*Diary*, III, p. 208)

A conundrum remains: Virginia Woolf disclaims having 'read' her father. Yet in this essay I have emphasized consonances between their written works. The answer may be that here she purposes a full reading, that act of intimacy, homage, and appraisal in which we subject ourselves to a writer's complete work. She defers any such task, setting it in that warm never-never-land of reading we hope 'some day' to fulfil. The evasion persists. She must delay reading the father. Her earlier familiarity with his work had taken the form of dipping, scanning, listening, a flighty and intrigued resistance which allows rereading and pillaging and avoids immersion.

The wise act of writing in *To the Lighthouse* disperses parenthood and all its symbolic weight. Want and will give way, the want and the will of the fisherman's wife, of Lily Briscoe, of Mrs Ramsay, Mr Ramsay, of Cam and James. Subject ceases to dominate object. We are left with 'the waves rolling and gambolling and slapping the rocks', 'the frail blue shape which seemed like the vapour of something that had burned itself away', the line in Lily's picture which enters and holds 'all its green and blues, its lines running up and across, its attempt at something'. The line is at last freed from the referential. The picture can be completed.

The end of *To the Lighthouse* performs the experience of ending which has already happened in Mrs Ramsay's reading aloud of Grimm's tale of the fisherman's wife. The end of a story allows annihilation and perpetuity at the same time. Things fall apart and – being written – for a time, endure.

So Mrs Ramsay equably reads the apocalyptic conclusion to James:

> 'Houses and trees toppled over, the mountains trembled, rocks rolled into the sea, the sky was pitch black and it thundered and lightened, and the sea came in with black waves as high as church towers and mountains, and all with white foam on top'.
>
> She turned the page; there were only a few lines more, so that she would finish the story, though it was past bedtime. It was getting late. ... It was growing quite dark.
>
> But she did not let her voice change in the least as she finished the story, and added, shutting the book and speaking the last words as if she made them up herself, looking into James's eyes: 'And there they are living still at this very time'. 'And that's the end', she said.

The elegiac triumph of the novel is to sustain entity. People survive when you are not there, when they are not there, in contradiction of Hume's assertion quoted at the beginning of this essay ('were all my perceptions remov'd by death ... what is farther requisite to make me a perfect non-entity'). But they survive here in a kind of writing which eschews permanence. The last part of the book escapes from symbolic raising, placing its parental figures 'on a level with ordinary existence', with the substance of a chair, a table, a house, with the depths of the sea which (as Mr Ramsay at last thinks) are 'only water after all'.

Notes

1. David Hume, *A Treatise on Human Nature* (1736), ed. T. H. Green and T. H. Gross (London, 1874), vol. I, p. 534. All further references are to this edition and appear in the text in parentheses.
2. *The Diary of Virginia Woolf*, ed. Anne Olivier Bell (London, 1980), vol. III, p. 208. Further page references appear in the text in parentheses.
3. Leslie Stephen, *English Thought in the Eighteenth Century*, 2 vols (London, 1876). Page references appear in the text in parentheses.
4. Virginia Woolf, *To the Lighthouse* (London, 1927). All page references are to this first edition and appear in the text in parentheses.
5. For discussion of this topic, see Allen McLaurin, *Virginia Woolf: The Echoes Enslaved* (Cambridge, 1973).
6. Bertrand Russell, *The Analysis of Matter* (London, 1927), p. 7.

3

The Body of the People:
Mrs Dalloway to *The Waves*

As Virginia Woolf began imagining the work which was to become *Between the Acts*, she foresaw the enterprise. She implored herself not to 'call in all the cosmic immensities' or 'force my tired and diffident brain to embrace another whole – all parts contributing'. Instead she wanted 'a centre: all lit[erature] discussed in connection with real little incongruous living humour; & anything that comes into my head; but "I" rejected": "We" substituted: to whom at the end there shall be an invocation?'[1] The alternation between 'I' and 'We' is the living quarrel of Virginia Woolf's art, particularly in her later career. Her subject-matter is often isolation, and she excels at recording the repetitive, fickle movements of an individual's thought and feeling at levels beneath self-criticism. But she was fascinated by communities: the family, groups of friends, the nation and history. These groupings control the form of her work in the novels from *Mrs Dalloway* on to *Between the Acts*. The need for a certain autonomy, 'a room of one's own', is set alongside the need to find a creative standpoint which will be less merely personal, less preoccupied with private relationships. To be alive on the same day in London may be a deeper bond, her writing in *Mrs Dalloway* suggests, than any of the individual choices of love and friendship which narrative fiction ordinarily privileges.

She saw the movement away from the particular to the broader inquiry as especially important for women writers. In 1929 in 'Women and Fiction' she predicts that future women writers will 'be less

First published in: Sue Roe (ed.), *Women Reading Women's Writing* (Brighton: Harvester, 1987), pp. 85–114.

absorbed in facts' ... 'They will look beyond the personal and political relationships to the wider questions which the poet tries to solve – of our destiny and the meaning of life'.[2] In 'The Narrow Bridge of Life' (1927) she wrote of the need to 'stand further back from life'.[3] We may temper these rather sibylline critical utterances with the evidence from her life of close involvement with the women's movement, with socialism and with the network of friends and ideas we call 'Bloomsbury'. And the process of the novels indicates that the 'standing further back' she recommends is not withdrawal but a means of observing patterns other than those formerly recorded. She made an early attempt at describing a new pattern, in an entry in her Diary on Monday, 21 February 1927, which plays third persons against each other, notably excluding the first person singular and plural, neither 'I' nor 'We' participating:

> Why not invent a new kind of play – as for instance:
>
> Woman thinks: ...
> He does.
> Organ Plays.
> She writes.
> They say:
> She sings:
> Night speaks:
> They miss
>
> I think it must be something in this line – though I can't now see what. Away from facts; free; yet concentrated; prose yet poetry; a novel & a play.[4]

Only subjects are recorded (woman, he, organ, she, they, she, night, they). The sentences have no object – the relation of subject and object appearing to her at this time, it seems, as the endorsement of 'facts'.

As she wrote *The Waves* and *The Years* she was steadily reading Dante, reading him in 'the place of honour' at the end of her own day's writing, quoting the Purgatorio at the end of the 1911 section of *The Years:*[5]

> Che per quanti si dice piu li nostro
> tanti possiede piu di ben ciascuno.
>
> (canto xv, ll. 55–6)
>
> So by so many more there are who say 'ours'
> So much the more of good doth each possess.[6]

The deep value which she accords to communality is not a matter only of her sincerely learnt and practised socialism or her forcefully written (if not always practised) solidarity with other women. It has to do with her practice of writing out of the mass and out of the body.

'We' is an elastic pronoun, stretching in numbers and through time. Its population ranges from the exclusive pair of lovers, now, to the whole past of human history. It can welcome or rebuff the hearer. It can also colonise. Virginia Woolf saw clearly that 'we' may be coercive and treacherous. It invites in the individual, the subset, the excluded, who once inside may find themselves vanished within an alien group claiming on their behalf things of no benefit or relevance to themselves.

Virginia Woolf was chary of the 'we' of patriotism, and of the self-gratifying claims of male writers to speak in universals which cover (in many senses) the experience also of women. Her reaction in writing to social communities was sceptical and wary; she needed to find ways of maintaining difference as well as constellation, lest clusters become ordered as hierarchies. Yet her writing emphasises communality and the body. Language itself drives, as Bernard remarks, 'roman roads across experience'. Living in an old linguistic culture burdens the speaker with shared and unshared experience. The autocracy of the inherited tongue may be at odds with the particular. So Mrs Ramsay resents being betrayed into uttering a belief she does not share ('We are in the hands of the Lord') through the power of language to stretch belief beyond reason. Woolf was attracted by assemblage rather than coherence: the slippage, repetition and reversal of oral elements within sentences and within words (the unstable movement of 'b' 'f' 'r' and 's' sounds in passages of which this is a brief example from the opening page of *The Waves:* 'Then she raised her lamp higher and the air seemed to become fibrous and to tear away from the green surface flickering and flaming in red and yellow fibres like the smoky fire that roars from a bonfire. Gradually the fires of the burning fibres were fused into one haze...'). This onomatopoeic emphasis is one means by which she represents the random communities of language, the waves of sound continuing on beyond sense. *The Waves*, in particular, explores various diads: the I/not I; the I/you and the I/we. For, paradoxically, 'we' always recognises separation even while it emphasises congruity. That recognition is epitomised in the line from Cowper's 'The Castaway' which Mr Ramsay obsessionally mutters at intervals throughout *To the Lighthouse:*

We perish each alone.

We/each/all/one: the systole and diastole of human experience is posed upon 'perish' and summarised in 'alone'. Yet only by means of 'the common life which is the real life', as she writes in *A Room of One's Own*, can change be brought about.

In *A Room of One's Own* (1929) she identifies first-person and its written sign 'I' with the phallic oppressiveness of the opinionated male writer, observed by the quizzical and insistent other 'I' of her narrator, who is also 'one'.

> Indeed, it was delightful to read a man's writing again. It was direct, so straightforward after the writing of women. It indicated such freedom of mind, such liberty of person, such confidence in himself. One had a sense of physical well-being in the presence of this well-nourished, well-educated, free mind, which had never been thwarted or opposed, but had had full liberty from birth to stretch itself in whatever way it liked. All this was admirable. But after reading a chapter or two a shadow seemed to lie across the page. It was a straight dark bar, a shadow shaped something like the letter 'I'. One began dodging this way and that to catch a glimpse of the landscape behind it. Whether that was indeed a tree or a woman walking I was not quite sure. Back one was always hailed to the letter 'I'. One began to be tired of 'I'. Not but what this 'I' was a most respectable 'I'; honest and logical; as hard as a nut, and polished for centuries by good teaching and good feeding. I respect and admire that 'I' from the bottom of my heart. But – here I turned a page or two, looking for something or other – the worst of it is that in the shadow of the letter 'I' all is shapeless as mist. Is that a tree? No, it is a woman. But ... she has not a bone in her body, I thought, watching Phoebe, for that was her name, coming across the beach. Then Alan got up and the shadow of Alan at once obliterated Phoebe. (pp. 149–50)

The humour of the passage is in the alternation of the identical first-person to signify two different views: one, the obliterativeness of the letter 'I' in whose shadow 'all is shapeless as mist. Is that a tree? No, it is a woman. But ... she has not a bone in her body'. The upright 'I' fillets the upright figure of Phoebe walking, into a softened receptacle of his own views and passions. The 'I' of the body is lost in the Lawrentian pastiche of passion. Phoebe is a lay-figure caught between the frank and sceptical 'I' of the insistently tart narrator 'But – I am bored!' and the imposing 'I' of the male author. At the end of the

paragraph Woolf asserts that she is describing the self-conscious viril-
ity of the male writer in the face of the women's movement. So the
doubling of the 'I' here and their mutual resistance makes for the
enclosure and limiting of each. But we will better understand the
awkwardness and allure of 'We' for Virginia Woolf if we group
together three works which came out of a single creative movement:
Orlando, *A Room of One's Own* and *The Waves*. First thoughts of *The
Waves* preceded the buoyant writing of *Orlando*, and her preparation
of *A Room of One's Own* accompanied that work. *Orlando* and *The
Waves* are the works in which she most trenchantly surveyed the
relationship between the subject and the self. She imagined *The Waves*
ending, perhaps, with a 'gigantic conversation'.[7]

Virginia Woolf is seeking a written 'I' which can also move out into
'We' and include a serenely and laterally shifting population. For that
she must do away with the insistent phallic 'I' and its blasting properties. She seeks a writing body which will be permeable and expansive:

> A very good summer, this, for all my shying & jibbing, my trem-
> ors this morning. Beautifully quiet, airy, powerful. I believe I
> want this more humane existence for my next – to spread care-
> lessly among one's friends – to feel the width and amusement of
> *human* life: not to strain to make a pattern just yet: to be made
> supple, & to let the juice of usual things, talk, character, seep
> through me, quietly, involuntarily, before I say – Stop & take out
> my pen. Yes, my thoughts now begin to run smooth: no longer is
> every nerve upright.[8]

She enjoys 'supple' and 'seep'; rejects 'strain' and 'upright'. 'We'
includes the body, and Virginia Woolf insisted on closeness to the body as
the primary source of humour and communality. She saw moreover that
creative writers do not write an ideolect in solitude: '*For masterpieces
are not single and solitary births; they are the outcome of many years of
thinking in common, of thinking by the body of the people, so that the
experience of the mass is behind the single voice*'.[9] (emphasis added)

Mrs Dalloway (1925) is the first of her works which moves about
within a community poised in a historical moment, and explores the
mass behind the single voice. Virginia Woolf was fascinated by place,
that condensing of past and present which subtly controls and changes
experience and establishes a common life. In *Mrs Dalloway* she sets
out the topography of London as precisely as does Defoe whom she so
much admired. Social territories are marked out (Lady Burton in
Brook Street, Sarah Bletchley in Pimlico); communal spaces are

lovingly articulated, particularly all the details of Regent's Park. The accounts of walks and of districts register the characters' social space as well as their separations. Elizabeth Dalloway 'looked up Fleet Street' and explores its sociogeography as if it were a strange house in which she was a shy visitor.

> She looked up Fleet Street. She walked just a little way towards St. Paul's shyly, like someone penetrating on tiptoe, exploring a strange house by night with a candle, on edge lest the owner should suddenly fling wide his bedroom door and ask her business, nor did she dare wander off into queer alleys, tempting by-streets, any more than in a strange house open doors which might be bedroom doors, or sitting-room doors, or lead straight to the larder. For no Dalloways came down the Strand daily; she was a pioneer, a stray, venturing, trusting.[10]

Alone of the characters, Septimus haunts an absolute world, bare of locality except for the dead places of the war.

The people in the book are inhabitants of the same city on the same day. They lightly bear the weight of a common past sealed in statues, buildings, roadways, and stored in the memories each privately preserves as they walk those open ways. The immediate trauma that unites them is that of the First World War, which for Virginia Woolf is also the deep historical separator, functioning as the line down the middle of the picture, represented also in the 'Time Passes' section of *To the Lighthouse* (which occupies the war years), and as the voiding topic of *Jacob's Room*. Septimus Smith endlessly and nihilistically recalls his lost experience of the war. But as we read, that experience is not confined to Septimus alone; it spreads *through our reading* into the whole community described.

The reader becomes the medium of connection, partly through our assumed familiarity with these same places and history, partly through the lateral entwining of the narrative and its easy recourse to the personal pasts of memory, the communal past of an imagined prehistory. Woolf uses several means of representing those impersonal intimacies of juxtaposition and association which usually go unrecorded. The closed car and the aeroplane are seen by the various figures in the book. More subtle and more mysterious are the two old women, of whom one, singing beside Regent's Park tube station, takes us back past language to a semiological cradle-land surviving into the present.[11]

Class and even gender may prove ultimately in her work to be ephemeral distinguishers. Nevertheless, alongside the emphasis on the common conditions of life, in *Mrs Dalloway* the two selves of gender are parted. Our response as practised readers is to recognise Septimus Smith and Clarissa Dalloway as the centres of intensity in the book's life, the 'major characters'. The shadow-plots derived from reading earlier fiction lead us to expect connection between them at the level of event. We are disturbed instead by slightness and separation, the connections being formed solely at the level of reading-process and, at the end, in Clarissa's musing consciousness of discrete lives. The contacts between Septimus and Clarissa are oblique and communal. They (like other inhabitants) share the day with the closed car, the commercial aeroplane. They share no personal history; they never meet, never have met. They belong to different social classes, have scarcely read the same books, but they are deeply embedded in common history – the recent past of the war, the longer past of English social stratification, the continuing presence of changing London.

Moreover Clarissa and Septimus are 'as one' in the book's imagination, standing in for each other in the reader's attention. We look for a contingent meeting, perhaps even for a rescue which never takes place. Clarissa cares about her roses not about the Armenians; Septimus about his revelation. Septimus knows nothing of Clarissa. Clarissa reaches out to make a one-way connection in her mind between his fate and hers, as she does also between herself and the woman in the room opposite. She feels his death in her body:

> He had killed himself – but how? Always her body went through it, when she was told, first, suddenly, of an accident; her dress flamed, her body burnt. He had thrown himself from a window. Up had flashed the ground; through him, blundering, bruising, went the rusty spikes. There he lay with a thud, thud, thud in his brain, and then a suffocation of blackness.

His death momentarily allows her absolute intimacy, which everywhere else eludes her: 'closeness drew apart; rapture faded; one was alone. There was an embrace in death'. The language is that of sexuality: Clarissa in fantasy feels the 'rusty spikes' invade her body as they had done Septimus. But the brief sentences succeed each other without lubricious dwelling on the event. Immediately afterwards she acknowledges her separateness, which now feels to her like a punishment:

> Somehow it was her disaster – her disgrace. It was her punishment to see sink and disappear here a man, there a woman, in this profound darkness, and she forced to stand here in her

evening dress. She had schemed; she had pilfered. She was never wholly admirable. (pp. 202–3)

This sense of desolate privilege is assuaged within the space of a page; at last the old lady in the room opposite, whom she had long observed, seems also to observe her: 'She parted the curtains; she looked. Oh, but how surprising! – in the room opposite the old lady stared straight at her! She was going to bed'. Even then it remains uncertain whether the other woman sees Clarissa.

By a magical transposition of persons that narrative can effect, Clarissa's hope of exchange and intimacy substitutes the old lady for Septimus in our experience as readers. But at the level of event Clarissa receives no recognition from Septimus; she simply claims him as her double, the enactor of her shadow-life and preserver of her and his unnamed treasure: 'A thing there was that mattered; a thing, wreathed about with chatter, defaced, obscured in her own life, let drop every day in corruption, lies, chatter. This he had preserved'.

The reader is likely, first, to feel affronted at her claim: much worse has happened to Septimus than to Clarissa. And who is she, society hostess, to claim the life of a shell-shocked, lower-middle-class person, to perceive his experience as somehow her own? The activity of the novel, however, sustains her claim, calmly receives our outrage and leads us to recognise some of its sources in stereotype. Kinship cannot be measured by event, by class, or even by gender, it seems. Separation may even be the condition for recognising kin. The two old women of the book are separate too, though they link London together; one privately goes on with her silent life in her solitary room, the other, open and derelict, sings a song which burrows beneath language and difference:

> ee um fah um so
> foo swee too eem oo.

'London has swallowed up many millions of young men called Smith' (p. 94): Septimus happens to be the recorded one among them. He and Mrs Dalloway are no mystic pair, but their poignantly repeated coldness allows Woolf in this novel to take the measure of a whole society in its historical moment.

The unforced likenesses between our reading experience of both characters reveals what is hidden far down beneath social event, personal relationship and individuality: the failure of feeling, and the fear of failing to feel, which marks the community of her time and writing.

That fear is registered in the process of thought which is Peter Walsh and Miss Kilman also. The novel creates the sense of an *atomistic gathering* through its piquant vignettes of people, its record of pathways; it has less recourse to the sustained analysis of established relationships. The work finds unity at a level other than that of discredited action, other even than analytical language. It gathers in upon the party-giving solitary, Clarissa Dalloway; and she has become, for a little while, also Septimus Smith and the unnamed beyond him: 'There she was'.

Orlando and *The Waves*, the books at the centre of Woolf's career, are, on the face of it, those most preoccupied with the self. One thing that sets them apart from the rest of her work is the absence of World War I from their pages: from *Jacob's Room* through to *To the Lighthouse* the war shapes, splits, and penetrates the works.[12] In *Orlando* it vanishes; in *The Waves*, despite its ruminating on imperialism and the city, the characters inhabit a world in which all that is traditionally central to narrative has been peripheralised or obliterated: Percival's adventures in India, Bernard's family, Louis' city career, Jinny's lovers, even the crisis of Rhoda's madness and the love affair between her and Louis are present only as fragmentary allusion. The characters inhabit a world devoid of close historical markers, though in a recognisable present day. The other work which forms a single creative flow with *The Waves* and *Orlando* is *A Room of One's Own*. Their composition weaves in and out of each other; but they are quite different, one from the other, each seeking to capture what has not been fully marked elsewhere.

Virginia Woolf much enjoyed biography and autobiography, even while she distrusted their evidences and their determinism. She distrusted the iconoclasm then in fashion in the biographical work of Lytton Strachey and liked autobiography because 'Almost always this comes from autobiography: a liking, at least some imaginative stir'.[13] In her essay on Christina Rossetti she remarked:

> As everybody knows, the fascination of reading biographies is irresistible. ... Here is the past and all its inhabitants miraculously sealed as in a magic tank; all we have to do is to look and to listen and to listen and to look and soon the little figures – for they are rather under life size – will begin to move and to speak, and as they move we shall arrange them in all sorts of patterns of which they were ignorant, for they thought when they were alive that they could go where they liked; and as they speak we shall

read into their sayings all kinds of meanings which never struck
them, for they believed when they were alive that they said
straight off whatever came into their heads. But once you are in a
biography all is different.[14]

The knowing biographer is on a par with the realist novelist in her
judgement: both claim an authority which stifles their awareness of life.

How to write lives became for Virginia Woolf a more inclusive
question: how to write life. In *To the Lighthouse* she had rewritten her
own family history, making of it something other than a 'historical'
record. At this period she became increasingly preoccupied with the
levels at which it is possible to describe life-process, and with the
exclusion of women from records which preoccupy themselves with
careers and historical triumphs and defeats.[15] She began the exploration novelistically in the twinned figures of Mr and Mrs Ramsay – he
so anxious for the survival of his fame: she so concerned for the
immediate – and for the survival of her children. How far are they at
odds? How much of human longing is wrapt into the longing for
survival?

In *Orlando* she elongated the arc of the individual's survival through
time; Orlando is not only continuously alive through many historical
periods; he never ages, she never ages, beyond thriving maturity. The
reader is jestingly made aware of how much we believe our reading.
Reading lets us live, apparently, through swathes of history. It allows
us, without danger, to take part in past tumult. We sleep it off, like
Orlando, and discover a new place, a new book, next day. In *Orlando*,
Woolf doubles our reading pleasure by making us aware of the gaps
between reading and living and also of how readily we confuse them.
In reading we readily shift gender – until the activity is pointed out to
us and then it seems strange. When Orlando with much hyperbolic
preamble becomes a woman, men and women readers equally are
made conscious of a constraint. The writing assumes that we will need
to change our relation to Orlando and yet points to the absurdity of
doing so, since we made no bones about participating in his earlier
adventures, whether reading with men's or women's eyes.[16]

Orlando rests on the surface of the ages she inhabits, teased by the
desire to write allayed by great possessions, experiencing as man and
woman without guilt or Tiresian pangs. The hedonistic ease with
which Orlando keeps just within the constraints of each society, and,
when she cannot do so, moves out or moves on is a tribute to Victoria
Sackville-West, the 'biographical' inspiration for the work. Its

lightheartedness is artfully to represent most things as possible. Its undertow of feeling is to remind us that, *au contraire*, in life, very many things are not. *Orlando* mitigates but also repeats the sad story of Shakespeare's sister which Woolf imagined, at about this same time, in *A Room of One's Own*. In *Orlando* the single self breasts the waves of society – moving at times almost without effort through the subsequences of event.

The triumph of the work is to offer epitomes not of Orlando him/herself, who soon becomes somewhat boring to the reader – transparent and foreknown – but rather of the societies s/he enters. History as Virginia Woolf tells it, becomes a form of biography: a biography of the land and sky as much as of the individuals who pass across its surface.

Orlando is a tale of the upper classes, of the inertia of the landed as much as the continuance of the land. It is in the vein of dream-work in which the reader, like the dreamer, identifies with royalty and has the freedom of strange lands. Wish-fulfilment here makes us turn our gaze back upon the wishes fulfilled and understand the impossibility of those wishes. The apparent entry which biography offers into another's life is, Virginia Woolf suggests, more often a self-gratifying spectatorship which diminishes the life observed. In *Orlando* she delights in breaking across the reader's expectations. Her work elsewhere, even in dialogue, does not much insist on the spoken voice, but here the clear tones of the assured narrative discourse mock the biographer's enterprise, the reader's choices, and the assumptions both writer and reader bring to the making of a life. By means of biography she explores the written and the bodily self, the self of biographer, reader, and subject. *Orlando* has at the centre of its discourse the body: Orlando's shifting sexual form, certainly, but also temperature, the heat and cold with which we most familiarly and with our whole body gauge the world. The Elizabethan age is characterised by hyperbolical weather:

> The age was the Elizabethan; their morals were not ours; nor their poets; nor their climate; nor their vegetables even. Everything was different. The weather itself, the heat and cold of summer and winter, was, we may believe, of another temper altogether. The brilliant amorous day was divided as sheerly from the night as land from water. Sunsets were redder and more intense; dawns were whiter and more auroral. Of our crepuscular half-lights and lingering twilights they knew nothing. The rain fell vehemently, or not at all. The sun blazed or there was darkness.[17]

Orlando survives, not in Tiresian disenchantment, but brilliantly engaged with the sensory world, even at the final collapse of her ancestral home merely into language. 'The gallery and all its occupants fell to powder. ... Her own body quivered and tingled as if suddenly naked in a hard frost'. Touch, most direct of contacts, breaks the sealed space between reader and subject. But the body is central to this book as humour, not earnestness: Virginia Woolf's riposte to the literary doggedness about 'natural desire' which she mocked in *A Room of One's Own* is to flaunt both language and body as joke.

> Hail! natural desire! Hail! happiness! divine happiness! and pleasure of all sorts, flowers and wine, though one fades and the other intoxicates; and half-crown tickets out of London on Sundays, and singing in a dark chapel hymns about death, and anything, anything that interrupts and confounds the tapping of typewriters and filing of letters and forging of links and chains, binding the Empire together. Hail even the crude, red bows on shop girls' lips (as if Cupid, very clumsily, dipped his thumb in red ink and scrawled a token in passing). Hail, happiness! kingfisher flashing from bank to bank, and all fulfilment of natural desire, whether it is what the male novelist says it is; or prayer; or denial; hail! in whatever form it comes, and may there be more forms, and stranger.[18]

The stereotypes of happiness are here jumbled together with the uncelebrated (but instantly recognisable) joys of 'singing in a dark chapel hymns about death'. The curious forms of happiness are less circumscribed than realism or lyricism would have us believe. This book mixes the pleasures of the impossible, 'It's a very fine boy M'Lady' said Mrs Banting, the mid-wife, 'putting her first-born child into Orlando's arms' with hyperbolic double-entendre:

> It was no longer so thick, so watery, so prismatic now that King Edward – see, there he was, stepping out of his neat brougham to go and visit a certain lady opposite – had succeeded Queen Victoria. The clouds had shrunk to a thin gauze; the sky seemed made of metal, which in hot weather tarnished verdigris, copper colour or orange as metal does in a fog. It was a little alarming – this shrinkage. Everything seemed to have shrunk. Driving past Buckingham Palace last night, there was not a trace of that vast erection which she had thought everlasting; top hats, widows' weeds, trumpets, telescopes, wreaths, all had vanished and left not a stain, not a puddle even, on the pavement.[19]

The inordinate fecundity of the Victorian age with its ponderous and imposing imperialist fertility leaves 'not a stain' from its vast erection.

Virginia Woolf wrote in *The Pargiters* of her difficulty in writing about her body, but in *Orlando* she freely moves across the inhabited and the imagined body in a way that challenges gender. Where do we live in our bodies? Can we give or take a few genitalia and remain ourselves, our desires not altered, our will hampered maybe, but the same? In *Orlando* the central self endures the vicissitudes of translation – through time, through gender, through changing language – not itself much changed. Primary allegiances (to 'The Oak Tree', to Sasha) are unmoved. The form of desire is peremptorily inscribed at the start.

In 1929 in Marshall and Snelgrove, Orlando smells a scent which 'curved like a shell around a figure' – and there she is, momentarily back again in Elizabethan England with Sasha. For, the narrator suggests, not only have we each many selves but many simultaneous times within us. Each human being is a full, fleeting history, incommunicable because made not out of public events but from sense-recall and private images. Yet this singularity is composed out of the shared materials of a community in time. How to discover the communal in this singularity is the poet's and, her work suggests, should be the fiction writer's task. In *Orlando* she offers us a sensory history of England: the size of the clouds, the smells, the differing intensity of colours, the weather and the natural growths. By this means she suggests the presence of the individual living in the body. In *Orlando* the two selves of gender alternate and oscillate: in comedy difference can be expressed as collision and joke.

Death is necessary to the economy of all Virginia Woolf's other novels. That is what makes *Orlando* remarkable: it is a jest in the face of death. The seamlessly en-gendered do not die. Death, it seems, finds its way in, at least in fantasy, by the separation of male and female. Orlando skirts death by changing dress. The force of the comedy here suggests anxiety. The biography of *Orlando* meditates on death by emphasising its absurd absence from the text: in this novel it is not the absence and death of a person (Jacob, Mrs Ramsay, Percival) which charges the narrative but the absence of death itself. 'Biography' – the writing of a life – is the form which ordinarily takes death for granted. At the beginning of *Orlando*, only, death is present in an appearance of life. The figure of the bumboat woman, sealed in ice as if in amber, locked beneath the fires burning on the frozen Thames, is a cruel and perfect reminder of the oppressions and extremes on which art builds.

Near London Bridge, where the river had frozen to a depth of some twenty fathoms, a wrecked wherry boat was plainly visible, lying on the bed of the river where it had sunk last autumn, overladen with apples. The old bumboat woman, who was carrying her fruit to market on the Surrey side, sat there in her plaids and farthingales with her lap full of apples, for all the world as if she were about to serve a customer, though a certain blueness about the lips hinted the truth. 'Twas a sight King James specially liked to look upon, and he would bring a troupe of courtiers to gaze with him. In short, nothing could exceed the brilliancy and gaiety of the scene by day. But it was at night that the carnival was at its merriest. For the frost continued unbroken; the nights were of perfect stillness; the moon and stars blazed with the hard fixity of diamonds, and to the fine music of flute and trumpet the courtiers danced.[20]

The poor provide a spectacle for the rich, the dead for the living. The book then uses this image of death as a punctuation mark, a sealed image of life-in-death and death-in-life from which to start its fugue. The narrative flight of this early episode is never quite fully matched again: the frozen Thames, the sumptuous fires and dances and furs, stark contraries which both represent the vigour of Elizabethan language and satisfy contrary needs in artist and reader: stability and flux. The episode ends with the stability of the ice (which provokes life and rapture) giving way to the death-dealing flow of the river. Time like an ever-rolling stream bears away the many: only Orlando and her faithful retinue back home survive to the end of fictional time. The imperious self cannot credit its own death and in this book it is comforted. Orlando is still there at the book's conclusion, in a thinner atmosphere.

If Orlando seems to have run out of steam at the end, that can be taken as the problem of making the present real on paper. The past is realised most fully in language. The present exists as body and as a semiological mass so current that our acts of interpretation are barely conscious. The past enlists consciousness: we recognise it as we do not do the present: the signs have been sorted, the cards dealt, the patterns established. The self may be known by others in the present, by ourselves in the past; that is the insight Woolf retrieves again in *Between the Acts*.

That is part of the explanation of why history is important to her. But there is another reason. The self is always insufficient. In *A Room of One's Own* she speaks of the communal self as a more enduring mode:

> For my belief is that if we [women] live another century or so – I am talking of the common life which is the real life and not of the little separate lives which we live as individuals –[21]

In her diary at around the same time she queried:

> Now is life very solid or very shifting? I am haunted by the two contradictions. This has gone on for ever; will last for ever; goes down to the bottom of the world – this moment I stand on. Also it is transitory, flying, diaphanous. I shall pass like a cloud on the waves. Perhaps it may be that though we change, one flying after another, so quick so quick, yet we are somehow successive, & continuous we human beings; & show the light through. But what is the light?[22]

In *Orlando* the male principle turns out to be less different from the female than it is portentously claimed to be. The whimsically unsexed biographer of Orlando discovers him and her not much changed by shifts in gender, though she experiences the constraints imposed on her sex. He is defined more by his class than his sex, it turns out. Incorrigibly an aristocrat with the confidence, blindness, and class-mobility flatteringly and traditionally ascribed to his clan, he can be ambassador, gypsy, blue-stocking and traveller. Orlando's male free-dom is *class* freedom and so is Orlando's female freedom. Orlando is privileged with wealth, beauty, androgyneity, and immortality. In such conditions differences of opportunity between men and women diminish, but they do not vanish. The aristocratic woman becomes for Virginia Woolf a necessary and comic symbol of the power to claim.

Orlando is exterior: the adamant central person is surveyed through-out in biographical third-person. The joke is on the ungendered biographer who seeks to plumb the depths of personality but finds the pen skimming on the surface. *The Waves* was to be her submarine adventure, a 'mystical eyeless book' in which the 'eye' and 'I' is multiplied and dissolved, written from within instead of from without. She began by thinking of the work as the multiple autobiography of a woman,[23] though that conception became less important as the writing advanced.

She had first imagined that roll beneath the waves through a true episode which she fictionalises in her diary in a way which is both menacing and farcical. Flight fascinated her. As always, in her work, humour has an undertow of the death of the body, a conjunction of human rigidity and human dissolution which she found artistically irresistibly comic and touching. The flying Princess seems like a haunting other imagination for her own fears of flying too high, as well as being a savage pastiche of aristocratic claims to dominance.

> The Flying Princess, I forget her name, has been drowned in her purple leather breeches. I suppose so at least. Their petrol gave out about midnight on Thursday, when the aeroplane must have come gently down upon the long slow Atlantic waves. I suppose they burnt a light which showed streaky on the water for a time. Where they rested a moment or two. The pilots, I think, looked back at the broad cheeked desperate eyed vulgar princess in her purple breeches & I suppose made some desperate dry statement – how the game was up: sorry; fortune against them; & she just glared; & then a wave broke over the wing; & the machine tipped. And she said something theatrical I daresay; nobody was sincere; all acted a part; nobody shrieked; Luck against us – something of that kind, they said, and then So long, and first one man was washed off & went under, then a great wave came & the Princess threw up her arms & went down; & the third man sat saved for a second looking at the rolling waves, so patient so implacable & the moon gravely regarding; & then with a dry snorting sound he too was tumbled off & rolled over, & the aeroplane rocked & rolled – miles from anywhere, off Newfoundland, while I slept at Rodmell, & Leonard was dining with the Craniums in London.[24]

The plane is lost; the bodies vanished; disappeared over the Atlantic without trace. With eerie glee Woolf pictures the scene: the absurdly small and proper statements; the cross-dressed princess in her purple breeches tumbling beneath the waves. The glassy calm of the pictured scene works as a disturbance in her mind which keeps drawing her awkwardly towards it, until at last writing it makes its hallucinating reality ebb and begin to be forgotten. The grandiose flight becomes absurd because failed. The mocked and admired figure of the Princess gives Woolf a means of trying out assertion, and vanishing, and submerging. The comic tone is disquieting but necessary: it provides a means of simultaneously letting go and holding on. As she writes *Orlando* she muses on her loss of the desire to have children.

> This insatiable desire to write something before I died, this ravaging sense of the shortness and feverishness of life, make me cling, *like a man on a rock, to my one anchor*. I don't like the

physicalness of having children of one's own. This occurred to me at Rodmell; but I never wrote it down. I can dramatise myself as a parent, it is true. And perhaps I have killed the feeling instinctively; as perhaps nature does.[25] (emphasis added)

In *The Waves* she lets herself roll under, no longer clinging 'like a man on a rock' to her 'one anchor', but fanning out into the manifold. She represents in Susan the desire for children, the having of natural happiness, and the ebbing of its fullness; she dramatises in Rhoda the fear of embraces, and it is to Bernard that she gives her own 'Fin, in a waste of waters' (p. 307) – the significant vision of the long summer of 1928 which she believed no biographer could retrieve. In retrospect we have a strong sense of the individual identities of her people in *The Waves*, even to the point of caricature. Their sinuously overlapping thoughts and images, however, emphasise the easy abrasions and floatings apart which occur in community. Waves are all the universe contains. The permeable human transmits and is composed by them. Towards the end of the book the separation between the various characters gives way and instead of a 'conversation', with which she first thought of ending, we have Bernard's inclusive monologue.

In *Orlando* the comedy is the immovability of the self as well as its dexterity. Beneath multiplicity there is a remarkable self-conformity: two thousand and fifty-two selves, the narrative reports, may have 'lodgment at one time or another in the human spirit'. The novel enjoys both the vacillations and the integrity of simple Orlando. Towards the end of the work the biographer blithely mulls over the order of selves and the excluding function of the conscious:

> these selves of which we are built up, one on top of another, as plates are piled on a waiter's hand, have attachments elsewhere, sympathies, little constitutions and rights of their own, call them what you will (and for many of these things there is no name) so that one will only come if it is raining, another in a room with green curtains, another when Mrs Jones is not there, another if you can promise it a glass of wine – and so on; for everybody can multiply from his own experience the different terms which his different selves have made with him – and some are too wildly ridiculous to be mentioned in print at all, 'the one she needed most kept aloof' ... 'as happens when, for some unaccountable reason, the conscious self, which is the uppermost, and has the power to desire, wishes to be nothing but one self'.[26]

In this fictional order, where the overweening self is king and queen, the whole community, even the shared discourse of the period, become figments of an organising singleness. In *The Waves*, on the contrary, we enter the iridescent play of communal selves. The spry zest of *Orlando's* language gives way to ruminativeness.

The Waves punctuates its multiple first-person form with sparse speech tags which become rarer as the book grows. 'Said Rhoda', 'said Neville': once the figures and their concerns are established even such interjections occur only every few pages. Virginia Woolf said that she wanted in *The Waves* to follow a rhythm not a plot: that rhythm is figured in the pressure of the waves moving beneath the surface of the sea, humping themselves momentarily at the shore to break in foam. The pattern can express both long continuity and ephemerality, the single and the common life. At death the waves of the individual break and are drawn back into the sea of shared memory, memory which then itself is loosed and scattered but never entirely lost, since the body of waters remains. That is the seismic level of the metaphor. The lengthening meditations of the people in the book, pitched beneath the level of speech, follow the same pulse.

Rhythmic organisation is far less referential than that of plot and may be seen as part of the movement towards impersonality in her work.[27] This impersonality does not imply a lack of concern with persons, but a dissipation of the intense analysis of developing individual relationships which had been the material of the English novel, and of her own early work in *The Voyage Out*. In *The Waves* characters speak with a liturgical separation, facing inward to the altar of the self or outward to the reader, but never in dialogue – though occasionally antiphonally ordered.

The absence of dialogue takes the reader deep into the submarine intimacy of the book's address. No one answers the diverse meditations, though they may hear and share. By this means Woolf forthwith moves outside binary oppositions. Instead of the two selves of gender, she creates a spectrum: six persons, three male, three female. They are separable, even highly distinctive, but 'at one', atoning for some irreparable loss which at once scatters and yet keeps life (the novel) going. They all lean towards the presence or memory of the lost hero: the unknowing, the clumsy and unreflective Percival who like his namesake Parsifal never asks questions at the right time. He goes, he performs, he plays cricket and rides, he sets out for imperial India and dies there in a fall from his horse.

'Now,' said Neville, 'my tree flowers. My heart rises. All oppression is relieved. All impediment is removed. The reign of chaos is over. He has imposed order. Knives cut again'.

'Here is Percival,' said Jinny. 'He has not dressed'.

'Here is Percival,' said Bernard, 'smoothing his hair, not from vanity (he does not look in the glass), but to propitiate the god of decency. He is conventional; he is a hero. The little boys trooped after him across the playing-fields. They blew their noses as he blew his nose, but unsuccessfully, for he is Percival. Now, when he is about to leave us, to go to India, all these trifles come together. He is a hero. Oh, yes, that is not to be denied, and when he takes his seat by Susan, whom he loves, the occasion is crowned,'[28]

Percival is the principle of death as well as of immediate living. He is the seventh, 'Septimus', who converted the six into a magical prime number and continues to make possible the seven-branched candelabra of friendship after his death. He is the male principle, idolised – and dead. He is given no discourse of his own. We know him only through the musings of others. The characters within the work are questioners, meditating on all they see and feel, suffering their insufficiencies and reaching out (save Rhoda) to other needed life. Percival represents the old narrative order. His story is simple: he is the young hero who goes out to the furthest reaches of his country's empire, though he finds not a grail but a grave. His fall is the stable ground on which the novel and the intermittent community of the six is built, the gravity that draws all together. With the death of classical narrative the book can become both an elegy and a release: a play-poem, in all senses. The death of Percival is the sole narrative event which we are allowed to record at its traditional scale. His death is the condition of the freedom to explore other kinds of 'I', permeable and transitive.

Although *The Waves* has many passages, particularly in the early part of the book, which are humorous, it has always been discussed in profoundly serious terms – and is referred to so by Virginia Woolf herself: a mystical eyeless book. Having no 'eyes' and multiple 'I's, the reader loses a steady quizzical distance.

Yet there is, though in a different mood, play in *The Waves* as much as in *Orlando*. The play of movement, the endless conjoining and dissipation of sea forms, is the rhythm of the characters' overlapping languages. As has often been observed, they have access to each other's thoughts and symbolic systems.[29] Woolf reconceives the act of writing fiction, not as novel but as play-poem, in which the silent voice upon the page allows consciousness to articulate itself with a clarity and panache rarely achieved in speech. Unchastened by the constraints of society, or of reply, the voices assert their presences with all the cadences of speech, so far as syntax can represent them, but without tone, sound or utterance. So they live alongside, dipping into each other's lore, assembling symbols from a common wealth, but always allowed their own full say.

The book points one speech against another and in the earlier parts of the work uses speech-tags to retard or disturb the sense of what is said. Read aloud, the humour of *The Waves* becomes manifest, as the gradings of voice point the distinctions between people and emphasise their inventiveness. But, enjoyable as such reading is, it does away with an important level of the work: its silencing of voice. We enter these speaking minds without satire, so close-in that judgments are never more than half-formed. Humour is there even in silent reading, of course, since humour is the form which makes room for identification and canniness at once. We experience incongruity as pleasure: Neville, even as a child, holds things apart and mocks the inclination to lyricism which is intrinsic to Woolf's work: 'I hate dangling things. I hate dampish things. I hate wandering and mixing things together'. The unwritten common life is essential to humour; it creates and delineates community. The shift from person to person within this books jogs our allegiance and our attention so that the multiple first-person controls our continued immersion in any single character. The movement of such humour can only be shown in a longer quotation:

> 'There is about both Neville and Louis a precision, an exactitude that I admire and shall never possess. Now I begin to be aware that action is demanded. We approach a junction; at a junction I have to change. I have to board a train for Edinburgh. I cannot precisely lay fingers on this fact – it lodges loosely among my thoughts like a button, like a small coin. Here is the jolly old boy who collects tickets. I had one – I had one certainly. But it does not matter. Either I shall find it, or I shall not find it. I examine my notecase. I look in all my pockets. These are the things that for ever interrupt the process upon which I am eternally engaged of finding some perfect phrase that fits this very moment exactly.
>
> 'Bernard has gone,' said Neville, 'without a ticket. He has escaped us, making a phrase, waving his hand. He talked as easily to the horse-breeder or to the plumber as to us. The plumber

accepted him with devotion. "If he had a son like that," he was thinking, "he would manage to send him to Oxford." But what did Bernard feel for the plumber? Did he not only wish to continue the sequence of the story which he never stops telling himself? He began it when he rolled his bread into pellets as a child. One pellet was a man, one was a woman. We are all pellets. We are all phrases in Bernard's story, things he writes down in his notebook under A or under B. He tells our story with extraordinary understanding, except of what we most feel. For he does not need us. He is never at our mercy. There he is, waving his arms on the platform. 'The train has gone without him. He has missed his connection. He has lost his ticket. But that does not matter. He will talk to the barmaid about the nature of human destiny. We are off; he has forgotten us already; we pass out of his view; we go on, filled with lingering sensations, half bitter, half sweet, for he is somehow to be pitied breasting the world with half-finished phrases, having lost his ticket; he is also to be loved'.[30]

Part of the pleasure of this passage is that Bernard, unnoticing, does achieve the perfect phrase for a mind-sensation that I have never seen described elsewhere: the impending knowledge that one must change trains which 'lodges loosely among my thoughts like a button, like a small coin'. Another pleasure is the speed and lucidity with which feelings and judgements shift: 'He tells our story with extraordinary understanding, except of what we most feel. For he does not need us. He is never at our mercy'. ... 'he is somehow to be pitied breasting the world with half-finished phrases, having lost his ticket; he is also to be loved'. The background of slapstick – the lost ticket, the missed train, the satisfying talk with the barmaid – is held quietly, though without austerity, at a level with all the other elements in Neville's musings.

This declarative discourse allows Woolf to include more and more, without crisis. She makes us acutely aware from time to time of the mass of unknown others among whom her named people move. Neville again: arriving at a mainline station in London:

What extraordinary adventure waits with me, among these mail vans, these porters, these swarms of people calling taxis? I feel insignificant, lost, but exultant. With a soft shock we stop. I will let the others get out before me. I will sit still one moment before I emerge into that chaos, that tumult. I will not anticipate what is to come. The huge uproar is in my ears. It sounds and resounds under this glass roof like the surge of a sea.

Jinny's exuberant story-making and speeding up of millions:

> 'Thus, in a few seconds, deftly, adroitly, we decipher the hieroglyphs written on other people's faces. Here, in this room, are the abraded and battered shells cast on the shore. The door goes on opening. The room fills and fills with knowledge, an-guish, many kinds of ambition, much indifference, some despair. In one way or another we make this day, this Friday, some by going to the Law Courts; others to the city; others to the nursery; others by marching and forming fours. A million hands stitch, raise hods with bricks. The activity is endless. And tomorrow it begins again; tomorrow we make Saturday. Some take train for France; others ship for India. Some will never come into this room again. One may die tonight. Another will beget a child. From us every sort of building, policy, venture, picture, poem, child, factory, will spring. Life comes; life goes; we make life. So you say.
>
> 'But we who live in the body see with the body's imagination things in outline. I see rocks in bright sunshine ... I must jump up and go ... I drop all these facts-diamonds, withered hands, china pots and the rest of it, as a monkey drops nuts from its naked paws'.[31]

Rhoda's horror at crowds takes over Bernard's 'pellets' and Jinny's 'monkey paws' and degrades them:

> 'Life, how I have dreaded you', said Rhoda, 'oh, human beings, how I have hated you! How you have nudged, how you have interrupted, how hideous you have looked in Oxford Street, how squalid sitting opposite each other staring in the Tube! Now as I climb this mountain, from the top of which I shall see Africa, my mind is printed with brown-paper parcels and your faces. I have been stained by you and corrupted. You smelt so unpleasant, too, lining up outside doors to buy tickets. All were dressed in inde-terminate shades of grey and brown, never even a blue feather pinned to a hat. None had the courage to be one thing rather than another. What dissolution of the soul you demanded in order to get through one day, what lies, bowings, scrapings, fluency and servility! How you chained me to one spot, one hour, one chair, and sat yourselves down opposite! How you snatched from me the white spaces that lie between hour and hour and rolled them into dirty pellets and tossed them into the wastepaper basket with your greasy paws. Yet those were my life'.[32]

To Bernard, 'general life' is the pre-language which he seeks and can never fully find, beset as he is with phrase-making. The image he uses for the satisfied loss of individuality is that of the baby replete: 'Having dropped off satisfied like a child from the breast, I am at liberty now to sink down, deep into what passes, this omni-present general life' (p. 122).

In *The Waves* repetition delineates personality, as in Louis's allusive closeness to T. S. Eliot's language of *The Waste Land:* 'I have read my poet in an eating-house, and, stirring my coffee, listened to the clerks making bets at little tables, watched the women hesitating at the counter. I said that nothing should be irrelevant, like a piece of brown paper dropped casually on the floor'.[33] Repetition also generates the relations of body to world. Certain obsessional cries persist: Rhoda's flowers: 'I made of them a garland and gave them – Oh, to whom?' Neville's 'Come closer, closer'. Words cling to particular people, 'blistered' to Louis, 'pear-shaped eyes' to Susan. The key relation of body to world is different for each person: Louis, later to be her lover, says of Rhoda: 'She has no body as the others have'; Susan, who will seek the 'natural happiness' of the farm and childbearing (and weary of it) observes an adult sexual encounter while the maid hangs out washing. The night-gowns are 'blown tight'; Ernest's mouth is 'sucked like a purse in wrinkles' and 'the pyjamas are blown out tight between them ... the urn roars as Ernest roared, and I blown out hard like the pyjamas'.[34]

Bernard, a child in the bath, feels the water from the sponge run down on him; knowing his body makes language simultaneously a primary pleasure to him:

> Water pours down the runnel of my spine. Bright arrows of sensation shoot on either side. I am covered with warm flesh. My dry crannies are wetted; my cold body is warmed; it is sluiced and gleaming. Water descends and sheets me like an eel. Now hot towels envelop me, and their roughness, as I rub my back, makes my blood purr ...[35]

At the end of the book, in the long meditation which replaced the 'conversation' she first expected to end with, Bernard feels the same physical well-being, like a loved gross animal within him:

> There is the brute, too, the savage, the hairy man who dabbles his fingers in ropes of entrails; and gobbles and belches; whose speech is guttural, visceral – well, he is here. He squats in me. Tonight he has been feasted on quails, salad, and sweetbread. He

now holds a glass of fine old brandy in his paw. He brindles, purrs, and shoots warm thrills all down my spine as I sip. It is true, he washes his hands before dinner, but they are still hairy. He buttons on trousers and waistcoats, but they contain the same organs. He jibs if I keep him waiting for dinner. He mops and mows perpetually pointing with his half-idiot gestures of greed and covetousness at what he desires. I assure you, I have great difficulty sometimes in controlling him. That man, the hairy, the ape-like, has contributed his part to my life. He has given a greener glow to green things, has held his torch with its red flames, its thick and smarting smoke, behind every leaf. He has lit up the cool garden even. He has brandished his torch in murky by-streets where girls suddenly seem to shine with a red and intoxicating translucency. Oh, he has tossed his torch high! He has led me wild dances![36]

That 'guttural, visceral' inner voice humorously represents the bodily community which is also the unreachable ideal language that Bernard always seeks. Such language is beyond or prior to words, 'a little language such as lovers use'; 'a bark, a groan'; 'a painful, guttural, visceral, also soaring, lark-like, pealing song to replace these flagging foolish transcripts – how much too deliberate! how much too reasonable' (p. 273).

Bernard seeks the deep stream: 'a rushing stream of broken dreams, nursery rhymes, street cries, half-finished sentences and sights – elm trees, willow trees, gardeners sweeping, women writing' (pp. 280–1). Bernard knows 'a howl, a cry'; at the end he has 'done with phrases'.

This communal world of the unrecorded – people, parts, cries – is the new writing world of the body, a world which can be represented only by language that is at once silenced and auditory, placing much emphasis on analogous elements. In *The Waves* Woolf explores a new form of communality and impersonality. Words and thoughts in this work move freely between people; sexual images are not reserved in mind to men or women only. Bernard is the man writing women's writing written by the woman writer; Jinny's 'senses stand erect' (p. 298); both pillar and pool are Rhoda's images; Susan's body is a tool: 'The blade is clean, sharp, worn in the centre'. Though each person lives within a separate configuration, gender and personal history converge only evanescently in individuality. Like the waves, the person and people come together, then sink 'into one of those silences which are now and again broken by a few words, as if a fin rose in the wastes of silence' (p. 299). The pressure of 'I' and 'We' have here formed a work at standing water, without tides. *The Waves* is dense on the page, intensely verbal and articulate, but it searches endlessly, through its rhythms of recounting, for a way of giving utterance to all that is unpossessed by writing. Virginia Woolf is not here creating simply an exploration of individualism; she seeks what is held in common – and as commonly lost.

Death is the undertow of the work: wave-forms dissipate as water. Social history as she explored it in *Mrs Dalloway* is unimportant in *The Waves*; finding a new discourse matters more. Social history, that invigorating element of the common life, will return as a sustaining force in *Between the Acts*, the novel in which 'we' is most fully substituted for 'I'. 'We' in *Between the Acts* does not attempt any sentimental knitting up into accord. 'We' remain 'orts, scraps and fragments', passing shows, skeins of gossip. The only common passions shown are those of sex, hunting, recall. But what profoundly connects all the figures in the book is the coming of the Second World War. 'We' becomes the only way to keep a future. The common future is under immediate threat: 'Unless we can think peace into existence we – not this one body in this one bed but millions of bodies yet to be born – will lie in the same darkness and hear the same death rattle overhead'.[37]

Notes

1. *The Diary of Virginia Woolf*, ed. Anne Olivier Bell (London: Hogarth Press, 1980), vol. V, p. 135.
2. *Collected Essays by Virginia Woolf* (London: Hogarth Press, 1966), vol. II, p. 147.
3. *Collected Essays*, vol. II, p. 224. 'It will give, as poetry does, the outline rather than the detail'. 'The psychological novelist has been too prone to limit psychology to the psychology of personal intercourse' (p. 225).
4. *Diary*, vol. III, p. 128.
5. *Virginia Woolf's Writing Notebooks*, ed. Brenda Silver (London: Hogarth Press, 1973) p. 244.
6. Ibid.
7. *Diary*, vol. III, p. 285 (Sunday, 26 January 1930); vol. V, p. 135.
8. *Diary*, vol. IV, p. 124 (16 September 1932).
9. *A Room of One's Own* (London: Hogarth Press, 1929) p. 98. See also 'Memories of A Working Women's Guild', *Collected Essays*, vol. IV, pp. 146–7; *Collected Essays*, vol. II, in 'Life and the Novelist', pp. 131–6 (1926). Virginia Woolf characterises the novelist's paradoxical need for immersion in 'life' and withdrawal from it, in terms of the body becoming writing: 'But at a certain moment he must leave the company and withdraw, alone, to the mysterious room where his body is hardened and fashioned into permanence by processes which, if they elude the critic, hold for him so profound a fascination' (p. 136). How much significance should we attach to the masculine gender here? Is the hardening of the body into writing to be set over against the passage quoted, or is it a description of a different imaginative phase: 'Stop, & take out my pen'. Her enjoyment of 'the company' of her own body needs to be set alongside the more solipsistic analysis of 'Virginia's Embodiment' in Roger Poole, *The Unknown Virginia Woolf* (Cambridge: Cambridge University Press, 1978), pp. 199–215.
10. *Mrs Dalloway* (London: Hogarth Press, 1925), pp. 151–2.
11. Pp. 90–1. See the first essay in this collection, 'Virginia Woolf and Prehistory', and for a

more detailed analysis of the semiotic signification of the song, Makiko Pinkney's *Virginia Woolf and the Problem of the Subject: Feminine Writing in the Major Novels* (Brighton: Harvester Press, 1987).

12. In *To the Lighthouse*, Virginia Woolf's most brooding meditation on the family community, about which I have written elsewhere, everything that happens in narrative representation occurs either before the war of 1914–18, in the rich childhood world of the Victorian family with its submerged tensions, or in the post-impressionism of the 1920s. In 'Time Passes' we have the major events of death and war summarised off-centre, flung into square brackets or past participles. With the mother, Mrs Ramsay, dead, the celibate woman artist, Lily Briscoe, now holds the narrative and pictorial line together. She does it by living askance from the family she observes and whom she celebrates at the end in the abstract forms of triangle and line.

    See 'Hume, Stephen, and Elegy in *To the Lighthouse*', in this collection.

13. *A Writer's Diary*, ed. Leonard Woolf (London: Triad/Panther, 1978). See, for example, 'The Art of Biography' and 'The New Biography', *Collected Essays*, vol. IV, pp. 221–35 as well as her many reviews of biographies and autobiographies.

14. 'I am Christina Rossetti', *Collected Essays*, vol. IV, p. 54.

15. 'The history of England is the history of the male line, not the female' ('Women and Fiction', *Collected Essays*, vol. II, p. 141.)

16. In *The Short Season Between Two Silences: The Mystical and the Political in the Novels of Virginia Woolf* (London: Allen & Unwin, 1984), Madeline Moore offers a celebratory reading of *Orlando* which places the work 'within the coherence of her radical political hopes' (p. 114). I find a darker undertow of pessimism in the work than her attractive reading acknowledges.

17. *Orlando, A Biography* (London: Hogarth Press, 1928), p. 27.

18. Ibid., pp. 264–5. Crowds characterise the modern age, their pleasures expressed in the dexterity of the body: 'Every inch of the pavement was crowded. Streams of people, threading in and out between their own bodies and the lurching and lumbering traffic with incredible agility, poured incessantly east and west' (p. 247).

19. Ibid., pp. 266–7.

20. Ibid., pp. 35–6.

21. *A Room of One's Own*, p. 171.

22. *Diary*, vol. III, p. 218 (Friday, 4 January 1929).

23. 'Yet I am now and then haunted by some semi-mystic very profound life of a woman, which shall all be told on one occasion'. *Diary*, vol. III, p. 118 (Tuesday, 23 November 1926).

24. *Diary*, vol. III, pp. 154–5 (Sunday, 4 September 1927). See also 'Flying Over London', *Collected Essays*, vol. IV, pp. 167–72.

25. *Diary*, vol. III, p. 167.

26. P. 277.

27. See 'A Letter to a Young Poet', *Collected Essays*, vol. III, p. 191, where she writes of 'the most profound and primitive of instincts, the instinct of rhythm … let your rhythmical sense wind itself in and out among men and women, omnibuses, sparrows – whatever comes along the street – until it has strung them together in one harmonious whole. That perhaps is your task – to find the relation between things that seem incompatible yet have a mysterious affinity'. (Written in 1932.)

28. *The Waves* (London: Hogarth Press, 1931), pp. 132–3.

29. A process more striking in *Virginia Woolf, The Waves: The Two Holograph Drafts*, ed. J. W. Graham (London: Hogarth Press, 1976).

30. *The Waves*, pp. 74–5.

31. Ibid., p. 77; pp. 190–1.

32. Ibid., pp. 221–2.

33. Ibid., p. 183.

34. Ibid., pp. 24–5.

35. Ibid., p. 26.

36. Ibid., p. 317.

37. '"Thoughts on Peace in an Air Raid" written in August 1940, for an American symposium on current matters concerning women', *Collected Essays*, vol. IV, p. 173. For discussion see Mark Spilka, *Virginia Woolf's Quarrel with Grieving* (Lincoln: University of Nebraska Press, 1980) and 'Virginia Woolf and Prehistory' *op. cit.*

4

The Waves: 'The Life of Anybody'

As she at last reached the final page of *The Waves*, on 7 February 1931, Woolf wrote in her diary: 'I have netted that fin in the waste of waters which appeared to me over the marshes out of my window at Rodmell when I was coming to an end of *To the Lighthouse*.' The arc through time of that glimpsed fin is remarkable. *The Waves* was conceived, brooded on, and written during a highly political phase in Woolf's career, when she was speaking at public and private meetings on issues of gender and of class. This was the period, too, when her love-affair with Vita Sackville-West was at its most intense. Yet the work is often described as if it were the product of a secluded disembodied sensibility. It might more aptly be described as seeking out the rhythms of the body.

To the Lighthouse was published in May 1927. Over the winter of 1927/8 Woolf wrote *Orlando: A Biography*. That work triumphs over death and over patriarchal succession, but not grandly: rather, in a speedy, lightfooted mode of satire, pastiche, and disrespect. The hero–heroine loosens the bonds of gender, evades history and the knowingness of the biographer's art, and collaborates mockingly with the class system. *The Waves* was meditated alongside the composition of *Orlando*, and of *A Room of One's Own* where Woolf more directly challenges the current ordering of society, particularly its disabling of women. *A Room of One's Own* issued out of papers she read to young women at Cambridge and it was finished in March 1929. At that same time Woolf began writing the first draft of *The Waves*. Towards the conclusion of the second draft, early in 1931, Woolf was seized by intense excitement over the project that was to issue in some of her

First published in: Virginia Woolf, *The Waves*, ed. G. Beer (London: Penguin, 1992), pp. xii-xxxvi.

most polemical writing, *The Pargiters* and *Three Guineas*.

> I have this moment, while having my bath, conceived an entire
> new book – sequel to a Room of Ones Own – about the sexual
> life of women: to be called Professions for Women perhaps –
> Lord how exciting! This sprang out of my paper to be read on
> Wednesday to Pippa's society. Now for The Waves. Thank God
> – but I'm very much excited. (*Diary*, 20 January 1931)

Her excitement is focused towards the new project, yet, as often happens in writing, it is as though at this late stage of composition she can
at last understand the project of the book on which she is at present
engaged. *The Waves*, also, has to do with the sexual life, with the six
persons of one woman.

In the paper she refers to above, 'Professions for Women', she
figures the imagination as a woman, fishing:

> lying sunk in dreams on the verge of a deep lake with a rod held
> out over the water. She was letting her imagination sweep un-
> checked round every rock and cranny of the world that lies sub-
> merged in the depths of our unconscious being.[1]

The unchecked, suffusive power of the imagination explores like fish
and fisher at once. The spatial image is that of descent into the depths,
just as she called *The Waves* a submarine book, every atom saturated.
The passage continues with an insight into how *The Waves* overcomes
what she saw as a central problem for women writing: expressing the
body and the passions.

> Her imagination had rushed away. It had sought the pools, the
> depths, the dark places, where the largest fish slumber. And then
> there was a smash. There was an explosion. There was foam and
> confusion. The imagination had dashed itself against something
> hard. The girl was roused from her dream. She was indeed in a
> state of the most acute and difficult distress. To speak without
> figure she had thought of something, something about the body,
> about the passions which it was unfitting for her as a woman to
> say. Men, her reason told her, would be shocked. The conscious-
> ness of what men will say of a woman who speaks the truth about
> her passions had roused her from her artist's state of uncon-
> sciousness.[2]

By going down in *The Waves* into 'the world that lies submerged in
our unconscious being' and by sustaining the evenness of a dream

75

state, 'her artist's state of unconsciousness', Woolf seeks to escape the narrow bounds of social realism which, she perceives, is functioning as a form of censorship. She has found a language and a rhythm that will be less 'impeded by the extreme conventionality of the other sex'. But it is not a language that excludes 'the other sex': the six speakers of the book, three male, three female, often stand separate from each other but are as often allied across gender. They share sensory experience, though they are later sorted socially.

Far from being a pallid retreat from political issues the project of *The Waves* is innovative and substantial. Its method is not that of confrontation. Instead the work brings into question the established hierarchies of what matters, what constitutes an event, how to write life – including knives and tables, and the presence of many people in a single street on a particular day. Woolf's writing in *Mrs Dalloway* had already suggested that the most fundamental form of connection between human beings is being alive in the same place at the same time, rather than the chosen friendships and love-affairs that fiction ordinarily privileges. *The Waves* sustains that perception but mixes it with an intense scrutiny of particular people. By the end of the book – and more and more in rereading – what has seemed at first oblique, hard to construe, proves to have provided intimate access to the individualities of Jinny, Susan, Rhoda, Bernard, Neville, Louis: though not to Percival. *The Waves* issues out of a vigorous phase of production and feeling and the language of the work is packed with sensory experience, highly sexualized, 'quivering within the wave's intenser day'.[3]

Woolf's hints and touches in her diary from 1925 on towards the work that became *The Waves* make it clear that this was to be experimental work, work that would fundamentally challenge the bounds of fiction. It would bring into question what gets left out when life is described. It would test the established demarcations between individual and communal experience. It would extend the reach of language and suffer its debilities. It would follow a rhythm, not a plot. It would also inhabit the body: 'Muscles, nerves, intestines, blood-vessels, all that makes the coil and spring of our being, the unconscious hum of the engine, as well as the dart and flicker of the tongue' (pp. 217–18)

This insistence on substantiality goes alongside a sense of how objects warp, bend, deliquesce and how the senses seize a world always irretrievably altered, endlessly contingent: at sunrise '*Everything became softly amorphous, as if the china of the plate flowed and the steel of the knife were liquid. Meanwhile the concussion of the waves breaking fell with muffled thuds, like logs falling, on the shore'* (p. 21).

The observation is exact. Waves are fluid, logs solid, yet the report of the waves' fall measures their weight. The ear registers a likeness lost on the eye. The eye's assurance wavers with the changes of light yet the mind remains determined to maintain distinctions: plates and knives are solid even while they are seen as amorphous. That double recognition permeates *The Waves*: of crusts, determined distances, carapaces, identities; of decay, shadows, accumulations, visceral softness, assembled cries.

Each of the books Woolf wrote around the time strained across genre, attempted to break through – or disturb – the limits of the essay, the novel, the biography, to touch realities denied by accepted forms. In all her work there was an astute awareness that apparently literary questions – of genre, language, plot – are questions that touch the pith of how society constitutes and contains itself.

In 'Women and Fiction' in 1929 Woolf connected the material conditions of women's lives with the forms of their expression, and saw that the two would change together: she hoped that in future women, like men, 'will deal with social evils and remedies. Their men and women will not be observed wholly in relation to each other emotionally, but as they cohere and clash in groups and classes and races.' Another, even more important, change will be that 'the greater impersonality of women's lives will encourage the poetic spirit, and it is in poetry that women's fiction is still weakest. It will lead them to be less absorbed in facts and no longer content to record ... their own observation. They will look beyond the personal and political relationships to the wider questions which the poet tries to solve of our destiny and the meaning of life.'[4] This may seem a paradoxical proposal, offering something like de-politicization as a political project for women. But her essay 'The Narrow Bridge of Art' (1927) attempts to analyse the relations between poetry and prose and takes things in a different direction. As she wrote ruefully to Vita Sackville-West on 19 July 1926: 'my God Vita, if you happen to know do wire whats the essential difference between prose and poetry – It cracks my poor brain to consider'.[5]

What she seeks for fiction is the possibility of detachment and feeling at once, an assaying of those experiences ordinarily reserved for poetry, avoiding the hubbub of demands, retaining humour. Instead of mirroring directly, this new form should be able to 'stand further back from life'.[6] But where the observer should be placed exercised her as she wrote:

I have thought of this device: to put

The Lonely Mind

separately in The Moths, as if it were a person. (*Diary*, 4 September 1929)

In the first draft an enigmatic figure, obscurely male or female, scrutinizes the scene from behind a veil. But this did not satisfy her. Again she writes in the diary, on 25 September 1929: 'Yesterday morning I made another start on The Moths, but that won't be its title. & several problems cry out at once to be solved. Who thinks it? And am I outside the thinker? One wants some device which is not a trick.' In the final work that device is the lady writing, the gardeners sweeping, at Elvedon, glimpsed once only in the children's elated and secret invasion of that foreign territory, yet perpetually present – and referred to – throughout the book (for example, on pp. 12, 224). The image is of absorbed, indeflectable activity. The lady is thinking and inscribing, not outwardly observing. The children watch, the lady writes, the gardeners sweep: the work turns its eyes upon itself, but entirely through the eyes of the actors. There is no outside place for the observer. The reader, too, must immerse in this submarine, eyeless (I-less) medium.

One of the first references in the diary to what will eventually form the enquiry of *The Waves* proposes a new kind of biography (or autobiography):

I am now & then haunted by some semimystic very profound life of a woman, which shall all be told on one occasion; & time shall be utterly obliterated; future shall somehow blossom out of the past. One incident – say the fall of a flower – might contain it. My theory being that the actual event practically does not exist – nor time either. But I don't want to force this. (*Diary*, 23 November 1926)

She has described this impulse at the end of October as 'a dramatisation of my mood at Rodmell ... an endeavour at something mystic, spiritual; the thing that exists when we aren't there' (*Diary*, 30 October 1926).

That first mood survives in the accomplished work, but it is lightened by her indefatigable sense of absurdity. Things will not stay still. The scale of experience constantly shifts. What looks large to one looks trivial to another. And in the same instant experience may be extended and doggedly contained. The pettiness of life may produce much of its meaning: trains and pillar-boxes, hide-and-seek and school lessons, jaunts and meals in humdrum cafés, walks through the streets of London, solitary suppers, belching and flowers.

Food is particularly vital to *The Waves*, functioning as ceremonial, aesthetic form, and rank appetite. Two dinner parties order the narrative: that before Percival leaves for India and that at Hampton Court when all the other characters meet again in middle age. The last scene, Bernard's consummating soliloquy, also takes place in a restaurant. Bernard, driven by the curiosity of language, the need to make phrases, is also the most primitive of the characters in his relation to food and drink. Language and appetite are fundamentally at one. In his young adulthood, newly engaged to be married, he reflects: 'Having dropped off satisfied like a child from the breast, I am at liberty now to sink down, deep, into what passes, this omnipresent, general life' (p. 92). Sexual fulfilment takes the individual back deep into the common life of first consciousness at the breast. At the end of the work Bernard thinks with pleasure of the appetites which live alongside the 'shadows of people one might have been; unborn selves'.

> There is the old brute, too, the savage, the hairy man who dabbles his fingers in ropes of entrails; and gobbles and belches, whose speech is guttural, visceral – well, he is here. He squats in me. Tonight he has been feasted on quails, salad, and sweetbread. He now holds a glass of fine old brandy in his paw. He brindles, purrs and shoots warm thrills all down my spine as I sip. It is true, he washes his hands before dinner, but they are still hairy. He buttons on trousers and waistcoats, but they contain the same organs. ... That man, the hairy, the ape-like, has contributed his part to my life. He has given a greener glow to green things ... (pp. 241–2)

Alongside this often ebullient emphasis on primary desires goes the evocation of temperature, touch (and the evasion of touch): 'Let me then feel pressing against me some human hand.'[7] Jinny's body,

> my companion ... is always sending its signals ... All my senses stand erect. Now I feel the roughness of the fibre of the curtain through which I push; now I feel the cold iron railing and its blistered paint beneath my palm. (p. 146)

While she was writing *Mrs Dalloway* Woolf copied a passage from Book VII of Wordsworth's *The Prelude* and added a comment:

The matter that detains us now may seem,
To many, neither dignified enough
Nor arduous, yet will not be scorned by them,
Who, looking inward, have observed the ties
That bind the perishable hours of life
Each to the other, & the curious props
By which the world of memory and thought
Exists & is sustained.

Good quotation for one of my books.

The quotation is quite as pertinent for *The Waves* as for *Mrs Dalloway*, and indeed Woolf copied exactly the same passage into her diary on 22 August 1929. The 'curious props' that memory selects, often apparently captiously, form the recurrent medium of experience for the reader of *The Waves*. Memory melds events and fantasies. Rhoda's bowl of petals and desert sands, Neville's knife blade and his spotless bookshelves, Louis's father 'a banker in Brisbane' and his humiliated memory of being given a Union Jack from the Christmas tree because no one had thought to prepare a present for him: recurrent phrases, intense knots of time, produce a rhythm that both partakes of everyday life and guides the reader through the welter of impressions. The new literary form that Woolf hoped for in 'The Narrow Bridge of Art' was to have 'something of the exaltation of poetry, but much of the ordinariness of prose. It will be dramatic, and yet not a play. It will be read, not acted.'[9]

This mingling of the humdrum with the high style, and particularly that dangerous word 'mystical' that Woolf associates with the work, may account for the relative neglect of *The Waves* in recent criticism. Although it has traditionally been treated as Woolf's 'masterpiece', it gets short shrift in a number of important recent studies. The comments of critics range from the cautious to the downright hostile, and several people skirt the problem that the book evidently presents to current thinking by leaving it out altogether, though often with a brief obeisance to its absence.

The demurrals and exclusions practised by these studies are in themselves revealing. Jane Marcus in her essay 'The Niece of a Nun: Virginia Woolf, Caroline Stephen, and the Cloistered Imagination' is forthright about the problem and imaginative in her response to it:

> As a feminist critic I had avoided the subject of Woolf's mysticism, and of *The Waves*, feeling that acknowledging her as a

visionary was a trap that would allow her to be dismissed as another female crank, irrational and eccentric. I was drawn to her most anti-capitalist, anti-imperialist novels, to Woolf the socialist and feminist, logical, witty, and devastating in argument.[10]

Marcus suggests that it may be possible 'to see the structure of *The Waves* as a Quaker meeting': that is, an occasion which gives particular value to communal silence and to individual utterance bearing profoundly shared concerns. This, she suggests, links the book to the particular exploration of silence and being silenced focused by Adrienne Rich and Tillie Olsen as part of women's experience. But Marcus has not, so far as I know, written at length about the book.

Perry Meisel makes briefly the telling point that 'Ironically, *To the Lighthouse* is a far more abstract account of the way the self is situated in the common life than *The Waves*, Woolf's apparently more oblique achievement. Here she is exceedingly concrete.'[11] In contrast, Alex Zwerdling asserts: 'The relentlessly elevated discourse of the book denied entry to the prosaic, the comic, the particular.'[12] This seems a surprising judgement in the light of the characters' preoccupation with the humdrum detail and the winning incongruities of daily life, 'the way some old woman sits, arms akimbo, in an omnibus with a basket' (p. 148). Louis relishes, with self-aware satire, his part in the business of the Empire:

> This is life, Mr Prentice at four; Mr Eyres at four-thirty. I like to hear the soft rush of the lift and the thud with which it stops on my landing and the heavy male tread of responsible feet down the corridors. So by dint of our united exertions we send ships to the remotest part of the globe; replete with lavatories and gymnasiums. The weight of the world is on our shoulders. This is life. (p. 140)

Susan describes her cooking with sensuous particularity, registering wet and dry, weight and temperature – and the live bodily forms of yeasty bread: 'I go then to the cupboard, and take the damp bags of rich sultanas: I lift the heavy flour on to the clean scrubbed kitchen table. I knead; I stretch; I pull, plunging my hands in the warm inwards of the dough' (p. 80). Zwerdling's outstanding study of Woolf's 'real world' takes *The Waves* as his adverse point of departure rather than exploring it fully.

Zwerdling cites to support his view of the work's insubstantial bias Woolf's own comment that 'there's no quite solid table on which to put it'. Woolf was here very probably responding also to contemporary scientific and philosophical writing. The distinguished physicist and writer Arthur Eddington observed in *The Nature of the Physical World* (1928):

> we have seen that substance is one of the greatest of our illusions ... Perhaps, indeed, reality is a child which cannot survive without its nurse illusion. ... In the world of physics we watch a shadowgraph performance of the drama of familiar life. The shadow of my elbow rests on the shadow table as the shadow ink flows over the shadow paper. It is all symbolic, and as a symbol the physicist leaves it.[13]

Doubting substance and solidity does not make work insubstantial. The overlaps and contradictions between substance and shadow that are so passionately explored in *The Waves* are (as I argue in a forthcoming book) part of the mainstream of enquiry in Woolf's time, not a limitation on her responsiveness to life.

The very unfamiliarity of Woolf's presentation of 'reality' in the work is tonic. It is not an issue that can be settled out of some secure position of observation. The then popular and highly regarded novelist Hugh Walpole complained that: 'Much of it beat me because I couldn't feel it to be real.'[14] Woolf counter-attacked with a shaft against Walpole's new novel, *Judith Paris*:

> Well, I'm very much interested about unreality and the Waves – we must discuss it I mean why do you think *The Waves* unreal, and why was that the very word I was using of Judith Paris – ... 'These people aren't *real* to me' ... But unreality does take the colour out of a book of course; at the same time, I don't see that it's a final judgment on either of us. You're real to some – I to others. Who's to decide what reality is?[15]

Many of the objections to *The Waves* as an image of reality resolve into questions of tense. The interludes, which describe the progress of the sun through a single day and across the world, are put in past tense. The episodes are chiefly in the present, and not always even the progressive present. 'I go to the bookcase' ... 'I come back from the office'; 'I detect; I perceive': such statements suggest habitual and repeated acts and avoid placing the event in a single moment of time. The pure present tense also implicitly suggests self-observation and a kind of instantaneous act of memory, the activity of the watching mind.[16] Only Bernard's concluding soliloquy is in the past tense, supposedly addressed to a listener casually encountered (someone first met long ago on board ship on a journey outside the narrative). That listener is also the reader who at last resolves and orders the group's lives through time, sharing them anew, recognizing stark individualities as well as the overlap of identities.

The Waves, as Makiko Minlow Pinkney well observes in one of the few extended recent discussions, maintains for most of its length 'a precarious dialectic between identity and its loss, the symbolic and its unrepresentable Other – an unsettling ad unsettable alternation prefigured in the sexual metamorphoses of *Orlando*'.[17] Elizabeth Abel, however, in her otherwise excellent study of the psychoanalytic context of Woolf's working community, surprisingly decides to 'omit *The Waves* (1931) whose experiment in dissolving identity sets it outside my concerns'. The omission is the more surprising since she continues, suggestively: 'the very disembodiment that characterizes the text, however, suggests a heightened ambivalence toward the body's origin. *The Waves* marks the terminus of Woolf's progression through the 1920s towards an ambivalent engagement with maternal origins.'[18]

Her comments focus the need now for a fuller study of the movement from the early drafts to the final version of the work. The first version of *The Waves* includes, very near the opening, the image of the maternal sea:

> Many mothers, & before them many mothers, & again many mothers, have groaned, & fallen ~~back, while the child crowed~~. Like one wave, ~~& then~~ succeeding each other. Wave after wave, endlessly sinking & falling as far as the eye can stretch. And all these waves have been the prostrate forms of mothers, in their ~~flowing~~ nightgowns, with the tumbled sheets about them holding up, with a groan, as they sink back into the sea, ~~infin innumerable~~ children.[19]

Labour, self-loss, origins prolonged beyond memory: the anonymity of childbirth and succession in this passage lends further resonance to Woolf's often-cited remark that women 'think back through their mothers'. In the finished novel the inchoate is replaced by the specific. Susan becomes the living presence who is typified by maternal conflict and maternal pleasure and who, late in the book, seeks to be free of that identification.

The most antagonistic recent comments on *The Waves* are those of Mark Hussey who sees *The Waves* as 'useful as a store-house of typical ideas, but not much more than this. It is a kind of warehouse in which are found the materials from which novels such as *To the Lighthouse* or

Between the Acts may be created.'[20] Hussey's principal objection, apart from this suggestion of discrete parcels awaiting delivery, is to the novel's resistance to the reader. Woolf herself was anxious about the reader's skills in this new form. She wrote to Ethel Smyth on 28 August 1930:

> What question in particular was it about the Waves that delicacy forbade? ... I think then that my difficulty is that I am writing to a rhythm and not to a plot. Does this convey anything? And thus though the rhythmical is more natural to me than the narrative, it is completely opposed to the tradition of fiction and I am casting about all the time for some rope to throw to the reader. This is rough and ready; but not wilfully inaccurate.[21]

If the rope the reader needs is information, it is there. (Readers may prefer to read the novel before considering the list of events I offer later in this paragraph, so be warned!) We are given a considerable number of statements about what are usually considered key events and emotions. What makes those statements strange, indeed difficult to read, is that they are presented dead-pan, as part of a sentence, in the midst of a paragraph, without comment or emphasis. Susan loves Louis, Percival loves Susan, Neville loves Percival. Percival leaves for India, Susan is married to a farmer, Bernard is engaged. His son is born just as he hears the news of Percival's death. Jinny has many lovers. Neville seeks the one, and after Percival's death finds him in a succession. Louis is successful in business, Neville distinguished. Louis writes poems, perhaps of lasting value. Louis and Rhoda are lovers. She leaves him. Bernard goes to Rome for ten days. At some time, Rhoda has killed herself. Rhoda was fatherless (the children's parentage is laconically summarized by Louis on p. 14).

In sexual orientation the six characters are fanned across a spectrum that includes Neville's heartfelt and unwavering homo-eroticism, Susan's passionately maternal preoccupation, Jinny's promiscuous and cheerful narcissism, Bernard's heterosexual marriage and fatherhood, Louis and Rhoda's twinned isolations, celibacies. This, then, is the 'semimystic, very profound life of a woman', the rhythm through which at that time Woolf found it possible to speak of 'the body, the passions'.[22]

The turning-point of the book is Percival's death and here Woolf pays death the tribute of narrative pattern. Woolf removed from the final version the particular irony that his horse stumbled over a mole-hill, which is much dwelt upon in the earlier drafts. Percival remains opaque, a figure whose consciousness the reader never enters. Percival is cricket captain, and later rows, rides, and hunts. He appears to be entirely unreflective and like his namesake Parsifal is both pure and ignorant. He is the man at ease in the world of Empire and action, beloved, absurd, mocked and adored by the other characters in their youth. Like Parsifal he is the perfect knight who is also maladroit, unable to ask the right question at the right time. He is also *past*, a focus for memory and community, but no saviour. In the complicated cross-allusions to T. S. Eliot's work in *The Waves* his name may have significance too. In Arthurian legend Parsifal found the Holy Grail at Chapel Perilous. In *The Waste Land* the chapel is empty: 'There is the empty chapel, only the wind's home.' Woolf may also have had Wagner's drama moving in her mind. She had already visited the Bayreuth festival in 1909 and remarks in her diary on 20 September 1927, as she is thinking her way into *The Waves*, that the young Quentin Bell 'wont let us play him Wagner: prefers Bach'. Be that as it may, Percival is an obscured, even blanked-out figure whose passage to India as part of the apparatus of Empire results in his pointless death.

The treatment of his death is remarkably different from that of Rhoda. We never know when that has occurred. Rhoda is absent for the length of two episodes but is present again at Hampton Court, the last episode before Bernard's summation. It is only from Bernard's last speech that we know that she has killed herself. From the outset she has been at odds with time; as a child, left behind to do her sums, the figures on the blackboard 'fill with time'. When she joins up the o, the zero, her reverie becomes nightmare: 'The world is entire, and I am outside of it, crying, "Oh save me, from being blown for ever outside the loop of time!"' (p. 15).

Rhoda is particularly closely associated with the language of Shelley, whose work forms so strong a strand in the elegiac allusions to other poets that I gloss in the notes. This submerged level of intertextuality in the book has not, I think, previously been brought to light. It bears on Woolf's feelings for her dead brother Thoby, friend of her youth, whose presence she longed to mark by writing his name on the first page, but did not.[23] Instead she drew upon the elegiac poems of Catullus and Shelley, Arnold and Milton, Ben Jonson, Shakespeare, and an anonymous medieval writer fleetingly to mark her tribute. Many of the fugitive literary allusions in *The Waves* are to scenes of death or mourning. They vary from the initial image of an arm rising through water that glancingly conjures Tennyson's 'The Passing of Arthur': 'an arm/Clothed in white samite, mystic, wonderful', to the reference to Arnold whose elegy for his friend Clough, 'Thyrsis', is organized around his search for a remembered tree, in *The Waves* the 'immitigable tree' (p. 18).[24]

Some of these allusions are indirect and wavering, but many others are quite precise and placed in quotation marks. Some have a proleptic function, suggesting Percival's journey to India before it has occurred or been mentioned. Shelley's poem 'The Indian Serenade' becomes part of Rhoda's physical experience long before Percival's journey is announced. Catullus is frequently invoked: his 'Odi et amo', I hate and I love, becomes Susan's recurring phrase. Her passionate and unquestioning immediacy is sustained by

> Odi et amo: quare id faciam, fortasse requiris.
> nescio, sed fieri sentio et excrucior.

> I hate and I love. Why I do so, perhaps you ask. I know not, but I feel it, and am in torment.[25]

That poem might also, for a reader saturated as Neville and Louis are said to be in Catullus's language, summon up other nearby poems from his works:

> Friends, who profess your ardour to explore
> The ends of the earth with me, on India's shore
> The long wave breaking calls for evermore
> > Clamorously.[26]

Shelley is directly and pointedly quoted on a number of occasions in the text. His presence is crucial beyond the elegiac, although of course Shelley did die young and tragically. In her rewriting of 'life' Woolf responded to the energy of his writing, and its constant shifting of scale and distances. Indeed, the opening image of the sun rising may include a response to his final, unfinished, and deeply equivocal poem 'The Triumph of Life' with its vigorous first lines when 'the Sun their father rose':

> Swift as a spirit hastening to his task
> Of glory and of good, the Sun sprang forth
> . Rejoicing in his splendour.[27]

Woolf's sun is no Apollonian figure but a woman, no father but a girl.

In September 1927, Woolf records in her diary, she was working on a review of Walter Peck's biography of Shelley. His poetry provides a language at once sensorily intense and intellectually distanced that in particular reinforces Rhoda's abstruse relation to life. Rhoda's reading of his poem 'The Question' as a child provides the yearning phrase that becomes Rhoda's leitmotiv, just as 'Odi et amo' is Susan's. The poem describes a dream where 'Bare Winter suddenly was changed to Spring' and the dreamer gathers 'wild roses, and ivy serpentine'. The poem ends:

> then, elate and gay,
> I hastened to the spot whence I had come,
> That I might there present it! – Oh! to whom?[28]

As the child Rhoda falls asleep just after this passage, phrases from another Shelley poem merge into the physical symptoms of the sleep-state:

> I die! I faint! I fail!
> Let thy love in kisses rain
> On my lips and eyelids pale.[29]

Rhoda's language as a child and adolescent is everywhere erotically charged. In adulthood she is in flight from intimacy, though she and Louis are for a time lovers. When Bernard goes to visit them (though they prove to be absent) the line 'Away! the moor is dark beneath the moon' comes into his mind as he mounts their stairs. Shelley's melancholy poem of loss and ghostly presences ends with a stanza equivocally connected here with the narrative of Percival's death and the lovers' absence:

> Thou in the grave shalt rest – yet till the phantoms flee
> Which that house and heath and garden made dear to thee
>   erewhile,
> Thy remembrance, and repentance, and deep musings are not
>   free
> From the music of two voices and the light of one smile.[30]

However that harmonious last line may mock the outcome, Rhoda and Louis, alone among the characters, address each other on one occasion by name and converse. They are said to be 'conspirators': they share private knowledge and they con-spire, that is, breathe together.

The language associated with Louis is perhaps the most allusively charged of all, since it shares so many of the qualities of T. S. Eliot's verse (as passages such as those on pages 168 and 211 demonstrate). Circumstantially, also, Louis bears some resemblances to Eliot: in his non-English ('colonial') background, in his banking career, classical learning, and fascination with the poetics of history and 'vile and famished' humdrum life. Tiresias-like, he remembers the ancient Nile 'and the women carrying pitchers on their heads' synchronically with chimney cowls, loose slates, slinking cats, and attic windows (p. 168). Though Bernard is the story-maker of *The Waves*, Louis is the poet and the one whose work the other characters expect will last. T. S. Eliot was born in St Louis.

Louis, the Australian whose father's bank failed in Brisbane, has political ambitions. (Woolf seams his pretensions in this direction with allusions to British politicians and lawmakers who were preoccupied with the Indian imperial enterprise, Chatham, Pitt, Burke, and Peel.) Alone among the characters Louis understands the 'third term' between literature and politics – the Industrial Revolution – and can avenge through business the 'beatings and other tortures' (p. 139) inflicted on him in his youth by the British upper classes.

Rhoda's childhood fantasies and images, like those of each of the other characters, revive persistently throughout her later life: the bowl of petals, the pillar, the pool, the zero. Music and geometric forms must supplement language if these experiences are to be registered, Woolf's characters discover. Life's ordered sequences are 'a convenience, a lie', Bernard thinks, 'always deep below' is 'a rushing stream of broken dreams, nursery rhymes, street cries, half-finished sentences and sights – elm trees, willow trees, gardeners sweeping, women writing' (p. 213). Within the book the 'Ah' of the singer (p. 133), the 'little language' that lovers use, pain itself (p. 246), the string quartet's instruments placing a square upon an oblong (pp. 134, 170): such are Woolf's means of reaching beyond the exigencies of prose and its tendency to drive Roman roads across unnoticed territory (p. 216). Jinny, alone of the characters, lives perfectly at home in each present moment, waving her scarf, alive in her body, the alternative story-teller who under- stands the sign-language of clothes and physical presence:

> I see what is before me. ... This scarf, these wine-coloured spots. This glass. This mustard pot. This flower. I like what one touches, what one tastes. I like rain when it has turned to snow and become palpable, I do not temper my beauty with meanness lest it should scorch me. I gulp it down entire. It is made of flesh; it is made of stuff. (pp. 183–4)

In the image of the waves, which succeeded to her first thoughts of moths or farmyard noises, Woolf found a form that perfectly ex- pressed at once the different measures of chronological and of psychic time. She knew the writing of the Victorian physical chemist John Tyndall and may have had passages such as this already in her imagination:

> The particles in front reach in succession the crest of the wave, and as soon as the crest is passed, they begin to fall. They then reach the furrow or sinus of the wave, and can sink no further. Immediately afterwards they become the front of the succeeding wave, rise again until they reach the crest, and then sink as before. Thus, while the waves pass onward horizontally, the individual particles are simply lifted up and down vertically. Observe a seafowl, or, if you are a swimmer, abandon yourself to the action of the waves; you are not carried forward, but simply rocked up and down.[31]

So, the wave-form flows onwards but the substance is not transferred. Psychic life remains fluid yet strangely unchanging. Individuals do not move much: they reach the crest and then fall back. That same image of a wave-like movement is repeated through the sequence of the interludes, when the sun rises, comes to full height, and at last sets. As Diane Gillespie suggests, the descriptions of the sun can probably best be read like the impressionist painter Claude Monet's series-paintings, in which different lights transform objects such as haystacks, cathedrals, trees – and light itself becomes the topic. Woolf's verbal equivalents for the changes wrought by light are here supplemented by 'the movement of light rays and waves as well as the sounds of the sea and the chirping of birds'.[32]

Certainly, the reader of *The Waves* needs to swim, to trust to the buoyancy of the eye and the suppleness of the understanding. It is no good panicking when sequence seems lost or persons are hard to pick out. The rhythms of the work will sustain us comfortably as long as we do not flounder about trying to catch hold of events. The events are there, sure enough, but they are not sundered from the flow. This is to say that the form of the waves is acted out in the actual reading experience, and the reader must trust the medium. The rhythmic patterns of the book, this 'play-poem', provide the clues for performance.

For, despite the uncertain status of the character's soliloquies as thought or utterance, the auditory is an important component in the work's effect. Indeed, it was the area where Woolf most recognized her own limits, here, of class. Because of her uncertainty about the sounds of other kinds of voice and her fear of condescending, Woolf made her one major concession as she worked to the contemporary social order.

She recognized that she had internalized some voices and not others. She drew back from her first intention to include working-class speech. She decided to concentrate her final version on middle-class people, a loss in a book that was to be, according to the title-page of the first draft, 'the life of anybody':

> Albert, who would look, if you only saw his head in a crowd ~~much~~ like ~~other pe~~ Roger; but ~~had~~ then there was a patch on his trousers & his boots were shabby – He was apprenticed to a ... linen draper – no single person could follow lives so opposite; could speak two languages so different; The light came gradually into the room.[33]

Notes

1. 'Professions for Women', in *The Death of the Moth* (London: Hogarth Press, 1942), p. 152.
2. Ibid.
3. My allusion to Shelley's 'Ode to the West Wind' is not casual. Woolf quotes Shelley directly at a number of moments in *The Waves*, particularly his elegiac poems, and his cosmic images of seas, suns, stars, waves, mingled with flowers and passionate outcry are crucial in the imaginative economy of the book's vocabulary.
4. *Collected Essays*, 4 vols (London: Hogarth Press, 1966–7) vol. II, p. 147.
5. *The Letters of Virginia Woolf*, ed. Nigel Nicolson and Joanne Trautmann, 6 vols (London: Hogarth Press, 1975–84), vol. III, p. 281.
6. *Collected Essays*, vol. II, pp. 224–5.
7. Virginia Woolf, *The Waves: The Two Holograph Drafts*, transcribed and edited by J. W. Graham (London: Hogarth Press, 1976), p. 7.
8. Brenda R. Silver, *Virginia Woolf's Reading Notebooks* (Princeton: Princeton University Press, 1983), p. 30.
9. *Collected Essays*, vol. II, p. 224.
10. Jane Marcus (ed.), *Virginia Woolf: A Feminist Slant* (Lincoln: Nebraska University Press, 1984), p. 27.
11. Perry Meisel, *The Absent Father: Virginia Woolf and Water Pater* (New Haven: Yale University Press, 1980), p. 200.
12. Alex Zwerdling, *Virginia Woolf and the Real World* (Berkeley: University of California Press, 1986), p. 12.
13. Eddington, *The Nature of the Physical World* (Cambridge: Cambridge University Press, 1928), p. xvi.
14. Quoted in Quentin Bell, *Virginia Woolf: A Biography*, 2 vols (London: Hogarth Press, 1972), vol. II, p. 162.
15. 8 Nov. 1931; *Letters*, vol. IV, p. 402.
16. For a fuller discussion of tense and point of view, see J. W. Graham, 'Point of View in *The Waves*: Some Services of the Style', in Thomas Lewis (ed.), *Virginia Woolf: A Collection of Criticism* (New York: McGraw-Hill, 1975).
17. Makiko Minow Pinkney, *Virginia Woolf and the Problem of the Subject* (Brighton: Harvester Press, 1988), p. 155.
18. Elizabeth Abel, *Virginia Woolf and the Fictions of Psychoanalysis* (Chicago: Chicago University Press, 1989), Notes, p. 132.
19. *The Waves*, ed. Graham.
20. Mark Hussey, *The Singing of the Real World: The Philosophy of Virginia Woolf's Fiction* (Columbus, Ohio: Ohio State University Press, 1986), p. 82.
21. *Letters*, vol. IV, p. 204.
22. See quotations on p. 75.
23. Thoby Stephen died of typhoid contracted when they and other members of the family were on holiday together in Greece. When he died he was 26 and Virginia 24.

24. *The Poems of Tennyson*, ed. Christopher Ricks (London: Longman, 1969), p. 1750. Lines 312–13; *The Poems of Matthew Arnold*, ed. Kenneth Allott (London: Longmans, 1965), p. 506.
25. *Catullus*, ed. F. W. Cornish, Loeb Classical Library (Boston, Mass.: Harvard University Press, 1962), pp. 162–3.
26. E. A. Havelock, *The Lyric Genius of Catullus* (Oxford: Basil Blackwell, 1939), p. 67.
27. *The Complete Poetical Works of Percy Bysshe Shelley*, ed. Thomas Hutchinson (Oxford University Press, 1934), p. 507.
28. Ibid., p. 614.
29. Ibid., p. 579.
30. Ibid., p. 521.
31. John Tyndall, *Six Lectures on Light* (London, 1873), p. 53.
32. Diane Filby Gillespie, *The Sisters' Arts: The Writing and Paintings of Virginia Woolf and Vanessa Bell* (Syracuse: Syracuse University Press, 1988), p. 303.
33. *The Waves*, ed. Graham, p. 68.

5

The Victorians in Virginia Woolf: 1832–1941

Where did Victorian writing go? What happened to those piled sentences of Ruskin's, those Carlylean metaphors, the lyrical grotesqueries of Dickens, aspirated for the speaking voice but lodged between covers? One answer is that they went into the writing of Virginia Woolf – and some very strange things happened to them there.

In May 1882 Adeline Virginia Stephen was born into what she later described as 'that complete model of Victorian society', the family of Leslie Stephen, editor of the *Cornhill Magazine* and of the *Dictionary of National Biography*, literary essayist, mountaineer, and Victorian man of letters and intellectual par excellence.[1] In that same year of 1882 (the last of his editorship of the *Cornhill*) there appeared, among articles on 'The Sun as a Perpetual Machine' and 'The World's End', an anonymous piece on 'The Decay of Literature', which looked back to the great days of Dickens and Thackeray, Elizabeth Gaskell and Kingsley, failed even once to mention George Eliot, and bemoaned the decline in novelistic achievement of the years between 1850 and 1880. The writer does unbend a little after observing that realism does not suit the English genius:

> We can only say in the vaguest way that in the mental as in the physical world there are periods of sudden blossoming, when the vital forces of nature are manifested in the production of exquisite flowers, after which it again passes into a latent stage. ... Perhaps the Shakespeare of the twentieth century is already learning the rudiments of infantile speech, and some of us may live to greet

First published in Joanne Shattock (ed.), *Dickens and Other Victorians: Essays in Honour of Philip Collins* (London: Macmillan, 1988).

his appearance, and probably ... to lament the inferiority of the generation which accepts him.[2]

If the writer of that essay had any immediate family hopes it might have been of his son Thoby, then rising two and 'learning the rudiments of infantile speech'. As it turned out, the gender and the model are wrong (Shakespeare is not quite the fitting comparison). Like Dombey and Son, Stephen and Son (for Leslie Stephen was the writer) proved to be Stephen and Daughter after all.

Leslie Stephen, who was born in 1832, died in 1904, only just outliving the Victorian age. He did not live to see the emergence of Adeline Stephen as Virginia Woolf, who in November 1928 mused in her diary: '1928–1832. Father's birthday. He would have been 96, 96, yes, today; and could have been 96, like other people one has known: but mercifully was not. His life would have entirely ended mine. What would have happened? No writing, no books; – inconceivable.' But despite the gloom of that judgement she realizes in the next paragraph that her own writing has changed her relationship to her parents, freeing them as well as her. The burden of the parental is laid aside and she can respond to the previous generation anew, as contemporaries: 'I used to think of him and mother daily; but writing the *Lighthouse* laid them in my mind. And now he comes back sometimes, but differently. ... He comes back now more as a contemporary.'[3] This process of resistance, exorcizement, transformation, and a new levelling relationship expresses also Woolf's relations with Victorian culture and writing.

The Victorians are not simply represented (or re-presented) in her novels (and in her last novels *The Years* and *Between the Acts* they are so with peculiar intensity); the Victorians are also *in* Virginia Woolf. They are internalized, inseparable, as well as held at arm's length. They are mimicked with an art of parody so indebted to its material that it sometimes, as in *Orlando*, seems at a loss to measure the extent of its own subversion or acquiescence. Wrestling with the angel in the house is a more protracted struggle even than that of the biblical wrestling match of Joseph and the angel.[4] For this angel is indoors, inside the self, a maternal figure whose worsting and expulsion might prove to have an intolerable creative cost. In *The Pargiters* Virginia Woolf acknowledges that dilemma and distinguishes the woman writer from the hero.

Virginia Woolf grew up a Victorian. She was already a young adult before the twentieth century. One of the tropes of modernism is its insistence on its own novelty, its disconnection from the past. 'In 1910 human nature changed', as Virginia Woolf asserted. But that assertion should not mislead us: Woolf did not simply reject the Victorians and their concerns, or renounce them. Instead she persistently rewrote them. Surviving our parents is a hard lesson to learn (parent-texts as well as parent-people), but essential if we are to survive at all. One way is to ignore them, another way is elegy, a third is to liberate them so that they become elements in a discourse and an experience which, bound in their historical moment, they could not have foreseen. Rewriting sustains and disperses, dispels, restores, and interrupts.[5] These observations are essential to my current enterprise of tracking Woolf's argument with the culture within which she grew, out of which she grew, and which she never quite grew out of.

Virginia Woolf grew up imbued with the literary culture of late-Victorian life, familiar with the major writers as books, acquaintance, and, in some cases, kin. But she was always peripheralized educationally. She had the run of her father's library, supplemented by the books he brought home for her from the London Library, but she did not – unlike her brothers – go to school or university. She rightly and profoundly resented this exclusion. She did not take part in the history of the women's colleges. She was never a student at Girton or Newnham and took a wry look at them only in her middle age. She had no experience of institutions. The school scenes in *The Waves* are as distant from her own autobiographical experience as are the university scenes. Writing to Vita Sackville-West, Woolf suggests that she had missed therefore, not learning, but the slapstick of ordinary experience: 'But then think how I was brought up; mooning about alone among my father's books; never any chance to pick up all that goes on in schools – throwing balls; ragging; slang; vulgarity; scenes; jealousy.'[6]

In her essay on Elizabeth Barrett Browning, the summary that Woolf offers of Barrett Browning's early life has an undertow of self-reference, a suppressed congruity from which she must break free.

> Her mother died when she was a child; she read profusely and privately; her favourite brother was drowned; her health broke down; she had been immured by the tyranny of her father in almost conventual seclusion in a bedroom in Wimpole Street.[7]

Virginia Woolf's mother died when she was 12; her brother Thoby died of typhoid on a visit to Greece; her health repeatedly broke down; and, although the tyranny was of a different kind, any reader of Stephen's *Mausoleum Book* and of Virginia Woolf's own accounts will recognize the tyrannical tenderness of the husband–father. It is not surprising that the Barrett Browning letters Woolf chooses to quote include one where Elizabeth Barrett Browning complains that her upbringing has made her too inward, too inexperienced in human nature. One task that Virginia Woolf set herself was necessarily that of how to escape from the education described by Aurora Leigh, Barrett Browning's first-person woman poet. Aurora remarks that women's rapid insight and fine aptitude are approved:

> As long as they keep quiet by the fire
> And never say 'no' when the world says 'ay',
> For that is fatal, – their angelic reach
> Of virtue, chiefly used to sit and darn,
> And fatten household sinners, – their, in brief,
> Potential faculty in everything
> Of abdicating power in it.[8]

The description seems more apt, perhaps, to Julia Stephen, Virginia's mother, or to Mrs Ramsay (in *To the Lighthouse*), than to Virginia herself. But she is obliged to repeat the rebellion already described in *Aurora Leigh* in the 1850s and to pry apart that fatal compacting of 'potential', 'abdication', and 'power'. This she had to do in her writing. 'Power' is a word she very rarely uses in her own work. Instead she peripheralizes many of the imposing categorizations of narrative and renders frail and absurd those claims to authority which emanate from family or past literature.

In his severe obituary of Leslie Stephen for the *Cornhill*, Frederic Harrison, after setting Stephen alongside the mid-Victorian masters, ends by emphasizing his limitations: he wrote without much poetry, only of literature; he was really only interested in the eighteenth and nineteenth centuries; he had no awareness at all of the Middle Ages and he was incorrigibly English in his preferences – never wrote of Dante or Molière or Goethe or other great European writers.[9] Woolf explored many of the writers who lay outside her father's sympathies: she had a particular responsiveness to the incandescent intelligence of Elizabethan and seventeenth-century language; she read Dante 'in the place of honour' while her mind was still red-hot at the end of each day's work on *The Waves*; probably she too did not read Goethe, to judge by the nature of her allusions to him.[10] Isa, in *Between the Acts*, is haunted by the line from Racine's *Phèdre*: 'Vénus toute entière à sa proie attachée'. But Woolf did not eschew her father's pleasures, reading Sterne particularly with admiration. To them she added the roll, the rise, the carol, the creation (though Hopkins is a poet she only twice and passingly refers to, however closely her feeling for the 'thisness' of things runs to his). All this is to say that she had a more shifting and scintillating sense of the fugitive presences of literature in our experience than had her father. Yet she shared the fascination of her parents' generation with 'Englishness', even if the definition differs.

Despite her abhorrence of the imperialism and patriarchy of English society past and present – and particularly of their forms as she experienced them in late-Victorian England – she is yet attracted by the idea of English history and of England. She tries to find a distance from which it will be possible to observe what is unmarred by disagreeable opinions or out-of-date politics, to find a language and a rhythm by which to measure what persists without faltering in land and people.

From our present vantage-point, which emphasizes the invention of tradition and the fictionality of all celebrated pasts, this enterprise may seem as romantically unprincipled as any imperialist dream, but it is nevertheless one to which Woolf brought the instruments of linguistic analysis and recall in all their refinement. To find a linguistic rhythm by which to express England without false patriotism she must work through parody and pastiche, fracturing and conjuring the verbal traces of the past – as we see particularly in *To the Lighthouse*, *Orlando*, *Flush*, *The Pargiters*, *The Years*, and *Between the Acts*. She works too, through what is communal: architecture, clouds, cows, street scenes. She is appalled by permanence when it is the permanence of heavy objects or relationships. She is heartened by the permanence of shifting and fleeting manifestations which recur: the day passing; cows bellowing; clouds; the sound of voices and of feet brushing the pavement; and writing, which again and again lends itself to fresh reading.

Looking back on her own early family life she emphasized its seeming permanence and bruising enclosure. The house 'seems tangled and matted with emotion. ... It seemed as if the house and the family which had lived in it, thrown together as they were by so many deaths, so many emotions, so many traditions, must endure for ever. And then suddenly in one night both vanished.'[11] Loss and freedom became hard to distinguish. Everyday life, whose familiarity makes it seem permanent, vanishes even fecklessly, the heavy furniture more fleeting than the residual forces of emotion. In another passage Woolf expresses her relations to Victorian society in terms which invoke the Gradgrinds and the horseriders in Dickens's *Hard Times*, where Mr Gradgrind comes upon his children, 'his own metallurgical Louisa' and 'his own mathematical Thomas' 'abasing' themselves to peep into the circus tent. Woolf writes:

> I felt as a tramp or a gypsy must feel who stands at the flap of the tent and sees the circus going on inside. Victorian society was in full swing. George was the acrobat who jumped through the hoops and Vanessa and I beheld the spectacle. We had good seats at the show, but we were not allowed to take part in it. We applauded, we obeyed – that was all.[12]

The circus has here become the central image for society, instead of representing an alternative world of amusement and skill opposed to the regulated workaday one. In this passage Virginia Woolf first figures herself as tramp or gypsy, but then – more prosaically – as bourgeois spectator: 'we had good seats'. The peeping Thomas and Louisa have been given good seats at the circus and required to admire its self-congratulatory and competitive antics. Sissie Jupe was a worker in the circus family, but the Stephen daughters were kept outside the ring. By a rearrangement of Dickensian hyperbole Woolf condenses the garish Grand Guignol of family and public life as circus. This impacting yields a comic image of Victorian society at its exercise.

Woolf's writing, indeed, everywhere suggests that hyperbole was the principal stylistic and psychological mode of Victorian experience, despite its dowdy surface. It was manifested in their hubristic desire to run the world in imperialism, in their uncontrolled procreativity, and in the besotted plenitude of their natural world:

> And just as the ivy and evergreen rioted in the damp earth outside, so did the same fertility show itself within. The life of the average woman was a succession of childbirths. She married at nineteen and had fifteen or eighteen children by the time she was thirty; for twins abounded. Thus the British Empire came into existence; and thus – for there was no stopping damp; it gets into the inkpots as it gets into the woodwork – sentences swelled, adjectives multiplied, lyrics became epics, and little trifles that had been essays a column long were now encyclopaedias in ten or twenty volumes.[13]

Like, one may say, the assembled volumes of Leslie Stephen's *Dictionary of National Biography*, the nation's memorial boast of its curious and manifold distinction.

With hyperbole goes promiscuity, so that a statue of Queen Victoria is transmogrified by a sunbeam into a 'conglomeration ... of the most heterogeneous and ill-assorted objects, piled higgledy-piggledy in a vast mound ... seemingly calculated to last for ever'. 'The incongruity of the objects, the association of the fully clothed and the partly draped, the garishness of the different colours and their plaid-like juxtapositions afflicted Orlando with the most profound dismay' (p. 209). Woolf's technique is to display the obverse of the Victorian ideal intellectual fiction of *synthesis*. As she demonstrates, synthesis more often founders as clutter than discovers true relations. Its intellectual acquisitiveness becomes indistinguishable from material greed.

Yet the medium for the opening of her satire on the Victorian age in *Orlando* is a version of Ruskin's prose: Ruskin both represents the idealistic mode of Victorian polymathism and the Victorian response to the particular. Of Ruskin's writing she said elsewhere: '*Modern Painters* takes our breath away. We find ourselves marvelling at the words, as if all the fountains of the English Language had been set playing in the sunlight for our pleasure, but it seems scarcely fitting to ask what meaning they have for us.'[14] In *Orlando* she takes up Ruskin's late sad vision of 'the storm-cloud of the nineteenth century' and interpenetrates it with the language of chapter 26 of *Modern Painters*, 'Of Modern Landscape'. The most striking thing about modern landscapes, argues Ruskin, 'is their *cloudiness*'.

> Out of perfect light and motionless air, we find ourselves on a sudden brought under sombre skies, and into drifting wind; and with fickle sunbeams flashing on our face, or utterly drenched with sweep of rain, we are reduced to track the changes of the shadows on the grass, or watch the rents of twilight through angry cloud. ... The aspects of sunset and sunrise, with all their attendant phenomena of cloud and mist, are watchfully delineated; and in ordinary daylight landscape, the sky is considered of so much importance, that a principal mass of foliage, or a whole foreground, is unhesitatingly thrown into shade merely to bring out the form of a white cloud. So that, if a general and characteristic name were needed for modern landscape art, none better could be invented than 'the service of clouds'.[15]

To Ruskin 'the service of clouds' brings with it the loss of '*stability*, *definiteness*, and *luminousness*, we are expected to rejoice in darkness and triumph in mutability'. Woolf opens her chapter thus:

> The great cloud which hung, not only over London, but over the whole of the British Isles on the first day of the nineteenth century stayed, or rather, did not stay, for it was buffeted about

constantly by blustering gales, long enough to have extraordinary consequences upon those who lived beneath its shadow. A change seemed to have come over the climate of England. Rain fell frequently, but only in fitful gusts, which were no sooner over than they began again. The sun shone, of course, but it was so girt about with clouds and the air was so saturated with water, that its beams were discoloured and purples, oranges, and reds of a dull sort took the place of the more positive landscapes of the eighteenth century. (p. 205)

Woolf sympathetically appropriates Ruskin's analysis, but to his afflicted, creatively agitated description she adds a single term: damp. Whereas in Ruskin's account words like 'flashing', 'drenched', 'angry' suggest the drama of extremes, Woolf continues her description thus:

But what was worse, damp began to make its way into every house – damp, which is the most insidious of all enemies ... damp steals in while we sleep; damp is silent, imperceptible, ubiquitous. Damp swells the wood, furs the kettle, rusts the iron, rots the stone. So gradual is the process, that it is not until we pick up some chest of drawers, or coal scuttle, and the whole thing drops to pieces in our hands, that we suspect even that the disease is at work. (pp. 205–6)

In Woolf's comic version of Ruskin the transacting words are 'insidi-ous', 'silent', 'imperceptible', 'gradual'. Instead of turmoil and dash, she expresses the dowdiness of swollen continuity which at last, in a new hyperbole, simply 'drops to pieces in our hands': the traditional phrase attributed by the middle classes to hapless servant-girls who have broken valuable objects. Here, the (absurd) explanation is given: damp. The lexical play is extreme: objects have lost all weight ('we pick up some chest of drawers, or coal scuttle') even while they are permeated with chill damp.

So the passage functions as pastiche: she brings out the repressed humdrum 'damp', to supplement and undermine the mythic aggran-dized account of Victorian weather in Ruskin, what he later calls, quoting Aristophanes, 'the coronation of the whirlwind'. But the pas-sage functions also as collusion and celebration. Ruskin attracts her as the writerly medium for expressing the Victorian age perhaps because of his antagonistic relationship to the powers of his society, as well as, I think, his capacity for self-contradiction. She opens her essay on Ruskin by enquiring, 'What did our fathers in the nineteenth century do to deserve so much scolding?', and she observes the teacherly tone which so often takes over from poet or prophet in Carlyle and Ruskin. But another reason for her responsiveness to Ruskin is his countervailing immersion in the specific: his joyous zeal in particularizing gives life to his writing in the modernist era, particularly to Virginia Woolf in her search for the 'moment', both evanescent and fully known. Ruskin's hyperaesthesia matched Woolf's own: his helpless openness to the sensory world alternated with a severe and minatory closing of the self against the follies and injustices of the age. He is askance from his generation, even while we take him as typifying much in Victorian literature and society. The fountainous and the crabbed alternated in his writing, often within a sentence.

Perhaps, too, Virginia Woolf appreciated the androgynous in Ruskin. He was never merely a patriarchal figure, though his fatal over-identification with women had results as disastrous to his happiness as his ignorant idealizing of them. It will be remembered that the Victorian husband of Orlando, Shelmardine, is 'really' a woman, to the degree that she is 'really' a man. Seeking the woman's sentence, as Woolf did, she might have glimpsed it among the Victorians in the agglomerative, impressionistic, ranging movement of Ruskin's sentences. In her rewriting of that sentence she interrupted its hyperbolic drive, scissored its afflatus, and yet, as in *The Waves*, swam with its tide. His emphasis on change and sameness in his description of waves, and his metaphors, certainly accord with Woolf's project in *The Waves*.

> Most people think of waves as rising and falling. But if they look at the sea carefully, they will perceive that the waves do not rise and fall. They change. Change both place and form, but they do not fall; one wave goes on, and on, and still on; now lower, now higher, now tossing its mane like a horse, now building itself together like a wall, now shaking, now steady, but still the same wave till at last it seems struck by something; changes, one knows not how, becomes another wave.[16]

Fortunately, in the whimsical good sense of the unconscious, fathers can be mothers, and so in looking back through our mothers, as she says women must do, Ruskin may be among them. Perry Meisel, in *The Absent Father*, has made a case for Pater as her obliterated kin and I have argued the case for Darwin in Chapter 1.[17] There is no contradiction in such multiplicity. In literary relationships parents are not restricted to two, nor need their gender be stable. Moreover, they may be most valuable when they come back as contemporaries. Despite his moralism, Ruskin represents a world alive to Woolf, opposed to that of

Arnold – a world of acute sensation, of passionate involvement with the anonymous life of unrecorded people: as she puts it, 'an eagerness about everything in the world'. His effects can sometimes even be seen, perhaps, in that condescension, the opening of *The Years* (though even here it is difficult to mark how far the plurals are parodic). Equally, though, he provides an example of 'impassioned prose' where there is nothing 'unfused, unwrought, incongruous, and casting ridicule upon the rest'. Seeking 'saturation' in her own writing in *The Waves*, she finds it in Ruskin, as she could find also a description of the action of waves which answers to her own need for the *permanently changing*, the untransformed.

The hyperbole in Ruskin's writing both amuses and empowers her; his feeling for detail lies alongside her own, yet it is distanced from hers by his nostalgic preference for the discrete and stable particularity of medieval observation, where acorns, fishes, faces, each are given their full record in the picture. Though this is Ruskin's declared preference, Woolf's writing has learnt more from the shifty evanescence of detail in Ruskin's prose, even while he seeks to analyse in fullest spectrum all the changes of colour and to list their sequences.

Ruskin's struggle to record and value 'life' though language, to render the visual world through the symbolism of letters, offered Woolf also a displaced understanding, a place from which to assess her own project. It would be a mistake to read the figure of Orlando as a self-portrait. Orlando is her hero-ine, not herself. Orlando is close to Vita Sackville-West and participates in the swashbuckling inertia of the landed classes who survive, not greatly changed by historical forces or even by simple onward movement of time. Virginia Woolf, on the other hand, is the writer whose hyperaesthesia forces her close into the welter of circumstance, and who controls that closeness by appropriating and recasting writing of the past as pastiche and celebration. In *Orlando*, in particular, her writing of others' writing is audacious. She can clutch, jettison, repossess those sombre, turgid sentences of the Victorians. The panache of *Orlando* helps her to break out of those 'seclusions' which she shares with Elizabeth Barrett Browning and which result, according to her description of Barrett Browning, in another form of hyperaesthetic hyperbole:

> The tap of ivy on the pane became the thrash of trees in a gale. Every sound was enlarged, every incident exaggerated, for the silence of the sick-room was profound and the monotony of Wimpole Street was intense. ... Ordinary daylight, current gossip,

the usual traffic of human beings left her exhausted, ecstatic, and dazzled into a state where she saw so much and felt so much that she did not altogether know what she felt or what she saw.[18]

This reading of Elizabeth Barrett Browning seems self-admonitory; it certainly does not pay sufficient attention to the wit of *Aurora Leigh*. It is by means of wit that Barrett Browning channelled heightened observation into often caustic poetry, as in her account of the over-interpretative scrutiny of Aurora's slightest acts as the household waits upon the outcome of her rejection of Romney. The humour both of Barrett Browning and of Woolf becomes much more marked when read aloud. On the page the eye glides without incongruity from level to level of discourse. Read aloud, the same passage registers the awkwardness of a syntax which seeks to yoke unlike, the collusive asides muttered within the public sentence. It is in the light of her endangering kinship with Barrett Browning (the sensibility of the sick-room, the writer's recalcitrance too quick consumed, the unstaunched lyric effusion) that we should measure also Woolf's admiration for this poet who was a woman and thereby trod across the categories of expectation, and who had for company her own creation, 'Aurora Leigh', a woman poet, and Flush, a spaniel. Virginia Woolf's choice of a dog as her second subject for biography, after the man/woman of *Orlando*, and before Roger Fry, has been a source of puzzlement, not to say embarrassment, to many of her professional readers.

In *Flush* Woolf finds a new means of measuring and limiting Victorian hyperaesthesia and hyperbole. Flush's doggyness means that the early Victorian age is experienced through different senses, its description made strange through hearing, touch, but particularly through smells. Woolf relishes the new configurations which emerge from the Browning letters when the encounters they record are reperceived as a racy mixture of coarse and delicate textures yielding smells, scents, stench, odours. She brings out playfully the censored version of the past we usually accept as true by offering us supplementarily a smell repertoire. It is impossible, this method paradoxically suggests, to regain the physical welter of life. Even the subtle naming of smells cannot communicate their pungency:

Mixing with the smell of food were further smells – smells of cedarwood and sandalwood and mahogany; scents of male bodies and female bodies; of men servants and maid servants; of coats and trousers; of crinolines and mantles; of curtains of tapestry, of curtains of plush; of coal dust and fog; of wine and cigars. Each

room as he passed it – dining-room, drawing-room, library, bedroom – wafted out its own contribution to the general stew.[19]

The bourgeois world stinks and so does the world of the poor.

Flush, like Elizabeth Barrett, like Adeline Virginia Stephen, is a
prisoner always on the edge of escape in Victorian bourgeois society.
When he is stolen and his mistress goes to Whitechapel to rescue him,
she sees for the first time the world of the poor:

> They were in a world where cows were herded under bedroom
> floors, where whole families sleep in rooms with broken windows;
> in a world where water is turned on only twice a week, in a world
> where vice and poverty breed vice and poverty. ... They had
> come to a region unknown to respectable cab-drivers. ... Here
> lived a woman like herself; while she lay on her sofa, reading,
> writing, they lived thus.

The next sentence reads: 'But the cab was now trundling along between
four-storeyed houses again' (p. 89). This episode alone is shown
through the eyes of Miss Barrett, rather than those of Flush, as though
Woolf needed to move outside the arch device of the animal observer
(whose subversiveness is limited by its quaintness) and to observe
human chagrin more directly, though still through that securing and
mocking device of the carriage-window within which the reader trun-
dles safely through the dangers of Victorian London.

It would probably be too much to claim on Woolf's behalf any
specific project in *Flush* of socially disquieting her reader about conditions still current in England. Rather, this small and lightly learned
work suggests the fictionality of our imagined Victorian England, even
by its use of documents and known personages. The spaniel's nose and
eyes and ears yield us intimacies with the sensory material of that past
world, but it remains fictional, irrecoverable. In her essay on 'Geraldine
and Jane' (Geraldine Jewsbury and Jane Carlyle) Woolf presents a
poignant appreciation of the impossibility of knowing other people
fully. Knowing them across time in letters sometimes gives the illusion
of full intimacy, but she ends by quoting Geraldine Jewsbury:

> Oh, my dear (she wrote to Mrs Carlyle), if you and I are
> drowned, or die, what would become of us if any superior person
> were to go and write our 'life and errors'? What a precious mess a
> 'truthful person' would go and make of us, and how very differ-
> ent to what we really are or were![20]

Virginia Woolf's method in her quasi-biographies is to suggest that we can know the past and its people best, not through opinions, but through textures, sounds, smells, sight (though rarely taste), through bodily impersonation – a method which, at the same time, shows up the absurd though necessary mismatch between writing and being. Her methods mock the ponderously achieved apparatus of the 'life and opinions' biography, and the assumption that the individual's success is the criterion for making record worthwhile, which is harboured by much Victorian biography.

Woolf enjoyed reading biography and, especially, autobiography. Her own method mocked the hagiographic style of many Victorian 'lives and letters', the summary accounting of the *Dictionary of National Biography*. She repudiated the insistence on action and event as the biographer's main resource. But she abjured equally the demystifying iconoclasm of Lytton Strachey. She liked delicately to bring to the surface mislaid lives, particularly those of women, excluded from historical record.

In her essay 'I am Christina Rossetti' she remarks on the fascination of reading biographies:

> Here is the past and all its inhabitants miraculously sealed as in a magic tank; all we have to do is to look and listen and to listen and to look and soon the little figures – for they are rather under life size – will begin to move and to speak, and as they move we shall arrange them in all sorts of patterns of which they were ignorant, for they thought when they were alive that they could go where they liked.[21]

The image of the controlling biographer and the knowing reader surveying the belittled figures of the past 'sealed as in a magic tank' seems aimed at Lytton Strachey and his accounts of Victorian figures. Strachey, indeed, had remarked in a letter to Maynard Keynes in 1906 that the Victorian age was one in which people 'were enclosed in glass'. He adds: 'it's damned difficult to copulate through a glass case'.[22] Woolf suggest that the glass is a product of the biographer's distance and it is he, not his subjects, who finds it difficult to copulate. (Strachey's formulation revealingly suggests his balked desire sexually to invade his subjects.) In Woolf's judgement the biographer, like the realist novelist, claims too much authority – an authority which stifles their awareness of the spontaneity and aimlessness of life: 'as they move we shall arrange them in all sorts of patterns'. The joke at Strachey's expense grew sad when he died while she was in the midst of writing *Flush*, in which she demonstrates how to release the Victorians from the stodginess of self-approval without simply transferring that self-approval into modernist knowingness.

In 1929, in 'Women and Fiction' she remarks that future women writes will 'be less absorbed in facts. ... They will look beyond the personal and political relationships to the wider questions which the poet tries to solve – of our destiny and the meaning of life.'[23] Woolf is seeking an impersonality which will not be alienation and a permanence which will not be statis. Frederic Harrison, in his obituary of Leslie Stephen, singled out for praise Stephen's essay 'Sunset on Mont Blanc' (1873). The essay opens thus: 'Does not science teach us more and more emphatically that nothing which is natural can be alien to us who are part of Nature? Where does Mont Blanc end, where do I begin?'[24] This is certainly a grandiose and emphatic way of presenting the problem of the frontiers of identity. But put in less massive, less hyperbolic style it is a question that Woolf's writing, like that of her father, constantly poses. And Victorian scientific writing presented her, as much as him, with a language in which to muse upon such issues.

In *Mrs Dalloway* Peter meditates with whimsical recollection on Clarissa's possible thoughts, 'possibly she said to herself, as we are a doomed race, chained to a sinking ship (her favourite reading as a girl was Huxley and Tyndall, and they were fond of these nautical metaphors)'.[25] Let us take up the hint that this passage's allusion offers us and consider the reading that Woolf must herself have had in her background to make the point here. The problem of 'where Mont Blanc ends and I begin' was presented by Huxley in a way which seems much closer than Stephen's formulation to Virginia Woolf's language, with its rapid shifts of scale and perturbation between metaphor and substance. Huxley is arguing, against appearance, for 'community of faculty' between living organisms quite unlike in complexity and scale: between 'the brightly-coloured lichen' and the painter and botanist.

> Again, think of microscope fungus – a mere infinitesimal ovoid particle, which finds space and duration enough to multiply into countless millions in the body of a living fly; and then of the wealth of foliage, the luxuriance of flower and fruit, which lies between this bald sketch of a plant and the giant pine of California, towering to the dimensions of a cathedral spire, or the Indian fig, which covers acres with its profound shadow, and endures while nations and empires come and go around its vast circumference. Or, turning to the other half of the world of life, picture to yourselves the great Finner whale, hugest of beasts that live, or

have lived, disporting his eighty or ninety feet of bone, muscle, and blubber, with easy roll, among waves in which the stoutest ship that ever left dockyard would flounder hopelessly; and contrast him with the invisible animalcules – mere gelatinous specks, multitudes of which could, in fact, dance upon the point of a needle with the same ease as the angels of the Schoolmen could, in imagination.[26]

These alternations imply unity by proposing only diversities: 'what is there in common between the dense and resisting mass of the oak, or the strong fabric of the tortoise, and those broad disks of glassy jelly which may be seen pulsating though the waters of a calm sea, but which drain away to mere film in the hand which raises them out of their element?' The word 'pulsating', set with faintly shocking energy between words indicating stability and immovability ('disks', 'glassy', 'calm'), is typical of the imaginative allure of Huxley's style which here finds its point of intervention in the tactile: the hand enters the water and changes pulsating life to 'mere films'. The fibrous connectedness of bodily life and physical world, the recognition of other forms as our 'unacted parts', which inform this and other Huxley passages, may be compared to the language of self-discovery in the childhood section of The Waves: 'My body is a stalk'. Rhoda rocks her petals as boats in a basin:

> On we sail alone. That is my ship. It sails into icy caverns where the sea-bear barks and stalactites swing green chains. The waves rise; the crests curl; look at the lights on the mastheads. They have scattered, they have foundered, all except my ship which mounts the wave.[27]

The 1927 commentary in Orlando ponders with some element of pastiche of the earnest enquiring Victorians:

> even now (the first of November 1927) we know not why we go upstairs, or why we come down again, our most daily movements are like the passage of a ship on an unknown sea, and the sailors at the mast-head ask, pointing their glasses to the horizon: 'Is there land or is there none?'

Froude in his life of Carlyle describes the Victorian age as one with 'the compasses all awry and nothing left to steer by but the stars'.[28] 'A doomed race, chained to a sinking ship': Clarissa's supposed images of empire and of degeneration register the darkest thoughts of the Victorians about themselves – and of Virginia Woolf's quarrel with them. At the heart of that quarrel was her rejection of their masculinism, their Mont Blanc self-image.

But within Victorian scientific writing was to be found release from such glacial impersonality. It is signalled in that other favoured name in *Mrs Dalloway*: John Tyndall. Tyndall's principal scientific work was on radiant heat, and he wrote at large concerning the 'use of the imagination in science', not only in the essay of that title but in his lectures on light, on heat, and on sound. Waves compose the universe and are endlessly in motion, as light-waves, heat-waves, water-waves, sound-waves.

Darkness might then be defined as ether at rest; light as ether in motion. But in reality the ether is never at rest, for in the absence of light-waves we have heat-waves always speeding through it. In the spaces of the universe both classes of undulations incessantly commingle. Here the waves issuing from uncounted centres cross, coincide, oppose, and pass through each other, without confusion or ultimate extinction. ... Its waves mingle in space without disorder, each being endowed with an individuality as indestructible as if it alone had disturbed the universal repose.[29]

In such a theory individuality is indestructible, but part of an endlessly fleeting pattern of coincidental crossing of waves. Interpretation rather than interaction is emphasized, and motion and stasis are hard to distinguish. The individual particles remain, the form changes. As Tyndall wrote in *On Light* of wave-motion: 'The propagation of a wave is the propagation of a *form*, and not the transference of the substance which constitutes the wave.'[30] Thus we have simultaneously form and dissolution, onward motion and vertical rocking. The parallels with the community of life-histories in *The Waves* are striking. The passage is worth quoting in full:

> The central difficulty of the subject was, to distinguish between the motion of the wave itself, and the motion of the particles which at any moment constitute the wave. Stand upon the seashore and observe the advancing rollers before they are distorted by the friction of the bottom. Every wave has a back and front, and, if you clearly seize the image of the moving wave, you will see that every particle of water along the front of the wave is in the act of rising, while every particle along its back is in the act of sinking. The particles in front reach in succession the crest of the wave, and as soon as the crest is passed they begin to fall. They then reach the furrow or sinus of the wave, and can sink no

further. Immediately afterwards they become the front of the succeeding wave, rise again until they reach the crest, and then sink as before. Thus, while the waves pass onward horizontally, the individual particles are simply lifted up and down vertically. Observe a sea-fowl, or, if you are a swimmer, abandon yourself to the action of the waves; you are not carried forwards, but simply rocked up and down. The propagation of a wave is the propagation of a form, and not the transference of the substance which constitutes the wave.

Tyndall, too, it was who in 'The Use of the Imagination in Science' brought to public knowledge that the blue of the sky was distance, not colour; and this assertion of his provoked considerable hostility in the 1870s. We know that the Tyndalls were friends of the Stephens. More important, Tyndall's exercise of the imagination in the oceans of the universe continued to have meaning for Woolf through to the end of her writing life. Near the beginning of *Between the Acts* she describes the 'blue that has escaped registration' in words close to those of Tyndall.[34]

When we consider Virginia Woolf's relations to the Victorians we scant their meaning if we fail to recognize how widely imaginative was her continuous reading and her rewriting, how broad a knowledge she drew on. Victorian physics may have come more strongly to her mind again in the 1930s because of the intervention of Einstein's theories, which fascinated her, and her reading of Eddington and Jeans. I have discussed that probability elsewhere. The Victorian reading bases of her imagination were not simply expunged, outdated by modernist writing and science. They were, as probably, reawakened by such interventions.[32]

In *Between the Acts* Victorian England re-emerged as a not quite dislodged present, no longer represented, as in *The Years*, as past family and national history. Instead, *Between the Acts* is preoccupied with synchrony as a new form (perhaps the only feasible remaining form) for permanence. When she wrote this work Woolf was nearing 60 years old, closer in age to the old people in the book than the young. Isa looks 'at Mrs Swithin as if she had been a dinosaur or a very diminutive mammoth. Extinct she must be, since she had lived in the reign of Queen Victoria.'[33] As had Virginia Stephen.

In *Between the Acts* she shows the whole community of England poised, only half aware, on the brink of national disaster (it is an afternoon of mid-June 1939). In the village pageant the past is summoned up, in the form of caricature, celebration, and reminiscence, 'Home' and ''Ome' epitomize Victorian expansion and repression together.

> BUDGE. ... Home, gentlemen; home, ladies, it's time to pack up and go home. Don't I see the fire (he pointed: one window blazed red) blazing ever higher? In kitchen; and nursery; drawing-room and library? That's the fire of 'Ome. And see! Our Jane has brought the tea. Now children where's the toys? Mama, your knitting, quick. For here (he swept his truncheon at Cobbet of Cobbs Corner) comes the bread-winner, home from the city, home from the counter, home from the shop. 'Mama, a cup o' tea.' 'Children, gather round my knee. I will read aloud. Which shall it be? Sinbad the sailor? Or some simple tale from the Scriptures? And show you the pictures? What none of 'em? Then out with the bricks.' (pp. 200–1)

Budge, the constable, guards 'respectability', 'prosperity', 'the purity of Victoria's land'. But it is 'going home': giving way like an old garment. Mrs Lynn Jones, watching the representation of Victorian family life, protests inwardly against the parody, but muses:

> Was there, she mused, ... something – not impure, that wasn't the word – but perhaps 'unhygienic' about the home? Like a bit of meat gone sour, with whiskers, as the servants called it? Or why had it perished? (p. 202)

Does the past simply 'go off', like a piece of meat, too closely connected to appetite to endure? Was the Victorian home particularly corruptible? Woolf here moves in on our irremediable confusions between language and body. She separates out for attention the word 'unhygienic', itself a Victorian coinage and crucial to the anxieties of that culture. So 'perished' exhibits both the sense of irremediable individual death and of technical material decay which operates within different linguistic registers ('We perish each alone', we recollect, but rubber perishes.)

The old imperialist Bart and the Christian lady Mrs Swithin, by virtue of old age, live in a shifting time in which prehistory, the Victorian age, and the present are all in synchrony, but as 'orts, scraps, and fragments'. Woolf places all her people this time in a possible final moment (as she wrote the book the bombers moved overhead and the boats set out for their rescue mission to Dunkirk just across the water). Budge's gesture towards Pointz Hall has a double meaning: 'Don't I see the fire (he pointed: one window blazed red) blazing ever higher?'

It is sunset, the war is about to begin. She shows a group who seem to go back uninterrupted to prehistory, but the constant references to the History of Civilization and the dinosaurs remind us, lightly, that civilizations end and the dinosaurs are no more.

She changes the image of 'orts, scraps, and fragments' from its signification in *Troilus and Cressida* as the greasy remains of a meal, into an archaeological image of vestiges, shards. The scraps of the communal and personal past are recuperable only *as* gossip and pastiche, a flotsam of significant fragments. The fragments, significantly, never collapse again into 'synthesis', that Victorian ideal of mind and writing. She jostles Victorian language into new patterns, establishing her separation from them. And that makes it possible for her to acknowledge them as kin.

Notes

1. For discussion of Woolf's Victorian upbringing, see Noel Annan, *Leslie Stephen: The Godless Victorian* (London: Weidenfeld & Nicolson, 1984), and Phyllis Rose, *Woman of Letters: A Life of Virginia Woolf* (Oxford: Oxford University Press, 1978). Woolf was called Adeline after her mother's sister, Adeline Vaughan, who died the year before Virginia's birth: see Leslie Stephen, *The Mausoleum Book*, ed. A. Bell (Oxford: Clarendon Press, 1977), pp. 59, 66–70. 1832 is the year of Stephen's birth, 1941 of Woolf's death.

2. *Cornhill Magazine*, XLV (1882), pp. 585–93, 481–90; XLVI (1882), pp. 602–12 (quotation from pp. 611–12).

3. *The Diary of Virginia Woolf*, ed. Anne Olivier Bell (London: Hogarth Press, 1980), vol. III, p. 208.

4. Woolf uses Coventry Patmore's title, *The Angel in the House*, for her own oppositional purposes. See *The Death of the Moth* (London: Hogarth Press, 1941), pp. 150–1, where a close relation between her mother and the angel is suggested.

5. Gillian Beer, 'Virginia Woolf and Prehistory', reproduced in this volume.

6. Quoted in Annan, *Leslie Stephen*, p. 119.

7. Virginia Woolf, *Collected Essays* (London: Hogarth Press, 1966), vol. I, pp. 212–13.

8. Elizabeth Barrett Browning, *Aurora Leigh* (London, 1857), book I, l. 426.

9. Frederic Harrison, in the *Cornhill Magazine*, XVI (n.s.) (1904), pp. 432–43.

10. *The Diary of Virginia Woolf* (1982), vol. IV, p. 5; *Virginia Woolf's Reading Notebooks*, ed. Brenda Silver (Princeton, NJ: Princeton University Press, 1983), LI, p. 243, and LVIII, pp. 255–73.

11. Virginia Woolf, *Moments of Being: Unpublished Autobiographical Writings*, ed. Jeanne Schulkind (Brighton: Sussex University Press, 1976), p. 161; see also 'Since the war', in *A Haunted House and other Short Stories* (London: Hogarth Press, 1943), p. 44, where she remarks that it was 'shocking and wonderful to discover' that these 'real things, Sunday luncheons, Sunday walks, country houses, and tablecloths, were not entirely real, were indeed half phantoms'.

12. Virginia Woolf, 'A sketch of the Past', in *Moments of Being*, p. 132.

13. Virginia Woolf, *Orlando* (London: Hogarth Press, 1928), p. 207. Further page references to this edition are included in the text.

14. *Collected Essays*, vol. I, p. 206.

15. John Ruskin, *Modern Painters* (New York, 1881), vol. III, containing part IV, 'Of Many Things', p. 248–9.

16. Ibid., vol. III, part IV, p. 161.

17. Perry Meisel, *The Absent Father: Virginia Woolf and Water Pater* (New Haven, Conn., and London: Yale University Press, 1980); Beer, 'Virginia Woolf and Prehistory'.

18. *Collected Essays*, vol. I, p. 214.

19. Virginia Woolf, *Flush: A Biography* (London: Hogarth Press, 1940), p. 19. Further page references are included in the text. Woolf's most rumbustious representation of chosen Victorians is *Freshwater: A Comedy* (London: Hogarth Press, 1976).
20. *Collected Essays*, vol. IV, p. 39.
21. *Collected Essays*, vol. IV, p. 54.
22. Quoted in Michael Holroyd, *Lytton Strachey: A Biography* (London: Heinemann, 1970), p. 312.
23. Virginia Woolf, 'Women and Fiction', in *Granite and Rainbow* (London: Hogarth Press, 1958), p. 83.
24. Frederic Harrison, *Cornhill Magazine*.
25. Virginia Woolf, *Mrs Dalloway* (London: Hogarth Press, 1925), p. 88.
26. Thomas Henry Huxley, 'On the Physical Basis of Life', *Lay Sermons, Addresses and Reviews* (London, 1870), pp. 104–27 (quotation from pp. 105–6). Huxley's volume is dedicated to John Tyndall.
27. Virginia Woolf, *The Waves* (London: Hogarth Press, 1931), p. 8.
28. James A. Froude, *Thomas Carlyle: a History of his Life in London, 1834–1881* (London, 1884), vol. I, pp. 289–91.
29. John Tyndall, *On Radiation* (London, 1865), pp. 9–10.
30. John Tyndall, *Six Lectures on Light* (London, 1873), p. 53.
31. See for example, 'The scientific use of the imagination', in John Tyndall, *Use and Limit of the Imagination in Science* (London, 1870), p. 26, and the responses collected in that volume, for example, *The Times*, 19 September 1870.
32. For a rather general discussion of the possible effects of Woolf's reading in twentieth-century popular physics, see Alan J. Friedman and Carol C. Donley, *Einstein as Myth and Muse* (Cambridge: Cambridge University Press, 1985).
33. Virginia Woolf, *Between the Acts* (London: Hogarth Press, 1941), p. 203. Further page references are included in the text.

6

Physics, Sound, and Substance: Later Woolf

'Like the symbolic world of physics, a wave is a conception that is hollow enough to hold almost anything: we can have waves of water, of air, of aether, and (in quantum theory) waves of probability.'

Arthur Eddington, *New Pathways in Science*

Virginia Woolf was not a university graduate and her relations with Cambridge were always awkward, sideways on, marking the degree of women's exclusion precisely because her family's history in the male line was so bound into the life of Cambridge colleges. Her grandfather was head of house, her father a don, her brother a graduate, but, *unlike* many intellectual women of her generation, Virginia Stephen never went to college. (Her sister-in-law, Karen Stephen, was at Newnham.) All her kin were classicists and scholars of the humanities. So it is particularly intriguing that when in *A Room of One's Own*, that classic of women's claims, Woolf tried to find an image for the future of women's friendship and identity, she chose that of two women scientists, co-workers in a laboratory.

Strikingly, the passage was changed to include this image after her visits to Girton and Newnham to deliver the lecture from which the book emerged. Yet it has been customary to argue that the writers associated with Bloomsbury, and Woolf in particular, were absolutely ignorant of and uninterested in science. Perhaps that insistence also has to do with a particular idea of how science functions: autonomous, separate from culture, untouched by it. It may be hard to recognise how scientific innovation flares out in different zones if we look only for a technical completeness. The process of reception is interactive, scientists also being driven by the concerns and thought resources of the historical period they share with contemporaries.[1]

In this essay I shall argue that for Woolf in the 1930s the language and ideas of the new physics helped to provide pathways out of the impasse of realist fiction. The physicists did not simply introduce ideas to her; rather, their insights and their language coalesced with hers. She saw realist fiction as an impoverishment of the real and in her own writing sought at once to condense and (as she put it) 'insubstantise'. In the late 1920s and early 1930s science – particularly physics – fascinated non-scientists, and the writings of Arthur Eddington and James Jeans were best-sellers. In part this fascination was because these physicists declared themselves discontented with closed epistemologies.[2]

'Modern physics is off the gold standard' wrote Eddington in *New Pathways in Science*:[3] that is to say, there is no single authoritative referent, no 'gold'; exchange rates vary between currencies; we are out in an unstable world of possibilities, statistics, waves.[4]

Just as chaos theory at present teases and stimulates non-scientists, so wave-particle theory at the end of the 1920s and through the 1930s caught the imagination. Newspapers and journals of the time contain frequent material and reports, as a glance at *The Times* and, particularly, the then new radio journal *Listener* will show. Indeed, from its inception in 1929 through to about 1934 up to 40 per cent of the articles in the *Listener* are by scientists and about science. And certain scientists developed a rhetoric by whose means the epistemological puzzles of the new physics could be communicated to a wider audience. In particular, Arthur Eddington and James Jeans (both later knighted) achieved high success, and Eddington especially was also an important original worker.[5] Eddington, professor in Cambridge of astrophysics and living at the university observatory, was Woolf's exact contemporary, born like her in 1882. Though, unlike her, as a fellow he could walk on the grass at Trinity and use the Wren Library, his work, beliefs and personality always made him something of an outsider in the establishment. He sought ways of combining science and mysticism. He was a Quaker and a conscientious objector. His father died before he was two, still an infant – without language – and he lived throughout his life for most of the time with his mother and sister. He was a rather unusual man. Three of his books in particular were immensely popular, admired by philosophers such as Bertrand Russell and ordinary readers alike, widely read and discussed: *The Nature of the Physical World* (Cambridge 1928, Gifford Lectures 1927), *Science and the Unseen World* (London 1929) and *New Pathways in Science* (Cambridge 1935). He was also one of the first to make use of radio for communicating complex ideas. Radio – itself one of the technological outcomes of the work of late nineteenth-century physicists such as Hertz and Maxwell – fascinated Woolf also, disjoining body and voice. In a couple of lines in her diary at the end of 1930 Woolf conjures the new gallimaufry of intimacies that radio brings: 'That bedroom voice, singing Bach, talking of the weather, has come in handy.'[6]

Both Eddington and Woolf would have been available to the other not as text only but as voice, across the airwaves, as also were James Jeans and Gerald Heard,[7] Bertrand Russell and Vita Sackville-West. Like Woolf, Eddington was sceptical about the worship of sacred words such as 'life' and 'reality'. He himself wrote like an angel, and funnily: 'There is still the tendency to use "reality" as a word of magic comfort like the blessed word "Mesopotamia".'[8]

While she was writing *The Waves* and just before she began writing the summation of the work, Bernard's last soliloquy, Woolf was reading James Jeans. His three most influential books of popular explication appeared during and just after the period that Woolf was thinking through *The Waves* (1931): *The Universe Around Us* (Cambridge 1929), *The Mysterious Universe* (Cambridge 1930) and *The New Background of Science* (Cambridge 1933). Conversation with David Cecil, Lytton Strachey and Clive Bell connects Jeans's mysterious universe and rhythm in prose: ('Talk about the riddle of the universe (Jeans' book) whether it will be known; not by us; found out suddenly: about rhythm in prose').[9] She worked at imagining the bending back of space as she read Jeans's description, and wrote about it in a letter to her friend the composer Ethel Smyth.[10] Jeans's thoughts about the nature of time continued to haunt her and became part of her thought on human emotions:

> You know what Jeans says? Civilization is the thickness of a post-age stamp on the top of Cleopatra's needle; & time to come is the thickness of postage stamps as high as Mont Blanc. Possessive-ness is the devil.[11]

Reading Jeans again in August 1937 ('I bought a 6d. Jeans on the Mysterious Universe') Woolf was inspired to buy a telescope. Through it she saw, like many amateurs, obscurely disappointing objects. She describes them with testy wit: 'Jupiter minus the waiting women: & a plaster cast of the moon' ... 'We saw the Ring of Saturn last night, like a cardboard collar.'[12]

By the late 1920s when Woolf was working on *Orlando* and *The Waves*, waves in motion were – according to the new physics – all the universe consists in. And they are probably fictitious, 'ondes fictives' as the French physicist de Broglie called them. In 1928, Eddington wrote in *The Nature of the Physical World*:

> In the scientific world the conception of substance is wholly lacking ... For this reason the scientific world often shakes us by its appearance of unreality. It offers nothing to satisfy our demand for the concrete. How should it, when we cannot formulate that demand? I tried to formulate it; but nothing happened, save a tightening of the fingers. (p. 274)

Or as Woolf wrote in 1929:

> Now is life very solid or very shifting? I am haunted by the two contradictions. This has gone on for ever; will last for ever; goes down to the bottom of the world – this moment I stand on. Also it is transitory, flying, diaphanous. I shall pass like a cloud on the waves. Perhaps it may be that though we change, one flying after another, so quick, so quick, yet we are somehow successive and continuous we human beings, and show the light through. But what is the light?[13]

James Jeans suggested in *The Mysterious Universe* that 'the ethers and their undulations, the waves which form in the universe, are in all probability fictitious – they exist in our minds' (p. 79). Jeans is thus led, long before Baudrillard, to equalise representation and enactment:

> The motion of electrons and atoms does not resemble those of the parts of a locomotive so much as those of the dancers in a cotillion. And if the 'true essence of substances' is for ever unknowable, it does not matter whether the cotillion is danced at a ball in real life, or on a cinematograph screen, or in a story of Boccaccio. (p. 136)

In 'The Narrow Bridge of Art', Woolf had argued at the end of the 1920s that the future for fiction, particularly for women writers, must lie in 'greater impersonality':

> the greater impersonality of women's lives will encourage the poetic spirit, and it is in poetry that women's fiction is still weakest. It will lead them to be less absorbed in facts and no longer content to record ... their own observation. They will look beyond the

personal and political relationships to the wider question which the poet tries to solve of our destiny and the meaning of life.

High words – and chilling. There may seem something vatic, and vague, about 'our destiny and the meaning of life' divested of the personal and political. Woolf thus imagined widening the scope of fiction half-way through her career. It was one way out of trapped sensibility, schematic plotting. In the event, though, she seeks throughout the 1930s for ways of letting poetry into her work – not through shifty expansiveness so much as through particularity, simultaneity, what she later calls (in quotation marks) 'seeing'. Above all, she works to a rhythm, not a plot ('the riddle of the universe' and 'rhythm in prose'). She finds ways between *The Waves* and *Between the Acts* of bringing comedy, politics, people, and perception into touch. That movement need not ape stability. It must find modes of thinking and representation that are limber, shifty, contingent: 'as if the china of the plate flowed and the steel of the knife were liquid'.[14]

In this turn of her thinking, both physics and poetry help. And neither of them in the 1930s was cut away from politics. Each suggested ways of energising the connections between everyday experience and long arcs of meaning. And Woolf worked, or as she said of *Between the Acts*, 'frisked' across these connections. The word 'frisk' includes 'risk'. Rhyme peculiarly levels hierarchies, refuses the dominance of semantic meaning, uncovers improbable likeness and affinity. One thing that she particularly enjoyed was frisking and risking, combining the serious and the wayward, first in *The Waves*, then in *Three Guineas* and *Between the Acts*. The materialising and deliquescing of words in rhyme function as an undertow or cryptic guide to connection. The fictive waves of physics, as she understood them, and of rhyme overlap in her creativity. To stay, first, with her response, loose and fascinated, not close honed, to the physics of the time.

As Woolf works in the 1920s the boundary between the actual and the fictional is no longer securely policed: presenting his argument concerning wave-particle dualism to the Parisian Academy of Sciences in September 1923, de Broglie emphasised that he was not speaking of material waves but of an 'onde fictive'.[15] Max Born wrote in Einstein's *Theory of Relativity* (tr. 1924): 'In the flood of invisible light that is accessible to the mental eye of the physicist, the material eye is almost blind, so small is the interval of vibrations which it converts into sensations' (p. 8). The minutiae of difference, the grains of sensation that make up what may be called an event, are in *The Waves* the process of the writing. *The Waves*, wrote Woolf, is an 'abstract, mystical, eyeless book'. The world of the physicist is, wrote Born, that of 'inaudible tones, invisible light, imperceptible heat' (Born sees that as at the opposite end of the spectrum from poetry). But the common topic of poetry and science is, in his view, 'the part that each doctrine assigns to the ego in the world'. Such speculations begin to offer a new shape for understanding Woolf's emphasis on 'standing further back from life'. 'We long for some more impersonal relationship. We long for ideas, for dreams, for imaginations, for poetry ... a novel that will give the relation of the mind to general ideas and its soliloquy in solitude ...'. Einstein's theory, Born argued, 'is a pure product of the striving after the liberation of the ego, after the release from sensation and perception'. 'Now, Einstein's discovery is that this space and this time are still entirely embedded in the ego, and that the world-picture of natural science becomes more beautiful and grander if these fundamental conceptions are subjected to relativization' (p. 5). The ego is etherialised, snatched away from a single base.

Woolf, like most educated people of the 1920s, was well aware of Einstein as an intellectual presence. And, like many others, she found his theories both baffling and magical. On Saturday, 20 March 1926 she went to a supper party: 'I wanted, like a child, to stay and argue. True, the argument was passing my limits – how, if Einstein is true, we shall be able to foretell our own lives.'[16] That dazzled appreciation (or misprision) of Einstein's work haunts the writing of the 1930s. In the main, her understanding came through newspaper articles and through the writing of Eddington and Jeans (though it is worth noticing that she also pasted in her scrapbook Einstein's denunciation of fascism). However, any too conscientious complete approximation of Woolf to the principles of relativity would have to cope with her amusement at any such idea. In May 1938, the first person to attempt to write a Ph.D. on Woolf came to visit her:

> Miss Nielsen came: a donnish bee haunted American lit. prof., entirely distracted by Einstein, and his extra mundane influence upon fiction. L. threaded the maze to the muddle in the centre. I gave up on the outskirts ...[17]

Still, Miss Nielsen perhaps had her effect. Woolf resists particularly her wholesale claim, but Einstein and Eddington are scattered in and named among other ideas in the gossip of *Between the Acts*.

I am not seeking to emphasise only *likeness* or to suggest one way debts between Woolf's work and the extraordinarily successful and popular writing of Eddington and Jeans. Rather, I want to indicate the speed of assimilation and reworking; to explore the resources ideas may provide for transformation, some moving out from the laboratory into apparently distant topics such as politics and poetry; and, at the same time, to indicate the degree to which, in explanation, scientists must think with the materials available to them in their culture: here, for example, the traditional instance of the 'table', derived from the philosophical tradition of British empiricism:

> 'Think of a table when you're not there.'
>
> Andrew to Lily in *To the Lighthouse*

> 'I do not see this actual table, except in flashes. I see a wave breaking upon the limits of the word.'
>
> Rhoda in the first draft of *The Waves*

> 'In the world of physics we watch a shadowgraph performance of the drama of familiar life. The shadow of my elbow rests on the shadow table as the shadow ink flows over the shadow paper. It is all symbolic, and as a symbol the physicist leaves it.'[18]

> I begin now to forget; I begin to doubt the fixity of tables, the reality of here and now, to tap my knuckles smartly upon the edges of apparently solid objects and say, 'Are you hard?'
>
> Bernard, in *The Waves* (1931)

> I have settled down to the task of writing these lectures and have drawn up my chairs to my two tables. Two tables! Yes; there are duplicates of every object about me – two tables, two chairs, two pens.
>
> Ibid., opening sentences

Woolf's preoccupations chimed in with those of the physicists who emphasised the universe as waves, the porousness of matter, 'the world moving through abysses of infinite space ... we are extinct, lost in the abysses of time, in the darkness', as Louis muses in *The Waves*. Yet is that abstracted insubstantial world *enough* for a novelist? How to find and sustain story? emotion? ordinary living without falling into the realist trap? In *The Waves* she takes up the tropes of table and waves in attempting to think what story can be, how it can begin and end and produce the consolation of containment in a world of ebbing tides, increasing entropy, and dissipating energy. The homely matters to her. The passage opens by musing on the dissolution of story, the sturdy present of appetite: table and wave.

Should this be the end of the story? a kind of sigh? a last ripple of the wave? A trickle of water to some gutter where, burbling, it dies away? Let me touch the table – so – and thus recover my sense of the moment. A side-board covered with cruets; a basket full of rolls; a plate of bananas – these are comfortable sights.

As the passage continues she draws in the failure of energy ('force ebbs away'), the debility of narrative, here revived by the endless reproduction of wave-form:

But if there are no stories, what end can there be, or what beginning? Life is not susceptible perhaps to the treatment we give it when we try to tell it. ... It is strange how force ebbs away and away into some dry creek. Sitting alone, it seems we are spent; our waters can only just surround feebly that spike of sea-holly; we cannot reach that further pebble so as to wet it. It is over, we are ended. But wait – I sat all night waiting – an impulse again runs through us; we rise, we toss back a mane of white spray; we pound on the shore; we are not to be confined. That is, I shaved and washed; did not wake my wife, and had breakfast; put on my hat, and went out to earn my living. After Monday, Tuesday comes. (p. 223)

Life rounds, runs on, is bathos and exaltation, routine and renewal. Indeed, routine *as* renewal.

In *Between the Acts* Isa seeks other forms of order and freedom from pain:

What remedy was there for her at her age – the age of the century, thirty nine – in books? Book-shy she was, like the rest of her generation; and gun-shy too. Yet as a person with a raging tooth runs her eye in a chemist shop over green bottles with gilt scrolls on them lest one of them may contain a cure, she considered: Keats and Shelley; Yeats and Donne. Or perhaps not a poem; a life. The life of Garibaldi. The life of Lord Palmerston. Or perhaps not a person's life; a county's. *The Antiquities of Durham; The Proceedings of the Archaeological Society of Nottingham.* Or not a life at all, but science – Eddington, Darwin, or Jeans.[19]

None of them, it will prove, stop her tooth-ache, but the ordering of the list is significant: from poems to lives, political and communal, to science. The movement is through and beyond the personal.

To return to Isa's list of possible salvation reading: 'not a life at all

119

but science: Eddington, Darwin, Jeans'. Darwin had always been one of Woolf's measures of 'greatness' – a concept which at the same time her writing persistently brings into question: Mr Bankes in *To the Lighthouse* doubts 'whether you could have your Darwin and your Titian if it weren't for humble people like ourselves' (p. 114). And the example of the humble figure that is used in *To the Lighthouse* is 'the liftman' – a figure whom Einstein in 1915 had also invoked, to clarify his discussion of relativity. More striking in Isa's list of possible salves for her consciousness are those names that now flank Darwin: Eddington and Jeans.

Towards the end of the book, when the play has ended and the audience are mulling over the afternoon, the hubbub of conversation yields vagrant talk of oracles and crêpe soles, physics, religion, the onset of war, red fingernails, and sex. It includes this passage:

> Oracles? You're referring to the Greeks? Were the oracles, if I'm not being irreverent, a foretaste of our own religion? Which is what? ... Crepe soles? That's so sensible ... They last much longer and protect the feet. ... But I was saying: can the Christian faith adapt itself? In times like these ... At Larting no one goes to church ... There's the dogs, there's the pictures. It's odd that science, so they tell me, is making things (so to speak) more spiritual ... The very latest notion, so I'm told is, nothing's solid ... There, you can get a glimpse of the church through the trees. ...[20]

From the 1920s on at least, Woolf found in the new physics dizzying confirmation of her sense that the real and the substantial are not the same. As early as 1923 she had invented a word for what she wanted to do: to 'insubstantise'. Eddington in 1928 describes a similar project. In the final chapter of *The Nature of the Physical World* Eddington turns to 'science and mysticism' and argues some of the relations between physics and poetry. Is the introjection of the ego into the external world an illusion (the example he gives is the phrase which moves associatively across – waves – ripples – laughter – gladness). Is it *more of* an illusion than substance?: 'the solid substance of things is another illusion. It too is a fancy projected by the mind into the external world'.

When Woolf comments wryly of *The Waves* that there is 'no quite solid table on which to put it', and when within the novel her thinkers doubt 'the fixity of tables ... are you hard?' (p. 240), she is taking part in a stressful debate at large in the world of her time, not engaging in solipsistic prose-poem musings on her own. Eddington suggests that substance is the hardest comfort to do without: 'we have seen that substance is one of our greatest illusion ... Perhaps, indeed, reality is a child which cannot survive without its nurse illusion'.[21]

Assonance, overlap between words, iteration and internal rhyme all, in that work, express the wave-like fluidity of a newly imagined universe. Indeed, stream of consciousness as she here effects it is an expression of a world organisation in which recurrent words are flow, engulf, waste, vast, wind:

> The roar of the traffic, the passage of undifferentiated faces, this way and that, drugs me into dreams; rubs features from faces. People might walk through me. And what is this moment of time, this particular day in which I have found myself caught? The growl of traffic might be an uproar – forest trees or the roar of wild beasts. Time has whizzed back an inch or two on its reel; our short progress has been cancelled. (p. 93)

In a virtuoso passage at the end of the chapter 'Science and Mysticism' Eddington describes the difficulties that the scientist experiences on the threshold in terms like those that Rhoda experienced as she approached the puddle she could not cross: for each of them the solid world dislimns. Elsewhere in *The Waves* Rhoda imagines herself as the foam scudding on the waves of the sea. Here:

> 'There is the puddle', said Rhoda, 'and I cannot cross it. I hear the rush of the great grindstone within an inch of my face. Its wind roars in my face. All palpable forms of life have failed me. Unless I can stretch and touch something hard, I shall be blown down the eternal corridors for ever.' (p. 130)

Each stands on a threshold. The difficulty and improbability of physical life declares itself. Eddington's imagining, quirky, humorous and compelling, is published four years after *The Waves*.

> I am standing on the threshold about to enter a room. It is a complicated business. In the first place I must shove against an atmosphere pressing with a force of fourteen pounds on every square inch of my body. I must make sure of landing on a plank travelling at twenty miles a second round the sun – a fraction of a second too early or too late, the plank would be miles away. I must do this whilst hanging from a round planet head outward into space and with a wind of aether blowing at no one knows how many miles a second through every interstice of my body.

121

The plank has no solidity of substance. To step on it is like stepping on a swarm of flies. Shall I not slip through? (p. 342)

Even the eye of a needle presents no greater difficulties for entry than the doorway to a room.

The great German Jewish thinker Walter Benjamin quotes this same passage of Eddington's in his second essay on Kafka in 1938, claiming that 'If one reads it one can virtually hear Kafka speak'. He comments on the tensions of 'physical perplexity' and 'mysticism' in Eddington and Kafka and swings his argument round into a blast of terrible foresight which includes his own individual death as part of 'the masses' ... 'being done away with':

> that reality of ours which realizes itself theoretically, for example, in modern physics, and practically in the technology of modern warfare. What I mean to say is that this reality can virtually no longer be experienced by an individual, and that Kafka's world, frequently of such playfulness and interlaced with angels, is the exact complement of his era which is preparing to do away with the inhabitants of this planet on a considerable scale.[22]

Benjamin here pinpoints ways in which the non-deterministic, relativised, ethereal world of play and representation in physics, and in its accounts of itself in the 1930s, are, ultimately, terribly yoked to the destructive outcomes of those same physics. The personal politics of Eddington are those of the conscientious objector, of the peace movement and Quaker humanitarianism. He finds that the work of physicists is fundamental to the conduct of the war, culminating in the atom bomb at its end. The politics of Virginia Woolf are anti-militarist, labour. Increasingly as the 1930s go on she clings to the frail hope of the Peace Pledge movement, and grits her teeth in the knowledge of the coming war. In *Three Guineas* she seeringly brings together gender politics and the politics of current rearmament and masculine aggression. At the same time she found herself accused in writing by her nephew Julian Bell as part of the quietist artistic world that had not acted politically when it was needed. Now the war was inexorably approaching which they had done too little to prevent.

The common danger for artists and physicists at the time is that of mentalism, a withdrawal from the social fray – particularly the political fray, in the light of an emphasis on emptiness, porousness, atomism, undecidability. Doing away with a stable nature 'out there' where 'there was no great difference between appearance and reality' and substituting a position in which the scientist must see nature not as 'entirely distinct from himself' rather: 'Sometimes it is what he himself creates, or selects or abstracts; sometimes it is what he destroys'.[23] Fascist art did not preoccupy itself with insubstantiality. Heads were substantial until the fascists got to them. Einstein and others were well aware of the quietism that could be the outcome of the loss of purchase for the physical world that physics could imply.

Of the writers on science in the 1930s Gerald Heard was the one who most knitted together theoretical science and its practical implications: politics and evolution, entropy and social conditions. He was anti-empire, anti-militarist; he emphasised that peace is a natural condition for advance, violence an interruption. Leonard Woolf while chief reviewer for *The Nation* paid him a good deal of attention. Woolf first read his work just as she was finishing *The Waves* in 1930; then his later more visionary writing while she was working at *Between the Acts*. She felt admiration and irritation for him. His reading of evolution insists that sensitivity has survival value, awareness is the specifying human virtue. She approved his anti-imperialism. Empire produces decay. 'Advance is accomplished by creative not destructive forces and, though such destructive forces exist, they do not help forward the life process but are sporadic interruptions, morbid aberrations.'[24] Because 'empire can have no frontiers' it is degenerative, overrunning its own strength. At the height of his argument in 1935 Heard, like Eddington, alludes to Mesopotamia. This time not a 'blessed word' but ravaged by war fought by intervening powers. Heard's chapter ends: 'Thy hand great anarch lets the curtain fall and universal entropy paralyses all.' Pope at the end of *The Dunciad*, here half-quoted, imagines civilisation overwhelmed not by chaos but dullness – the opposite of awareness. Listening to Hitler's a-rhythmic rant Woolf commented on this loss of bounds, of rhythmic sense.[25] By 1939 Woolf had largely lost patience with Heard's apocalyptic manner. Now she seeks to hold things together, fleetingly in rhyme and gossip, and at the end of *Between the Acts* insists: 'The curtain rose. They spoke.' After alienated silence Isa and Giles will at last, at least, speak to each other, reasonably use the human voice.

Why then did she need physics? As a medium of poetry? Certainly not to expunge the political. In the writing of the 1930s, *The Years*, 'The Pargiters', *Three Guineas* and *Between the Acts*, the politics of the family, the nation, of classes, sex and war are exposed, as well as implicit, in the texts. What she needed was the power of speaking in chords. She needed sounds and speech and the processes by which we experience sound. She needed 'the sound of a bell' and the realisation that 'the sensation which I describe as hearing the sound of a bell ... actually ... is feeling the effect of waves of condensation and rarefaction of the air inside my ears'.[26] It turned out that the language of physicists chimed with her search for rhythmic prose to give her new working freedoms. She used those freedoms to sound communal experience, even universal experience, and to reveal the lines of force that run through historical moments.

Notes

1. For a full discussion of the writing of Arthur Eddington see my essay 'Eddington and the Idiom of Modernism', in *Science, Reason and Rhetoric*, ed. Henry Krips (Pittsburgh, 1995). See also my essay '"Wireless": Radio, Physics and Modernism', in *Cultural Babbage*, ed. Francis Spufford and Jenny Uglow (London, 1996).

2. Of course, Woolf did not have access to the highly mathematical scientific writings of Eddington or Jeans but only to their popularisations.

3. A. S. Eddington, *New Pathways in Science* (Cambridge, 1935), p. 81.

4. Britain suspended the gold standard in September 1931. For Woolf's irreverent and exasperated comments on this event see *The Diary of Virginia Woolf*, ed. Anne Olivier Bell (London: Hogarth Press, 1980), vol, IV, p. 45.

5. See my essay 'Eddington and the Idiom of Modernism', in *Science, Reason, and Rhetoric*, ed. Henry Krips et al. (Pittsburgh, 1995), pp. 295–315. Sections of the present essay overlap with material published there.

6. *Diary*, vol. III, p. 343. See my essay '"Wireless": Radio, Physics, and Modernism', in *Cultural Babbage*, ed. Francis Spufford and Jenny Uglow (London, 1996).

7. From 1930 to 1933 Heard gave a series of radio broadcasts on scientific subjects called 'The Surprising World'; he also published widely, for example, *The Emergence of Man* (1931). Leonard Woolf reviewed him in *The Nation* and Virginia Woolf read him at intervals throughout the 1930s.

8. A. S. Eddington, *The Nature of the Physical World* (Cambridge, 1928), p. 327.

9. *Diary*, vol. III, p. 337 (8 December 1930).

10. James Jeans, *The Universe Around Us* (Cambridge, 1929), pp. 70–1 ff.

11. *Diary*, vol. IV, p. 65 (30 January 1932).

12. *Diary*, vol. V, pp. 107, 109, 110.

13. *Diary*, vol. III, p. 218.

14. *The Waves*, ed. Gillian Beer (Oxford, 1992), p. 21.

15. Quoted in Bruce R. Wheaton, *The Tiger and the Shark: Empirical Roots of Wave-Particle Dualism* (Cambridge: Cambridge University Press, 1983), pp. 290–1. In 1929 de Broglie received the Nobel prize in physics for his theoretical hypothesis of matter waves.

16. *Diary*, vol. III, p. 68.

17. *Diary*, vol V, p. 146.

18. Eddington, *The Nature of the Physical World*, p. 2.

19. *Between the Acts* (London: Hogarth Press, 1941), p. 26. All further page references to this edition are included in the text after quotations.

20. p. 232. The intervening dots are part of the text, not omissions.

21. Eddington, *The Nature of the Physical World*, p. 318.

22. Walter Benjamin, *Illuminations* (London, 1973), p. 145; first published in 1938.

23. James Jeans, *The New Background of Science* (Cambridge: Cambridge University Press, 1933), p. 2.

24. Gerald Heard, *The Source of Civilisation* (London: Jonathan Cape, 1935), p. 25.

25. At the Nuremberg Rally, live on radio, 13 September 1938: *Diary*, vol. V, p. 169.

26. Jeans, *New Background*, p. 22.

7

Between the Acts: Resisting the End

*B*etween the Acts is Woolf's final novel. She imagined, planned, and wrote it through the last days of a peace that seemed at times like a national hallucination, and into the period when England daily expected invasion. As she wrote and revised, the bombers passed nightly overhead. She and Leonard Woolf discussed what they would do if the German parachutes landed. They knew the fate of Jews throughout Europe. They would shut the garage doors and die.[1] When the work was more or less completed she died by her own will, but alone, drowning on 28 March 1941 in that same river where a man she described in a letter to Ethel Smyth shot himself just before the outbreak of war. Such an account of the circumstances of composition suggests a sombre work. But that would be to underestimate Woolf's vitality as a writer.

With *Orlando, Between the Acts* is Woolf's most mischievous and playful work, as well as one that muses much upon death and extinction. It is also a work where each word tells – sometimes at odds with its neighbour. Together these disparate words tell a resourceful history that jettisons ideas of development, discovers the remote past in the present moment, celebrates and mocks 'Englishness' and family life – and knows passion in all its improbability.

War

The novel is set quite specifically on a mid-June afternoon 1939. The Second World War will start only six weeks later. The characters in the book are preoccupied with the village pageant, with the weather and weather forecasts, with longing and lascivious fantasies: apparently

First published in: Virginia Woolf, *Between the Acts*, ed. G. Beer (Oxford: World's Classics, 1992), pp. ix–xxxv.

(save for Giles) with anything but the war. But the coming war broods over the whole community, 'the doom of sudden death hanging over us' (p. 70), changing the meaning of past and present, threatening even the possibility of repetition: 'The future shadowed their present, like the sun coming through the many-veined transparent vine leaf: a criss-cross of lines making no pattern' (p. 70).

The playfulness and the holiday atmosphere in the book are partly rituals of defence against that future; a future which in the sentence quoted above is figured pastorally ('like the sun coming through the many-veined transparent vine leaf'), but in words that refer also to the play of searchlights ('a criss-cross of lines making no pattern'). Likewise, the funds raised by the village pageant are to go towards, the vicar says, 'the illumination of our dear old church' (p. 114). But ironically, as Woolf and her first readers well knew, the blackout was about to be imposed just beyond the book's ending. The novel is sprung on such contingent ironies. The blackout is nowhere mentioned but Woolf wrote in it, her readers read in it, and the work ends in 'the heart of darkness, the fields of night'. Conrad's image of imperialism discovering the savagery at its own heart is combined with a side-long glance at Pope's *Dunciad*, which ends with the return of Chaos as the curtain falls on civilization.

> Thy hand, great Anarch! lets the curtain fall,
> And Universal Darkness buries All.

At the end of Woolf's work, however, the curtain will rise on a future that is also pre-history.

> Left alone together for the first time that day, they were silent. Alone, enmity was bared; also love. Before they slept, they must fight; after they had fought, they would embrace. From that embrace another life might be born. But first they must fight, as the dog fox fights with the vixen, in the heart of darkness, in the fields of night ... The house had lost its shelter. It was night before roads were made, or houses. It was the night that dwellers in caves had watched from some high place among rocks.
>   Then the curtain rose. They spoke.

In those final sentences a new act is set to begin: sexual, theatrical, war-like, yet suggesting continuance. What that communal future will contain the reader must come to know in history beyond the aid of this book.

The work itself humorously, sometimes sardonically, interleaves literature, gossip, and communal events actually occurring in the world beyond the fiction. It dwells on objects and emptiness, skews (and skewers) perceptions through puns and rhymes. The seized fragments of language are robust, demotic, evanescent; many of the people in the work – old Lucy Swithin, her brother Bartholomew, his son Giles, Isa married to Giles, their guests Mrs Manresa and William Dodge, and Miss La Trobe, creator of the pageant – are vividly characterized. The small change of domestic life brims out of a fund of long and deep experience. The book includes the very old as well as new generations: old Mrs Swithin broods on 'the iguanodon, the mammoth, and the mastodon; from whom presumably, she thought, jerking the window open, we descend' (p. 8). Isa 'looked at Mrs. Swithin as if she had been a dinosaur or a very diminitive mammoth. Extinct she must be, since she had lived in the reign of Queen Victoria' (p. 104). All these characters are set in the midst of the voices and names of the village community, whose words are shared, dispersed, and shorn away from particular mouths.

The idea for the book began to stir in April 1938, as Virginia Woolf worked on the proofs of her boldest feminist polemic, *Three Guineas*, and laboured still at her biography of her friend, the art critic and painter Roger Fry. News came of the ironic death of Ottoline Morell, struck down by a heart-attack on hearing that her husband was ill and might die. Woolf was obliged to write an obituary. She addresses herself in her diary that day:

> So I had to write; the horrid little pellet screwed my brain; leaves it giddy. Yet in spite of that here I am sketching out a new book; only dont please impose that huge burden on me again, I implore. Let it be random and tentative; something I can blow of a morning, to relieve myself of Roger: dont, I implore, lay down a scheme; call in all the cosmic immensities; & force my tired & diffident brain to embrace another whole – all parts contributing – not yet awhile. But to amuse myself, let me note: why not Poyntzet Hall: a centre: all lit. discussed with real little incongruous living humour; & anything that comes into my head; but "I" rejected: 'We' substituted: to whom at the end there shall be an invocation? "We" … composed of many different things … we all life, all art, all waifs and strays – a rambling capricious but somehow unified whole – the present state of my mind? And English country; & a scenic old house – & a terrace where nursemaids walk? & people passing – & a perpetual variety & change from intensity to prose. & facts – & notes; & – but eno'. I must read

127

> Roger: & go to Ott's memorial service, representing also T. S.
> Eliot at his absurd command. 2.30 at Martins in the Fields.[2]

The impulses set out in this passage are astonishingly close to the novel that actually emerged, in contrast, for example, to *The Waves* which underwent many transformations from conception to text.

Woolf's sense that the capricious and the fugitive may be the only way of holding things together abides throughout the composition of *Between the Acts*. 'Living humour' brings body and language into irresolute contact. Woolf is amused and irritated in this diary entry by Eliot's pompous command that she 'represent' him at Ottoline Morell's memorial service, partly because she sees bodily difference as more important than symbolic statement. Also she had, after all, only recently finished *Three Guineas* in which she mocked the masculine trappings of solemn social rituals. She is *not* T. S. Eliot: but now there he is, tangled into the start of her new project. He was to remain so, for *Four Quartets* and *Between the Acts* cite and sound each other repeatedly.

Ritual in *Between the Acts* emerges from the need for repetition and recurrence, but its forms are flighty. Woolf was familiar with the work of the anthropologist Jane Harrison and knew her as a friend. Harrison's work on ritual, like that of Ruth Benedict whom Woolf read as she wrote, has its effects in the work, but not, I would argue, by providing a system of interpretation.[3] Indeed, the work's partial, fugitive method of allusion and recall characteristically lets the reader brood or skim at will. Things go awry with interpretation here when the critic seeks, as some have done, to turn glimpses into systems.

Writing to her friend the composer Ethel Smyth in August 1939, just before the outbreak of the Second World War, Virginia Woolf describes impasse, dislocation, communal unreality, summer heat: 'Then there's the war – black outs: a man shot in the river where I walk; and the Labour party meeting here. I cant make a song of this, not a consecutive phrase, for I'm too hot.'[4] A few days later she writes to Vita Sackville-West as she packs up her house:

> whatever rung I'm on, the ladder is a great comfort in this kind
> of intolerable suspension of all reality – something real.
> But isn't it odd? – one cant fold it in any words.[5]

Woolf holds on to prosaic material objects like ladders, finding in them the continuing present. Language seems to promise continuance but, so responsive is it to the multiplicity of the moment, that it cannot be relied upon to provide the comforting sameness of ladders.

Virginia Woolf lingeringly hopes to find songs, phrases, words for overwhelming communal experience; but she knows that they must be words that acknowledge bafflement. Things broken apart, or lightly laid alongside, must take the place of fusion. Heteroglossia is here acted out by recording steadily what's thought, what's said, what's scrappily overheard. Isa, taking a cup of tea, broods on desire and drowning, through a remembered fairy tale:

> 'But what wish should I drop into the well?' She looked around. She could not see the man in grey, the gentleman farmer; nor anyone known to her. 'That the waters should cover me,' she, added, 'of the wishing well.'
>
> The noise of china and chatter drowned her murmur. 'Sugar for you?' they were saying. 'Just a spot of milk? And you?' 'Tea without milk or sugar. That's the way I like it.' 'A bit too strong? Let me add water.'
>
> 'That's what I wished,' Isa added, 'when I dropped my pin. Water. Water ...'
>
> 'I must say,' the voice said behind her, 'it's brave of the King and Queen. They're said to be going to India. She looks such a dear. Someone I know said his hair ...' (pp. 63–4)

What 'someone I know' said about the King's hair could be readily filled in by the contemporary reader who could join in the glee. Gossip stands in for dialogue. Gossip about the royal family is gleaned from the brouhaha of contemporary talk in the late thirties: 'about the Duke of Windsor. He landed on the south coast. Queen Mary met him. She'd been buying furniture – that's a fact. And the papers say she met him ...' (p. 64). And so indeed the papers of the time did say, just as Queen Mary's furniture-buying habits were part of ordinary malicious talk outside the action. The novel invokes the larger ordinary community of which the reader is a part and makes of that stuff the will to survive.

Dispensing and receiving tea, and the accompanying phrases ('Sugar for you?'), are here the forms that ritual takes, producing surface and depths alike. Woolf eschews grander invocations, of earth mothers or Isis. The community steadies itself through humdrum repetition, whose significance is in saying things again, more than in what is said. Saying things again implies that you are still there to say them. *Between the Acts* is preoccupied with communal survival, even as it glances across individual loss. It does not particularly praise the community it represents. That community typifies the attitudes that have brought the country to the brink of war and of fascism. But neither does the novel suggest any value in the community's possible obliteration.

Screaming past behind the tea-urn and the barn are the swallows who have returned endlessly over the centuries, since before humankind was here. Those same swallows have, by humankind, been made part of myths of rape and violation for which, as I shall show, Woolf uncovers a hideous and absurd recent parallel. This shifting overlay of contemporary life, natural recurrence, phatic language, and literary fragments, is the way Woolf's community survives. She chooses to show them gathered at leisure. That is her method of intensification.

Pastimes – gossip, play-acting, sociable meals – may make tolerable the inevitable passing of time, because they suggest that there is time in abundance. That fiction of time-to-spare becomes more important in periods of crisis. In the community and the historical moment that Woolf writes out of, and into, very little time seemed left. Europe stood on the edge of destruction and by the end of June 1940, a week after the disaster and amateur heroism of Dunkirk, Woolf wrote of the war: 'We pour to the edge of a precipice ... & then? I cant conceive that there will be a 27th June 1941.'[6] For her, there was not. She delayed finishing *Pointz Hall* (the working title), as much for the anchoring pleasure its writing gave her, as for any other reason. She toyed with delay to ward off defeat. People were killed nightly in nearby air-raids that passed overhead and she foresaw that she might be one of them. A few days earlier, in a different mood, she wrote in the diary: 'I feel, if this is my last lap, oughn't I to read Shakespeare? But cant. I feel oughn't I to finish off P.H.: oughtn't I to finish something by way of an end? The end gives its vividness, even its gaiety and recklessness to the random daily life.'[7]

Between the Acts comes to no conclusions, but it includes several endings: among them, the end of the village play, the dispersal of the audience, and the end of the day and coming of night with which scene the book itself comes to a close without closure: 'The curtain rose. They spoke.'

At the end of the village pageant that occupies so many pages of the book the audience begins to leave:

> The wheels scurred on the gravel. The cars drove off.
> The gramophone gurgled *Unity – Disperity*. It gurgled *Un* ... *dis* ... And ceased. (p. 119)

Opposites exist alongside, and cancel each other's meaning. Syllables disjoin. The gramophone runs down, 'And ceased.' At the same time the elements of dispersed words skein together to produce a word of a different sense: *undeceased*.

Throughout the novel the reader works with echoes, wraiths of words and forthright homely statements. Making noises makes sense in this writing. In this passage, for example, the nonce word 'scurred'or 'scrurred' (and its half-rhyme 'gurgled') mimic sounds as if the reader were there now in the drive;[8] the mimesis comes close, and falls pleasurably short, encouraging the reader to try the sounds out with the inner ear, yet acknowledging also that we are reading words and that words will not quite fold round actuality.

Words

The fascination with words, their depth and instability of reference, their capacity to survive into new circumstances, their interplay of allusion, is central to Woolf's examination of community. Words are always communal, particularly when set in grammatical relations. Words always include others than the self; they can figure what cannot be performed. People's proper names are quiddities but may express endurance and signify much within a close community:

> Again, had Figgis called the names of the villagers, they too would have answered. Mrs. Sands was born Iliffe, Candish's mother was one of the Perrys. The green mounds in the church-yard had been cast up by their molings, which for centuries had made the earth friable. (p. 47)

In a 1937 essay on 'Craftsmanship' Woolf muses on the street-wise resilience of words:

> Now, this power of suggestion is one of the most mysterious properties of words. Everyone who has ever written a sentence must be conscious or half-conscious of it. Words, English words are full of echoes, of memories, of associations – naturally. They have been out and about, on people's lips, in their houses, in the streets, in the fields, for many centuries.[9]

Strikingly, this discussion was part of a talk for the BBC, so that it was itself a part of the new oral culture that was rising around the written word. The radio, alongside newspapers, is the new communication system, carrying authoritative pronouncements that are scattered into shards of gossip.

What are the difficulties posed for the writer by the historical freight words carry? 'They are so stored, with meaning, with memories, that they have contracted so many famous marriages.' How to split one word apart from its expected partner is one difficulty, she suggests. Then, 'You cannot use a brand new word in an old language because of the very obvious yet mysterious fact that a word is not a single and separate entity, but part of other words. It is not a word indeed until it is part of a sentence.'[10] Fortunately, as we have already seen, Woolf did not always obey her embargo on new words. More striking is her assertion that words are not fully words until they are set in relationships with other words in a sentence, and that no word is a single or separate entity. Her final question on the same page is: 'How can we combine the old words in new orders so that they survive, so that they create beauty, so that they tell the truth?'

Survival; beauty; truth-telling; her question makes it clear that, for her, lexical play is no lightweight matter, though the play be airily deft. Such play ('combining the old words in new orders') seeks a communal *new order* as well as using the old as a bulwark against ruin. The effect of threnody is strong in much that Woolf writes at this time, sometimes mysteriously so:

> Voices interrupted. People passed the stable yard, talking.
> 'It's a good day, some say, the day we are stripped naked. Others, it's the end of the day. They see the Inn and the Inn's keeper. But none speaks with a single voice. None with a voice free from the old vibrations. Always I hear corrupt murmurs; the chink of gold and metal. Mad music ...' (p. 94)

Her writing is not nostalgic. It seeks to sustain life in the present, and does so through a singularly free-spoken use of words issuing from unnamed mouths, as gossip and aside. She writes out too the flow of individual half-consciousness in which words whimsically translate themselves, uncovering lateral kinships, saying and changing the unsayable. So Isabella cleanses the foul language of prejudice in the judgement that her husband Giles makes on William Dodge, whose homosexuality is indicated but never named (e.g. p. 65):

> Isabella guessed the word that Giles had not spoken. Well, was it wrong if he was that word? Why judge each other? Do we know each other? Not here, not now. But somewhere, this cloud, this crust, this doubt, this dust – She waited for a rhyme, it failed her; but somewhere surely one sun would shine and all, without a doubt, would be clear. (p. 39)

The word 'queer', hinted at in the outer rhyme of 'here' and 'clear' and reinforced a sentence later with 'I think I hear them', is conjured and evaded.

In this book, access to half-consciousness, communal and individual, is given by the anarchic neatness of rhyme, which pins together the unlike, making the ear the arbiter of significance. Woolf uses doggerel as much as high chime, figuring indignant exclamations as the music turns to jazz and the pageant ends without a grand finale:

> What a cackle, a cacophony! Nothing ended. So abrupt. And corrupt. Such an outrage; such an insult; And not plain. Very up to date, all the same. What is her game? To disrupt? (p. 109)

The rhyming game continues on down the page, and on other pages. In part, the effect is a tribute to music which alone, and briefly, can make things whole: 'Music wakes us. Music makes us see the hidden, join the broken. Look and listen' (p. 73). In part, it is a tribute to the human voice, which may belie the sense on the page, registering the tug between oral speech and written language. Woolf is exploring the way words 'cling' together. The effect though, is often less benign, suggesting the helpless staleness of an old community.

Words in this book also spring apart and re-order themselves in kaleidoscopic comedy (words like *sole*, which in the play of the text shifts vagrantly between fish, crepe soles of shoes, and spirit, and then flips backwards, reversing itself to become *lose* (p. 18), for example). The effect of such transformations is often lackadaisical, eschewing the vigorous urgings of Joycean word-play. The ability of words to come together and produce new ones a little later in the writer's consciousness makes for an easy motion between event and notation. Words shuffle between speech-acts. Frank Kermode has observed, for example, how the words 'prayer' and 'umbrella', contested between Bart Oliver and Lucy Swithin, produce the nurses wheeling a 'perambulator' several lines further on.

Woolf's writing always had this shiftiness at its edge (an ear that heard the auditory likeness between the most improbable concepts, as in *The Waves* the word 'tea-urn' generates 'eternity' a few lines down). But in *Between the Acts* such melding and interruption become crucial to the significance of the work. So Giles can begin a sentence, struggling to recall a line of poetry, and Albert, the idiot, end it (p. 53). Conversely, characters repeatedly break in on each other's reveries. Old Bartholomew dozes:

> seeing as in a glass, its lustre spotted, himself, a young man

helmeted; and a cascade falling. But no water; and the hills, like grey stuff pleated; ... a bullock maggot-eaten in the sun; and in the shadow of the rock, savages; and in his hand a gun ...

The door opened.

'Am I,' Isa apologized, 'interrupting?' (p. 13)

In this passage fragments of *The Waste Land* shade into Rider Haggard or Rudyard Kipling, the whole seen 'through a glass darkly'. The same sequence of interrupted mind-action is repeated for Mrs Swithin and for Isa. The only character who longs for interruption more than she finds it is Miss La Trobe who needs human company and drink to discover fertile words in the mud of the subconscious. In the pub she listens: 'Words of one syllable sank down into the mud. She drowsed; she nodded. The mud became fertile ... Words without meaning – wonderful words' (p. 125).

Woolf undoes the canon. Fragments from famous works wind in and out of people's consciousness, half-remembered, often misremembered, valued nonetheless. Like single words, single works are not autonomous. In memory they are shards scattered, or shared, among a community. That image of fragmentation becomes also a binding refrain in the book: 'orts, scraps, and fragments'. The lines from Shakespeare's most sceptical play *Troilus and Cressida* are persistently referred to, re-arranged, and riffled through the text. They express the scatter of identity, the absence of centre. Where in its original setting the strongest association of the metaphor is with the greasy remnants of a meal, Woolf (and Isa) re-invent the line so that it suggests instead archaeological findings and fragments – and the wisps of speech overheard. The book is not so much studded with quotation and allusion as combed through: sometimes mere sparks of reference remain, sometimes clandestine glories. Shakespeare is dispersed among limber sentences. *Lear*, the sonnets, *Macbeth*, *Troilus* and *The Tempest* all play their parts, in fragments often shorn of context or contextual urgency (never, never, never; the temple haunting martins; I fear I am not in my perfect mind; this insubstantial pageant faded). Sometimes streaks of reference are absurdly integrated into apparently inappropriate sentences: Mrs. Manresa, flirting with Giles, 'had him in thrall' (p. 68) and her make-up is not sufficiently 'deeply interfused' (p. 120). Wordsworth and Keats are *almost* there, for fun, part of the language of the tribe.

That tribe is capable of terrible things. Once only, when the shower comes as the audience survey themselves uneasily in the mirrors at the end of the pageant, is totality momentarily evoked as language. The rain pours 'like all the people in the world weeping. Tears tears tears'. The 'blots of rain ... were all people's tears, weeping for all people'. A little later an unnamed person remembers the poem (but not that Walt Whitman wrote it): 'There's a poem, *Tears tears tears*, it begins. And goes on *O then the unloosened ocean* ... but I can't remember the rest' (p. 119). Individual authors and whole poems are lost in the oceanic flow of language. Still, fragments welter and remain. Accepting the loss of the author is hard but necessary for Woolf. The writing, lightly, forms the figure of 'Anon'.

The pageant, like a masque, is performed once only. The day's news is recorded and jettisoned. The flowers fade. But words in their arrangements oddly do survive, often disturbed but called again into life. So, Keats's 'Ode to a Nightingale' can be seamed into a line from *Hamlet*. And when the characters confront the audience at the pageant's end with looking-glasses and reflective scraps of tin, they all simultaneously chant fragments of verse, from music hall songs to Dante (p. 110). The cacophony of western civilization is also a set of talismanic utterances: the flotsam of language absurdly bobbing loose from its moorings is also borne up on an ocean of human grief (p. 107). The unskeining of literature does not disavow it, though it sets it unhierarchically in among all the goings on of human behaviour; that human business which is irrelevant to the sky perpetually passing, the blue 'which resists registration'.

In the mind, things do not keep securely within classifications. In reading, everything is in the mind. In this book, the characters' passions are played out between the acts. Speech-acts and mind-acts create a turbulent medium in which the characters live, enjoy and suffer. The writing shifts under the reader's gaze between third-person narrative and free indirect discourse. In free indirect discourse the terms of the sentence, and its syntax, are recognizably the product of a particular consciousness within the book, though the sentence holds to the form of third-person description. Looking at such sentences the reader often cannot be certain of their provenance: who thinks? or do they speak? perhaps it is she? or they? or I, the generating reader? This casualness about source emphasizes the common tongue, the common reader.

The book is light on the eye. This is no non-stop stream-of consciousness. Instead the page is slightly pointed with remarks, in which cliché carries as much meaning as does meditation. The fragments shored against ruin here are no grand exotica as at the end of *The Waste Land*; instead they are little phrases, phatic sayings:

135

'He looks blooming,' said Mrs. Swithin.
'It's astonishing how they pick up,' said Isa. (p. 17)

The punctuating speech-tags here ('said Mrs. Swithin', 'said Isa') draw attention to the dance being performed between the two characters. Often such speech tags are interposed to disrupt the smooth run of the obvious and re-shape it into the odd:

'Marriages with cousins,' said Mrs.Swithin, 'can't be good for the teeth.' (p. 21)
'What's the origin,' said a voice, 'of the expression "with a flea in his ear"?' (p. 74)
'What's the object,' said Bartholomew, suddenly rousing himself, 'of this entertainment?'(p. 105)

The ritual repetitions that make up so much of the life of speech are likened earlier in the text to church bells: 'The words were like the first peal of a chime of bells. As the first peals, you hear the second; as the second peals, you hear the third' (p. 16). But though reiteration makes for a seemingly unchanged, resonating world, it also highlights change. The harmonics alter. Old Mrs Swithin remembers her mother speaking to her in that room, 'But in a different world' her brother Bart reminds her. *Between the Acts* is fascinated by change.

Words mean differently – *sound* differently – as they are spoken into new experience. This novel makes clear that though things are said many times they never mean quite the same. As a result, though opposites alternate they never pair simply as disappointment, as slack recurrence. It is not enough, as some recent critics have done, to note alternation as if the matter ended there. Language is capable always of tugging the reader through into unforeseen feeling.

Violence

Woolf in this novel, as in no other, puts violence near the centre of meaning. For Isa, listening to her elders reiterate their dialogue for the seventh year, the morning newspaper has just made her privy to horror, a horror surrounded by absurdity.

So when Isa heard Mrs. Swithin say: 'I've been nailing the placard on the Barn,' she knew she would say next:
'For the pageant.'
And he would say:
'Today? By Jupiter! I'd forgotten!' ...
Every summer, for seven summers now, Isa had heard the

same words; about the hammer and nails; the pageant and the weather. Every year they said, would it be wet or fine; and every year it was – one or the other. The same chime followed the same chime, only this year beneath the chime she heard: 'The girl screamed and hit him about the face with a hammer.' (p. 16)

The steady chime of alternation, the little liturgy of domestic life, is undermined by violence. The 'hammer and the nails' become also the instruments of Christ's passion, and the sevenfold repetition chimes with the seven last words on the cross. Those resonances are generated partly out of Lucy Swithin's intensely religious life but they start into consciousness here as Isa broods on an item she has read in the morning's newspaper.

The events described in the newspaper are, startlingly, not invented.[11] When Woolf proposed the book to herself she wanted to include 'facts' and the work hauntingly broods on the question of what's real: is it what's embodied? what's believed? or what's not acted? 'Real swallows' swoop across the stage set, 'Reality too strong,' mutters Miss La Trobe, as her play threatens to collapse into its artifice of present time and emptiness.

The episode of rape to which Isa flinchingly returns in the quotation above was undeniably real, as I shall explain, and was one of those 'facts' that Woolf sought. The identification Isa makes with the victim is altered, I would assert, by the knowledge that the bodies and persons in the case existed, just as the coming war was a 'real' war, communally experienced.

Isa tries to find in the library of the house a book that will satisfy her rage to ... what? understand? participate? be? The need is not specified. Isa, whose age is the same as the century's, thirty-nine, is, we are told, part of a generation 'book-shy', 'gunshy', for whom literature cannot 'stop her toothache' (pp. 14–15). Teeth and dentistry form part of the book's debate about what's savage, what civilized: savages could perform delicate operations, Isa remembers; while toothache is the most direct experience of violent pain common in European cultures, and dentistry, when Woolf wrote, still an excruciating practice. *Between the Acts* refuses the divisions between high and low examples, reaching instead for what comes close to hand since that is likely to be shared experience. So toothache and rape can be laid alongside without demeaning, and the fantasy of a horse with a green tail (*a green tale*) leads into real horror. The naïve, green girl believes the tale, and tragedy begins.

> For [Isa's] generation the newspaper was a book; and, as her
> father-in-law had dropped the *Times*, she took it and read: 'A
> horse with a green tail ...' which was fantastic. Next, 'The guard
> at Whitehall ...' which was romantic and then, building word
> upon word, she read: 'The troopers told her the horse had a green
> tail, but she found it was just an ordinary horse. And they
> dragged her up to the barrack room where she was thrown upon a
> bed. Then one of the troopers removed part of her clothing, and
> she screamed and hit him about the face ...'
>
> That was real; so real that on the mahogany door panels she
> saw the Arch in Whitehall; through the Arch the barrack room;
> in the barrack room the bed, and on the bed the girl was scream-
> ing and hitting him about the face, when the door (for in fact it was
> a door) opened and in came Mrs. Swithin carrying a hammer. (p. 15)

'That was real': that happened beyond fiction to the body and mind of
a human woman. In this event, purveyed by a newspaper's account,
Isa experiences the empathy she cannot find in literature. 'For in fact it
was a door': the Alice-in-Wonderland aside produces an interruption,
or juncture, for the reader between Isa's reverie and actuality (which is
also our reverie as readers). Is a newspaper different from a book? Is
one more real? How does fiction relate to known events? Woolf
implicitly places these questions within her own fiction. They are
questions intimately connected to a particular brutal happening that
occurred, like many other unrecorded brutal happenings, on an April
day in 1938.

The very day after Woolf first recorded her project for *Pointz Hall*
(in the passàge quoted at the start of the essay) a young girl of fourteen
was raped by guardsmen, on 27 April 1938. The soldiers asked her if
she would like to see a horse with a green tail, lured her into the
barracks, and raped her. On 28 April Woolf received the proofs of
Three Guineas. Woolf's fundamental argument in *Three Guineas* is that
men's upbringing and education breeds militarism and makes violence
inevitable. The eery contiguity of the conceiving of the novel and the
rape would not have been known to Woolf in that moment, but two
months later in June of the same year the trial of the soldiers and the
girl's testimony was reported in *The Times*:

> The girl said that she was crying and shouting, and he said if she
> shouted it would be the worse for her. She screamed and tried to
> push him away and punched him, and he said he would hit her
> back and hurt her, as he had been a champion boxer.

The girl in the case had no weapons but her hands. The hammer has got into Isa's fantasy enactment from Lucy Swithin's entrance carrying a hammer and interrupting Isa's reverie. The mild old lady becomes momentarily a figure of female vengeance – another of her 'unacted parts'.

The actual case had further consequences. The girl became pregnant and a respected gynaecologist Aleck Bourne performed an abortion and then drew the attention of the police to what he had done. Abortion at that time was illegal, save to preserve the mother's life. So Aleck Bourne was tried at the Old Bailey the month after the soldiers, July 1938, for procuring an abortion. The case became something of a *cause célèbre*. He was acquitted, after the judge extended the phrase 'preserve the mother's life' to mean that 'the probable consequence of the continuance of the pregnancy will be to make the woman a physical or mental wreck'. But the law was not changed until 1967.

Woolf here condenses the actual case of the previous year into the June day of 1939, and associates it with the approach of a war that will send guardsmen into action. The judge in the case had reproached the defendants: 'One would think that every Englishman, especially English soldiers, would be anxious to help her and protect her.' That had not proved to be so. In Miss La Trobe's pageant England is represented as a girl, who forgets her lines.

Woolf makes another condensation in this episode. The newspaper that Isa casually picked up was the one that her father-in-law had used that morning to pretend to be a monster, terrifying her three-year-old son George, and then reproaching him as a cry-baby and a coward. George is absorbed in the flower he is grubbing up out of the earth, and Woolf represents his concentration with febrile intensity, with a mixture of violence and rapture as membranes tear and 'a lambent light under a film of velvet ... filled the caverns behind the eyes with light' But:

> Then there was a roar and a hot breath and a stream of coarse grey hair rushed between him and the flower. Up he leapt, top-pling in his fright, and saw coming towards him a terrible peaked eyeless monster moving on legs, brandishing arms. (p. 10)

The old man is affronted by the child's fear. The child, further terri-fied by his grandfather's Afghan hound, bursts into tears. The old man is re-living his military days 'as if he were commanding a regi-ment' as he cows the 'wild beast' and mocks the 'coward'. The British Empire, to which old Oliver looks back as his youth, similarly saw itself as disciplining, or subjugating, other 'wild' breeds, or more 'primitive' peoples, justifying imperialism by the metaphor of cultural development in which 'other races' were viewed as children. The analogy is sharply present.

In this episode Woolf conjures the violence that adults' teasing phlegmatically imposes on children, and makes that insensitivity work also as a glancing critique of militarism and empire. Her concurrent reading of Freud's *Moses and Monotheism* may have made her even more aware of the prehistoric aggressions that, Freud argues, persist in present-day personality and give insight into early tribal formations.

The needling recognition forced on the willing or unwilling reader that militarism plays many parts is, if anything, reinforced by the suggestion that Bart Oliver is a nice enough old boy. The episode ends with Bart comforting himself by finding another item in the paper:

> 'M. Daladier,' he read finding his place in the column, 'has been successful in pegging down the franc ...' (p. 11)

Again, 'facts' enter the novel. Edouard Daladier, then Prime Minister of France, was present at the Munich agreement that gave Europe a delusive hope of peace with Hitler at the end of September 1938. The terms agreed were dishonourable, involving the sacrifice of Czechoslovakia, though at the time many people were for a while understandably overwhelmed with relief that the threat of war had withdrawn. Woolf felt both shame and relief, as her diary records.[12] In this passage, she draws attention to the market forces at work in diplomacy, and to the financial interests involved as war approached. Leonard Woolf in his analysis of the European political scene that same year, *Barbarians at the Gate* (London, 1939) characterized Daladier as being typical of the forces that weaken civilization, 'not the strength of the dictators and the barbarians' but 'the capitalist who wants liberty, justice, truth, and tolerance'.[13]

Between the Acts, which I earlier characterized as full of play, is, then, also full of violence: the violence of the coming war, of rape, of adults terrorizing children, of snake devouring toad, of Giles stamping on the impasse of toad and snake, of unrealizable passion, '*Vénus tout entière à sa proie attachée*'. The reader experiences also the violence of language awakened from a long sleep of repetition: Giles, outraged by his knowledge that war approaches and that he is powerless to prevent it, refusing to understand his own historical complicity in aggression, hears phrases concerning communal passivity in a new medium.

> 'We remain seated' – 'We are the audience.' Words this afternoon ceased to lie flat in the sentence. They rose, became menacing and shook their fists at you. This afternoon he wasn't Giles Oliver come to see the villagers act their annual pageant; manacled

to a rock he was, and forced passively to behold indescribable horror. (p. 38)

He becomes, in his own mind at least, a mythic hero chained to a rock: Prometheus; or, worse, Andromeda?

The work refuses to place these different forms of violence in a hierarchical order. It refuses, too, to privilege violence with the central place in our attention, though it may be central to the order of things in the world. The pageant eschews it altogether, concentrating on reconciliation and accord, save for the absurd figure of the Victorian policeman Budge with his truncheon. The play within the novel sorts language into simpler patterns as a series of copy-book tableaux and pastiches.

The swallows who sweep constantly across the barn recall the myth of Procne and Philomela in Ovid's *Metamorphoses*, but that allusion to rape, violation, and murder is kept as a distant echo, evoking Eliot's 'A Game of Chess' from *The Waste Land*, confirmed by the invocation of the *Pervigilium Veneris* and by the repeated reworking of the opening line of Swinburne's poem 'Itylus', based on the Philomela and Procne legend. Bartholomew murmurs:

> O sister swallow, O sister swallow,
> How can thy heart be full of the spring? (p. 70)

In this novel swallows are not coupled with nightingales – we are told, apparently rather purposively, on the novel's first page as the characters ruminate on sewage, old families, and bird-song, that 'nightingales didn't come so far north'. The swallows' own lives, dipping and wheeling, returning and leaving, are unencumbered by the mythic freight that human beings attach to them though they become for the audience part of the play. Signifying is a limited activity, this work suggests.

Emptiness matters as much. At different times we are told that the nursery is empty, the stage is empty, the barn is empty, the room is empty.

> Empty, empty, empty; silent, silent, silent. The room was a shell, singing of what was before time was; a vase stood in the heart of the house, alabaster, smooth, cold, holding the still, distilled essence of emptiness, silence. (p. 24)

The language of *Four Quartets* is conjured here. Emptiness may be song or distillation. It may also be active, full of all those other, unobserved, non-human inhabitants that human eyes dismiss. Waiting for the tea rush, 'the barn was empty'.

Mice slid in and out of holes or stood upright, nibbling. Swallows were busy with straw in pockets of earth in the rafters. Countless beetles and insects of various sorts burrowed in the dry wood. A stray bitch had made the dark corner where the sacks stood a lying-in ground for her puppies. All these eyes, expanding and narrowing, some adapted to light, others to darkness, looked from different angles and edges. (pp. 61–2)

Emptiness and silence are the shaping shadows behind language, or even music.

Acts

Sexuality and desire also pulse through the book. Woolf exempts none of her characters completely from the association with violence: even Mrs Swithin enters with a hammer. William Dodge and Lucy Swithin, across gender and generation, share a delicately intimate friendship for a single afternoon. Once Giles enters, William Dodge can see only him. Giles knows what William Dodge's 'left hand is doing'. In a world charged with sexuality *eros* is always agape. But Woolf does not allow the reader to become besotted with this discovery. Her gossips deal briskly with the question: 'Did she mean, so to speak, something hidden, the unconscious as they call it? But why always drag in sex?' (p. 118) Silence, emptiness, momentary accords, enduring kinships, are also part of the work's exploration, in characterization and in language itself.

One line from Racine's *Phèdre* haunts Isa and flashes across near the end of the book into William Dodge's mind: '"like Venus" he thought, making a rough translation, "to her prey ..."' (p. 123). Isa's passionate infatuation with Rupert Haines, the 'man in a grey suit' (with whom she scarcely exchanges a word) is as absorbing as Phèdre's tragic love for her stepson. But Isa's love finds neither expression nor outcome. The dart she feels in her flank is felt also by the cows:

From cow after cow came the same yearning bellow. The whole world was filled with dumb yearning. It was the primeval voice sounding loud in the ear of the present moment. Then the whole herd caught the infection. Lashing their tails, blobbed like pokers, they tossed their heads high, plunged and bellowed, as if Eros had planted his dart in their flanks and goaded them to fury. (p. 85)

The cows' outcry restores the emotion of the stage scene and Miss La Trobe is saved. These parallels between Phèdre, Isa, the cows, are not

142

mock-heroic or demeaning, though serenely absurd. The primal powers of sex and violence, appetite and loss, are always struggling free
within the everyday.

In keeping with the seam of reference to Racine that runs through
the work, the sequences of the book itself more or less hold to the neo-
classical three unities of place, time, and mood. Mrs Swithin argues
that:

> 'Actors show us too much. The Chinese, you know, put a dagger
> on the table and that's a battle. And so Racine ...'
> ''Yes, they bore one stiff,' Mrs. Manresa interrupted. (p. 85)

Mrs Manresa, the self-conceived 'wild child of nature', the townee
whose name is that of a Chelsea street as well as a pun on 'manraiser'
or cock-teaser, is always there to kick over the traces of too intellectual
a reading. Her sappy middle-aged sex is mocked and celebrated. She
alone of the characters is not confounded when the mirrors turn on
them at the end of the play: she powders her nose.

The novel's formal severity of contour contrasts with the plethora of
language and event in Miss La Trobe's sprawling, yet stylized, pageant.
So Woolf is able to evoke the characteristic forms both of French and
English drama – and the experience of play and of audience alike. Miss
La Trobe's village pageant displays widely separated moments from
English history and literary tradition. Lost heirs discovered, parted
lovers united, picnics with a purpose ('O has Mr. Sibthorp a wife'), a
final comic unravelling of Victorian domesticity: none of these events
matter, Miss La Trobe suggests, save to produce emotion. Love, hate,
and, Isa adds, peace. The pastiche languages of the pageant range
through lyricism, melodrama, and comedy without settling on any one
of them. By including the bustling yet static drama of the pageant and
the inward, dynamic drama of the audience's thoughts and feelings
Woolf is able to achieve a cross-grained play between acts, acting, and
the 'unacted part'.

Each of the characters discovers other parts of themselves. Seeing
the play makes chaste old Lucy Swithin feel that she 'might have been
– Cleopatra' while to William Dodge she appears 'like a girl in a
garden in white, among roses, who came running to meet him – an
unacted part' (p. 122). In the book's final scene 'For a moment she
looked like a tragic figure from another play' (p. 127). The village
store-keeper proves to be an imposing Queen Elizabeth; Isa is consumed with desire for the gentleman farmer Haines who merely hands
her a cup of tea; William Dodge percipiently acts several parts in

relation to the others of the party but experiences himself as 'a half-man'; the idiot is alarmingly himself, always on the verge of shocking the village elders, because for him there is no gap between acts and thought.

The 'acts' of the novel's title are of several kinds: the acts of a play; sexual acts; and the period between the two acts of twentieth-century European history, the First and Second World Wars. The brief time of the book also expands to include in simultaneity pre-history and what Woolf dreaded would prove to be post-history. The book ends with a scene in which present time grows indistinguishable from the remotest past when scarcely a human presence was established in the vastnesses of a natural world without need of the human. '"England," she was reading, "was then a swamp. Thick forests covered the land. On the top of their matted branches birds sang ..."'(p. 129).

Woolf here draws on a passage from the opening of G. M. Trevelyan's *History of England,* a work she mocked in *Orlando* for the absence of women from its social history. Throughout the book Isa is the medium of brooding awareness and reflexivity. She is also rather silly, as any displayed half-consciousness perhaps would seem. She and her husband address not one remark directly to each other. Only in the final sentence of the book 'They spoke'. What they said the audience is not to hear; but the reader knows that it is prelude to anger and to sexual congress, out of which 'another life might be born'.

The whole action of Woolf's work takes place within twenty-four hours, from evening to evening in mid-June. The place is Pointz Hall, the country house where several of the principal figures live. The mood is more questionable: it remains shifty, vacillating, but equilibrated, able to accommodate love, hate, peace without strident changes of linguistic register and with such slight shifts of pitch that the whole remains, as it were, within an octave. But like any good neo-classical drama, time, place, and mood condense extremes within their apparent constancy. The time zones of the novel range, within the characters' minds, from the pre-historic to the imminent future. Old Mrs Swithin reading her favourite 'Outline of History' has spent the morning hours 'between three and five thinking of rhododendron forests in Piccadilly; when the entire continent, not then, she understood, divided by a channel, was all one' (p. 8). Giles arriving home at lunchtime from the city 'came into the dining room looking like a cricketer, in flannels, wearing a blue coat with brass buttons; though he was enraged. Had he not read, in the morning paper, in the train, that sixteen men had been shot, others prisoned, just over there, across the gulf in the flat land which divided them from the continent?' (p. 30) Lucy Swithin seeks to resolve divisions and to find 'all one', through space as well as time. Giles is at odds with the pastoral complacency that refuses to recognize that even landscape need not last: 'At any moment guns would rake that land into furrows; planes splinter Bolney Minster into smithereens and blast the Folly. He, too, loved the view' (p. 34). Division, continuity, contiguity: all are phases of time.

Where land earlier joined Britain to the Continent, aeroplanes do so now. The vicar's attempted summation of meaning is scattered by the roar of military aircraft overhead. Again, the communal chatter says it: 'I agree – things look worse than ever on the continent. And what's the channel, come to think of it, if they mean to invade us? The aeroplanes, I didn't like to say it, made one think …'(p. 118). The outrage of the present burns through but is not allowed predominance within the novel.

The pageant stylizes a peaceable vision of England, re-cast as literature and tableau, landscape and cattle. Its language is busy with the clutter of human desires and their passing. Perhaps there is in its liberalism an allusion to E. M. Forster's village pageant, *England's Pleasant Land*, which was given at Milton Court, near Dorking in July 1938. Certainly the persistent anxiety in *Between the Acts* about a downpour of rain washing out the day (one shared by all organizers of outdoor events in Britain) is borne out by the fate of Forster's pageant: 'Wet, black cold – worst July on record – Morgan's pageant.'[14]

Miss La Trobe's is a revisionary play which cuts out the army and the Grand Ensemble to the discomfiture of some of the audience: 'Also, why leave out the Army, as my husband was saying, if it's history?' (p. 117) The pageant makes few concessions to that ritual patriotism that combines church, state, and armed forces:

> 'What's she keeping us waiting for?' Colonel Mayhew asked irritably....
>
> Mrs. Mayhew agreed. Unless of course she was going to end with a Grand Ensemble. Army; Navy; Union Jack; and behind them perhaps – Mrs. Mayhew sketched what she would have done had it been her pageant – the Church. In cardboard. (p. 106)

Instead, Miss La Trobe confronts her audience with silence and with mirrors: the present moment; emptiness; themselves; dispersal; diaspora.

It is an extraordinary liquidation of the expected triumphalist summary. Present readers, for whom the genre of the Empire Day pageant is unknown, do not perhaps fully grasp the comic and disturbing

145

impertinence of Miss La Trobe's conclusion. While she was first absorbed in imagining *Pointz Hall*, on 3 May 1938, Woolf visited St Albans: '& saw Roman pavements, guarded by men in overcoats, attending upon imbecile sons. Had tea, & heard the local ladies discussing the Empire Day celebrations, which are to include a red white & blue cake decorated with flags. What will they say to 3 Gs?[15]

Woolf, like La Trobe, is the outsider, averse to imperial celebrations (and also snooty about popular taste). By the next week Woolf had decided that *Pointz Hall* was to be a play: on 9 May she wrote of 'a patchy week': 'cant settle either to my Play (Pointz Hall is to become in the end a play) or to Roger's Cambridge letters.'[16]

Woolf felt herself an outsider in Sussex at the start of the war though she tried to find ways of involving herself in the village community at Rodmell. She was asked by the local Women's Institute to write a play for them. (As most British readers will know, the Women's Institute is a national organization devoted to rural skills within the home for women and at that time much involved in the war effort.) Though she refused to write, Woolf did become embroiled in village rehearsals of dull plays, about which she wrote in her diary with a venomous distaste: 'I'm bored: bored and appalled by the readymade commonplaceness of these plays: which they cant act unless we help. I mean, the minds so cheap, compared with ours, like a bad novel.' Recognizing her own middle-class insolence, she defends herself by arguing that what appals her is 'the simper'. ... 'the conventionality'. The battening-down of imagination in the material performed by the Women's Institute is what disgusts her. Elsewhere in the diary at the same time she is writing admiringly about individual workers in the village, picking up scraps of speech for her novel, and commenting on the imaginative power of rumour, which draws on a 'surplus of unused imagination'.[17]

The anger that Woolf experiences is ugly; some of it goes compellingly into Miss La Trobe who is always at odds with her cast, urging them on, gnashing her teeth, crushing her manuscript, hiding in the bushes, a loner who sees because she is separate, pugnacious, imaginative: the one who can imagine community because she is cast out (p. 74). Miss La Trobe has lost her lesbian partner and is distrusted in the village. Her name suggests *trope*, perhaps: those liturgical phrases whose frequent repetition makes it possible to embellish and re-order them without erasing communal meaning. As Mitchell Leaska points out in his useful annotations to the early drafts, her name also suggests a troubadour, and means 'invention'.

Isa at the end of the day broods: 'love and hate – how they tore her asunder! Surely it was time someone invented a new plot, or that the author came out from the bushes ...' (pp. 127–8). Neither Miss La Trobe nor Virginia Woolf will come out from the bushes. Woolf works by dispersal. At one moment in the text Miss La Trobe glimpses an idea for a new play, more scattered and domestic than her pageant, but she can't get it and shrugs it off. That other play is very like parts of *Between the Acts*:

> Miss La Trobe stopped her pacing and surveyed the scene. 'It has the makings ...' she murmured. For another play always lay behind the play she had just written. Shading her eyes, she looked. The butterflies circling; the light changing; the children leaping; the mothers laughing — 'No, I don't get it,' she muttered and resumed her pacing. (p. 40)

In the event, *Between the Acts* includes both play and audience, both acts and intermissions. By this move, Woolf is able to range across many voices, unnamed, and many desires, unknown, even while the play is watched communally in the open air. She recaptures the condition of 'Anon', that communal playwright she described in the new project she was developing alongside *Between the Acts*. But she made room also for the reader: 'There is a long drawn continuity in the book that the play has not. It gives a different pace to the mind. We are in a world where nothing is concluded.' So ends her draft chapter on the reader in her projected work 'Turning the Page'.[18] The resistance to conclusion had a particular political and emotional force at the outbreak of war. She is able to include the anxieties of authorship and the puzzled authority of the audience or reader. She is able also to include the uncontrollable, unforeseeable natural world: the rain that suddenly falls, the cow's bellow, the swallows sweeping between England and Africa.

Woolf wants to explore how England came to be; and how it came to be as she described it in *Three Guineas*, patriarchal, imperialist and class-ridden. *Between the Acts* acknowledges those characteristics, but faced with the probable obliteration of people, landscape, and history in the war, Woolf sought to produce another idea of England, one which might survive, but survive without portentousness – as mixture and common place.

VIRGINIA WOOLF: THE COMMON GROUND

Notes

1. *The Diary of Virginia Woolf*, ed. Anne Olivier Bell and Andrew McNeillie (London: Hogarth Press, 1982), vol. V, 15 May 1940, p. 284; 7 June 1940, p. 292; 9 June 1940, pp. 292–3.
2. *Diary*, vol. V, 26 April 1938, p. 135.
3. 'I'm reading Ruth Benedict with pressure of suggestions – about Culture patterns – which suggests rather too much' (*Diary*, vol. V, 26 July 1940, p. 306). The influential American anthropologist, Ruth Benedict was Woolf's close contemporary (1887–1948). Benedict worked with Franz Boas and influenced Margaret Mead. Woolf here refers to Benedict's *Patterns of Culture* (Houghton Mifflin, 1934). Her later book, *Race: Science and Politics* (NY: Modern Age Books, 1940) appeared while Woolf was writing *BA*. For extensive discussion of Woolf's possible debts to Jane Harrison see Patricia Maika, *Virginia Woolf's Between the Acts and Jane Harrison's Conspiracy* (UMI Research Press, 1987) and Jane Marcus, *Virginia Woolf and the Languages of Patriarchy* (Indiana University Press, 1987).
4. Letter to Ethel Smyth, 20 August 1939, *The Letters of Virginia Woolf*, ed., Nigel Nicholson and Joanna Trautmann, 6 vols (London: Hogarth Press, 1975–84), VI, p. 352.
5. Letter to Vita Sackville-West, 29 August 1939, *Letters*, vol. VI, p. 355.
6. *Diary*, vol. V, 27 June 1940, p. 299.
7. *Diary*, vol. V, 22 June 1940, p. 298.
8. This edition prefers 'scurred' to the first edition's 'scrurred'. Though 'scrurred' may be happy accident, its combination of *scrunch* and *whirred* is typical of Woolf's portmanteau words and provides a richer onomatopoeia.
9. 'Craftsmanship', Broadcast on 20 April 1937 in a series called 'Words Fail Me', *The Death of the Moth* (Hogarth Press, 1942), p. 129.
10. Ibid., p. 130.
11. Stuart N. Clarke, 'The Horse with a Green Tail', *Virginia Woolf Miscellany*, no. 34, 1990, pp. 3–4. See also *The Times*, 28, 29, 30 June, 20, 26, 30 July 1938.
12. *Diary*, vol. V, 29 September–2 October, pp. 176–8.
13. Mitchell Leaska, *Pointz Hall: The Earlier and Later Typescripts* (University Publications, 1983), p. 199.
14. *Diary*, vol. V, 17 July 1938, p. 156 and note.
15. *Diary*, vol. V, 3 May 1938, pp. 138–9.
16. *Diary*, vol. V, 9 May 1938, p. 139.
17. *Diary*, vol. V, 29 May 1940, p. 288; 31 May 1940, p. 291.
18. '"Anon" and "The Reader": Virginia Woolf's Last Essays', edited with an Introduction and Commentary by Brenda Silver, *Twentieth Century Literature*, XXV (1979), pp. 356–435.

8

The Island and the Aeroplane: The Case of Virginia Woolf

E ngland's is, so writers over the centuries have assured us, an island story. What happened to that story with the coming of the aeroplane? That larger question is central to my essay but my chosen example is a particular one: the writing of Virginia Woolf.

The advent of the aeroplane had profound political and economic consequences;[1] the object itself rapidly entered the repertoire of dream symbols, with their capacity for expressing erotic politics and desires. In the period between 1900 and 1916 Freud came to recognize the extent to which 'balloons, flying-machines and most recently Zeppelin airships' had been incorporated into two kinds of dream symbol: those which are 'constructed by an individual out of his own ideational material' and those 'whose relation to sexual ideas appear to reach back into the very earliest ages and to the most obscure depths of our conceptual functioning'.[2] His analysis of flying dreams is phallocentric (women can have them as the 'fulfilment of the wish to be a man', a wish which can be realized by means of the clitoris which provides 'the same sensations as men'). He identifies 'the remarkable characteristic of the male organ which enables it to rise up in defiance of the laws of gravity' as the reason for its symbolic representation as a flying-machine. If we pursue that line of argument what are we to make of Virginia Woolf's striking interest in her *Diary* in air crashes? Or of her description of the Zeppelin with an umbilical 'string of light hanging from its navel'?[3] Suffice it for the moment to say that the aeroplane in Woolf's novels is given a crucial presence in four of her works, *Mrs*

First published in Homi Bhabha (ed.), *Nation and Narration* (London: Routledge, 1990), pp. 265–90.

Dalloway, Orlando, The Years and *Between the Acts*, all of which are concerned with the representation of England and with difficult moments of historical national change.

The destructiveness and the new beauty generated by the possibilities of flight are realized by Gertrude Stein in her book, *Picasso* (1938), in which she comments on the formal reordering of the earth when seen from the aeroplane – a reordering which does away with centrality and very largely with borders. It is an ordering at the opposite extreme from that of the island, in which centrality is emphasized and the enclosure of land within surrounding shores is the controlling meaning. Stein writes of the First World War thus:

> Really the composition of this war, 1914–18, was not the composition of all previous wars, the composition was not a composition in which there was one man in the center surrounded by a lot of other men but a composition that had neither a beginning nor an end, a composition of which one corner was as important as another corner, in fact the composition of cubism.

Flying over America she thinks: 'the twentieth century is a century which sees the earth as no one has ever seen it, the earth has a splendor that it never has had, and as everything destroys itself in the twentieth century and nothing continues, so then the twentieth century has a splendor which is its own'.[4] The patchwork continuity of an earth seen in this style undermines the concept of nationhood which relies upon the cultural idea of the island – and undermines, too, the notion of the book as an island. Narrative is no longer held within the determining contours of land-space. Woolf's first novel is *The Voyage Out*, which opens with the ship leaving England – a journey from which its heroine never returns. *Between the Acts*, her last novel, takes up the multiple signification of the island, including that of the literary canon, and places them under the scrutiny of aeroplanes at the beginning and end of the work.

Woolf's quarrel with patriarchy and imperialism gave a particular complexity to her appropriations of the island story. At the same time her symbolizing imagination played upon its multiple significations – land and water margins, home, body, individualism, literary canon – and set them in shifting relations to air and aeroplane.

'If one spirit animates the whole, what about the aeroplanes?' queries a character in Woolf's last novel, *Between the Acts*, which is set on a day in mid-June 1939 and was written with the Battle of Britain going on overhead.[5] In the midst of its composition a last version of the island story as safe fortress was played out: an 'armada' (telling word) of little boats set out from England to rescue from the beaches of Dunkirk the British soldiers being strafed by German bombers. Woolf writes of the events with great intensity in her diary, as we shall see. In the public mythologization of that episode it has never been quite clear whether the topic is triumph or defeat.

Much earlier in the century H. G. Wells concluded his novel of coming events, *The War in the Air*, with Bert Smallways thinking that 'the little island in the silver sea was at the end of its immunity'.[6] Yet the myth of the fortress-island was sustained past the beginning of the Second World War, so that the sculptor and refugee Naum Gabo could note in his Diary in 1941:

> The sea lies stark naked between my windows and the horizon. ...
> The heart suffers looking at it and the contrast with what is hap-
> pening in the world ... how many more weeks will this peace last
> on this little plot of land? ... Our life on this island, in this last
> fortress of the old Europe, gradually enters ... into a state of siege.[7]

In *British Aviation: The Ominous Skies 1935–39* Harald Penrose reports a journalist as writing at the beginning of August 1939, a month before the outbreak of the Second World War: 'The dangers of air attack have been much magnified. This country is protected by stretches of sea too wide for the enemy to have an effective escort of fighters.'[8]

The advent of the aeroplane was by no means only a military phenomenon, of course. H. G. Wells was not far out when in the 1890s he wrote a forward fantasy, 'Filmer', in which the hero's mastery of the art of flying 'pressed the button that has changed peace and warfare and well nigh every condition of human life and happiness'.[9] In 'The argonauts of the air' he grimly foresaw the future of the flying machine: 'In lives and in treasure the cost of the conquest of the empire of the air may even exceed all that has been spent in man's great conquest of the sea'.[10] Later in his life, when he had experienced the pleasures of flying for himself, and when the diversity of uses for the aeroplane had become actual, Wells argues against the individualism of light aircraft and for large passenger airships in order that the freedoms and pleasures of flight should be opened to many. In 'The present uselessness and danger of aeroplanes. A problem in organization', in *The Way the World is Going* (1928), he writes:

> I know the happiness and wonder of flying, and I know that its
> present rarity, danger, and unattractiveness are not due to any
> defects in the aeroplane or airship itself – physical science and

mechanical invention have failed at no point in the matter – but mainly, almost entirely, to the financial, administrative, and political difficulties of aviation.[11]

Unlike H. G. Wells and Gertrude Stein, Virginia Woolf never flew, though she fantasized the experience vividly in her late essay 'Flying over London'.[12] But the aeroplane is powerfully placed in her novels. It typifies the present day, and beyond that it is a bearer and breaker of signification, puffing dissolving words into the air in *Mrs Dalloway* to be diversely construed by all the casual watchers of its commercial task. In *Between the Acts* its presence is more menacing, breaking apart the synthesizing words of the rector at the end of the village pageant, rumbling overhead towards the imminent war. *The Years* represents the whole period of the First World War by the 1917 air raid. ('The first mass aeroplane raid took place on London on June 13, 1917', Gibbs-Smith informs us.)[13] *Orlando* ends with the sea-captain-husband transformed into an aeronaut, 'hovering' over Orlando's head. Menace, community, eroticism, warfare, and idle beauty: the aeroplane moves freely across all these zones in her writing. The pilot's eye offers a new position for narrative distance which resolves (as at the opening of *The Years*) the scanned plurality of the community below into patterns and repeats. Woolf was not alone in her invocation of the aeroplane, of course: we think across immediately to Yeats and Auden. But she was, I think, particularly acute in her understanding of it in relation to the cultural form of the island, and extraordinarily economical in her appraisal.

The story of Daedalus and Icarus – the craftsman father who made the flying machine and the flying son whose wings loosened disastrously when he flew too near the sun which melted the wax that attached them – revives in twentieth-century literature, very possibly accompanying the coming of aeroplanes. In the last pages of *Portrait of the Artist*, written in 1914, such imagery seems still entirely mythological and is related to ships sailing rather than aircraft flying.

> *April 16.* Away! Away!
>
> The spell of arms and voices: the white arms of roads, their promise of close embraces and the black arms of tall ships that stand against the moon, their tale of distant nations. They are held out to say: We are alone – come. And the voices say with them: We are your kinsmen. And the air is thick with their company as they call to me, their kinsman, making ready to go, shaking the wings of their exultant and terrible youth.[14]

In 'Musée des Beaux Arts' (1938) Auden makes of Breughel's *Icarus* an image of the insouciance with which suffering is surrounded, 'its human position'.

> In Breughel's *Icarus*, for instance; how everything turns away
> Quite leisurely from the disaster; the ploughman may
> Have heard the splash, the forsaken cry,
> But for him it was not an important failure; the sun shone
> As it had to on the white legs disappearing into the green
> Water; and the expensive delicate ship that must have seen
> Something amazing, a boy falling out of the sky,
> Had somewhere to get to and sailed calmly on.
>
> *December 1938*[15]

The discreet clarity of description here distances the disaster and mutes its specific reference to Europe at the time of its inscribed date 'December 1938', keeping the discrepancy between acute suffering and humdrum life permanently disturbing. In another poem written in the same year (which Auden did not retain in 'Sonnets from China' but which appears in the original sequence, *In Time of War*, as sonnet 15) Auden concentrates on the pilots 'remote like savants' who are preoccupied only with skill as they approach the city. (Fuller reads this poem as being about politicians, surely mistakenly.)

> Engines bear them through the sky: they're free
> And isolated like the very rich;
> Remote like savants, they can only see
> The breathing city as a target which
>
> Requires their skill; will never see how flying
> Is the creation of ideas they hate,
> Nor how their own machines are always trying
> To push through into life. They chose a fate
>
> The islands where they live did not compel.[16]

Auden and Yeats dwell on the human pilots of such planes; the isolation and aggression of such a position is inimical to Woolf, for it is dangerously caught in to the militarism it castigates. But she, like them, does explore the paradoxes in flight:

> How their own machines are always trying
> To push through into life (as Auden writes.)

The glamour that pervades 'An Irish Airman Foresees his Death' in

The Wild Swans at Coole (1919) is riposted even within Yeats' own work in a poem called 'Reprisals', not printed in the definitive edition and first published after the Second World War, in 1948. It opens:

> Some nineteen German planes, they say,
> You had brought down before you died.
> We called it a good death. Today
> Can ghost or man be satisfied?[17]

One of Woolf's last essays, written as she was finishing *Between the Acts*, was 'Thoughts on peace in an air raid', prepared for an American symposium 'on current matters concerning women'.[18]

Woolf's opposition to patriarchy and imperialism, her determined assertion that she was 'no patriot', her emphasis on women's 'difference of view', all have their bearing on her figuring of the aeroplane and of flight in her writing. The diaries and the essays, as well as the novels, allow us, through her, to understand some of the ways in which the advent of the aeroplane reordered the axes of experience.

The Island

The identification of England with the island is already, and from the start, a fiction. It is a fiction, but an unwavering one among English writers and other English people, that England occupies the land up to the margins of every shore. The island has seemed the perfect form in English cultural imagining, as the city was to the Greeks. Defensive, secure, compacted, even paradisal – a safe place; a safe place too from which to set out on predations and from which to launch the building of an empire. Even now, remote islands – the Falklands Islands or Fiji – are claimed as peculiarly part of empire history.

The island is equated with England in the discourse of assertion, though England by no means occupies the whole extent of the geographical island; Scotland and Wales are suppressed in this description and Ireland is corralled within that very different group, 'the British Isles'. In this century, of course, the disjuncture has become more extreme, with the division between Ulster and Eire, one assertively within 'the United Kingdom', the other an independent state. But Ireland has for far longer been the necessary other in the English description of England, 'John Bull's other island' which is determinedly *not* John Bull's.

Shakespeare's *Richard II* provided the initiating communal self-description, alluringly emblematic and topographical at once. Gaunt calls England:

> This royall Throne of Kings, this sceptred Isle.
> This earth of Majesty, this seate of Mars,
> This other Eden, demy paradise,
> This Fortresse built by Nature for her selfe,
> Against infection, and the hand of warre:
> This happy breed of men, this little world,
> This precious stone, set in the silver sea,
> Which serves it in the office of a wall,
> Or as a Moate defensive to a house,
> Against the envy of lesse happier Lands,
> This blessed plot, this earth, this Realme, this England.
>
> (II. i. 42–52)

England is seen as supremely and reflexively *natural*: 'This Fortress *built by nature for her selfe'*. The 'insularity' of the island is emphasized in this part of the speech: it is a 'little world', a moated country house as well as a fortress. It is both a miniature cultivated place, 'this blessed plot', and an extensive 'Realme'. It is 'this England' (as the *New Statesman* fondly titles its collection of symptomatic newscuttings each week). The less-quoted second part of Gaunt's speech turns into an accusation against the present state of this favoured island. First, he represents the noble fecundity of the land, 'this teeming wombe of Royall Kings', who are renowned for their deeds:

> This Land of such deere soules, this deere-deere Land,
> Deere for her reputation through the world,
> Is now Leas'd out (I dye pronouncing it)
> Like to a Tenement or pelting Farme,
> England bound in with the triumphant sea,
> Whose rocky shore beates backe the envious siedge
> Of watery Neptune, is now bound in with shame.

The country house or fortress is become 'a Tenement or pelting Farme'. The binding in of the land by the sea – a natural battle of repulsion and attraction in which 'triumphant' curiously attaches both to land and sea and suggests a sustained and wholesome matching – is instead constrictingly 'bound in with shame'. It is easy to see why the latter part of this speech is less often ritually recalled than the first. Value ('this deere-deere Land') and price ('Leas'd out') are here set disquietingly close. Shame – the shame of bad government – mars the perfect order of the island.

The imagery which Shakespeare employs is defensive, not expansionist, though there is a suggestion of the depradations of the crusaders at the centre of the speech which speaks of the 'Royall Kings':

> Fear'd by their breed, and famous for their birth,
> Renowned for their deeds, as farre from home,
> For Christian service, and true Chivalrie,
> As is the sepulcher in stubborne Jury
> Of the Worlds ransome blessed Maries Sonne.

The punctuation in the first folio affirms that they are *renowned* 'far from home' rather than that their deeds took place far from home: but the ear receives both meanings. The passage has certainly been put to expansionist uses, though its insistence in context is on correcting the bad governance of the island so that its society may fulfil is demi-paradisal geography. In its later extracting from the play the passage has been repeatedly employed for self-congratulation rather than self-correction.

But the Shakespeare passage draws attention also to a fundamental tension in the idea of the island, one which has been to some extent concealed by the later phases of its etymology. The concept 'island' implies a particular and intense relationship of land and water. The *Oxford English Dictionary* makes it clear that the word itself includes the two elements: 'island' is a kind of pun. 'Isle' in its earliest forms derived from a word for water and meant, 'watery' or 'watered'. In Old English 'land' was added to it to make a compound: 'is-land': water-surrounded land. The idea of water is thus intrinsic to the word, as essential as that of earth. The two elements, earth and water, are set to play. An intimate, tactile, and complete relationship is implied between them in this ordering of forces. The land is surrounded by water; the water fills the shores. The island, to be fruitful, can never be intact. It is traceried by water, overflown by birds carrying seeds.[19]

The equal foregrounding of land and sea is crucial not only in understanding the uses of the concept in imperialism, but in the more hidden identification between island and body, island and individual. The tight fit of island to individual to island permits a gratification which may well rely not only on cultural but on pre-cultural sources. The unborn child first experiences itself as surrounded by wetness, held close within the womb. It is not an island in the strict sense since it is attached to a lifeline, an umbilical cord. It becomes an island, an isolation, in the severance of birth. Such conceptual power-sources are available for our speculation, even though they may not be directly represented. When Donne, in one of the most famous sentences in English, asserts that 'No man is an island' the words take their charge from their quality of paradox. They presuppose that the individual *is* ordinarily understood to be like an island.

In *The Tempest* Caliban's claim to the island condenses oedipal and land-descent discourses: '*by* Sycorax my mother'. The island is his progeny and his inheritance. It is also himself:

> This Island's mine by Sycorax my mother,
> Which thou taks't from me.
>
> (I. ii. 391)

His claim to possession is matrilineal. He is ab-original.[20]

The island has features of the female body; the map of the British Isles has sometimes been represented as taking the form of an old crone. But England is only intermittently a woman in the symbolic discourse of the nation. Britannia is a considerable displacement of the island idea, though she carries Poseidon's trident for pronging the fish and the foe. The sea, which encircles the land, can also bring enemies to its shores and occasionally, as when the Dutch sailed up the Thames in 1667, the island has been humiliated by foreign penetration. At such times the sexual imagery of invasion makes England for a while the 'mother-land' in the language of politics.

H. G. Wells astutely commented in 1927 on the contrast between the steamship and the aeroplane era: 'the steam-ship-created British Empire ... is, aerially speaking, decapitated. You cannot fly from the British Isles to the vast dominions round and about the Indian Ocean without infringing foreign territory' (*The Way the World is Going*, p. 131). In the Victorian period, he suggested, the sea-tracks of the long-distance steamships could foster the illusion that the British Empire dominated the entire world, because it was possible to set out from the central island and stay always within either British or international waters. This is an ingenious rationalization of the expansionist phase of the island story. Since the sea is as important as the land for the island concept, the sea offers a vast extension of the island, allowing the psychic size of the body politic to expand, without bumping into others' territory. The aeroplane, on the other hand, though offering access to almost limitless space, must overfly the territories of other nations. It cannot imitate the extension of the island, magically represented by the silver pathways in the wake of ships, threads linking imperial England to its possessions overseas.

To the Lighthouse is Woolf's island story. The family group and the house are themselves contracted intensifications of the island concept: and, in a further intensification, the final separation of the individual each from each is figured in the work: 'We perish each alone', Mr Ramsay obsessionally recalls. The island is displaced, a Hebridean place oddly like St Ives in Cornwall where Virginia Stephen spent her childhood summers and where the harbour island was much painted by the St Ives group at about the same time that Woolf was writing her novel. Throughout the book, sometimes louder, sometimes muted, the sound of the waves is referred to. The sea is as much the island as is the land. The fisherman's wife, in the story Mrs Ramsay read to James, longs for possession and for dominance, for control: that last wish is shared with Mrs Ramsay, and perhaps the other wishes too. 'That loneliness which was ... the truth about things' permeates the book (p. 186).[21] The lighthouse itself is the final island, the last signifying object, amidst the timeless breaking of the sea: 'it was a stark tower on a bare rock', thinks James as they finally come close to the lighthouse in the last pages of the book. At the end of the book the First World War is over; the family is fragmented: the mother is dead, a son, a daughter; the fishes in the bottom of the boat are dead. Cam and James, looking at their ageing father reading, renew their silent vow to 'fight tyranny to the death'. But Cam's musing continues:

> It was thus that he escaped, she thought. Yes, with his great forehead and his great nose, holding his little mottled book firmly in front of him, he escaped. You might try to lay hands on him, but then like a bird, he spread his wings, he floated off to settle out of your reach somewhere far away on some desolate stump. She gazed at the immense expanse of the sea. The island had grown so small that it scarcely looked like a leaf any longer. It looked like the top of a rock which some big wave would cover. Yet in its frailty were all those paths, those terraces, those bedrooms – all those innumerable things.

Distance and retrospect is achieved at the end of *To the Lighthouse*: 'It was like that then, the island, thought Cam, once more drawing her fingers through the waves. She had never seen it from out at sea before' (p. 174). The long backward survey to the politics of Edwardian family life, to England before the First World War, which began to unravel through the image of the abandoned house in 'Time Passes' here reaches conclusion: 'It is finished' – Lily's words – and those of the Cross – mean also what they say. Things have come to an end. The period of empire is drawing to its close. The book ends; the picture is done; the parents' England is gone. In laying the ghosts of her parents Woolf clustered them within an island, a solitary island which no one leaves at the end of the book save to accomplish the short, plain journey to that final signifier, the lighthouse, whose significations she refused to analyse. The island is here the place of intense life and the conclusion of that form of life, both private and the image of a community from whose values she was increasingly disengaged.

To the Lighthouse is an elegy for a kind of life no longer to be retrieved – and no longer wanted back. In *To the Lighthouse* Woolf frets away the notion of stability in the island concept. The everyday does not last forever. The island is waves as well as earth: everything is in flux, land as much as sea, individual as well as whole culture. The last book of *To the Lighthouse* looks back at the conditions of before 1914. Implicit is the understanding that this will be the last such revisiting for the personages within the book.

The Aeroplane

The absolute answering of land and sea to each other, which contributed ideas of aptness and sufficiency to the Victorians' understanding of 'England', will soon be disturbed by a change of axes: under water, in the air. Woolf is writing into the period at which the island could be seen anew, scanned from above. Her later writing shares the new awareness of island-dwellers that their safe fortress is violable. They look up, instead of out to sea, for enemies. Stephen Kern argues of the aeroplane:

> Its cultural impact was ultimately defined by deeply rooted values associated with the up-down axis. Low suggests immorality, vulgarity, poverty, and deceit. High is the direction of growth and hope, the source of light, the heavenly abode of angels and gods. From Ovid to Shelley the soaring bird was a symbol of freedom. People were divided in their response to flying; some hailed it as another great technological liberation and some foresaw its destructive potential.[22]

All felt its symbolic and its political power.

The old woman singing besides Regent's Park in *Mrs Dalloway* mouths a primal series of syllables which have persisted from the prehistoric realm, a sound composed out of 'the passing generations ... vanished, like leaves, to be trodden under, to be soaked and steeped and made mould of by that eternal spring –

> ee um fah um so
> foo swee too eem oo.[23] (p. 90)

The aeroplane in the same novel, writing its message in the air, seems at first equally unreferential. Earth and air, sound and sight, resist signification though not interpretation. The people of the book set to, reading their messages into the community and into private need. The aeroplane is sybaritic, novel, and commercial. Its intended message is nugatory: an advertisement for Kreemo toffee, but it rouses in the watchers, many of whom do not appear elsewhere in the novel, thoughts, pleasures, and anxieties both glancing and profound.

In *Mrs Dalloway* the aeroplane is set alongside, and against, the car. (Both are observed by most of the book's named and unnamed characters). The closed car suggests the private passage of royalty, and becomes the specular centre for the comedy of social class: the 'well-dressed men with their tail-coats and their white slips and their hair raked back' who stand even straighter as the car passes; 'shawled Moll Pratt with her flowers on the pavement'; Sarah Bletchley 'tipping her foot up and down as though she were by her own fender in Pimlico'; Emily Coates thinking of housemaids, and 'little Mr Bowley, who had rooms in the Albany and was sealed with wax over the deeper sources of life' (p. 23). All these briefly named characters respond to 'some flag flying in the British breast' and gaze devotedly on the inscrutable vehicle whose occupant is never revealed. The sharp description, as so often in Woolf's representations of the English classes and their rituals, inches its way towards hyperbole. At White's:

> The white busts and the little tables in the background covered with copies of the *Tatler* and bottles of soda water seemed to approve; seemed to indicate the flowing corn and the manor houses of England; and to return the frail hum of the motor wheels as the walls of a whispering gallery return a single voice expanded and made sonorous by the might of a whole cathedral. (p. 22)

The continuity of club and cathedral, of London institutions (White's and St Paul's), and of London typecast characters, mocks the self-esteem which expands from individual to nation, and which clusters upon an invisible and yet over-signifying personage inside the car.

In the next paragraph Emily Coates looks up at the sky. Instead of the muffled superplus of attributed meaning represented by the car, the aeroplane is playful, open, though first received as ominous. Its 'letters in the sky' curl and twist, offer discrete clues to a riddle whose meaning will prove trivial – and the writing teases the reader with the ciphering of 'K.E.Y.':

Every one looked up.

Dropping dead down, the aeroplane soared straight up, curved in a loop, raced, sank, rose, and whatever it did, wherever it went, out fluttered behind it a thick ruffled bar of white smoke which curled and wreathed upon the sky in letters. But what letters? A C was it? an E, then an L? Only for a moment did they lie still; then they moved and melted and were rubbed out up in the sky, and the aeroplane shot further away and again, in a fresh space of sky, began writing a K, and E, a Y perhaps?

'Blaxo,' said Mrs Coates in a strained, awe-stricken voice, gazing straight up, and her baby, lying stiff and white in her arms, gazed straight up.

'Kreemo', murmured Mrs Bletchley, like a sleep-walker. With his hat held out perfectly still in his hand, Mr Bowley gazed straight up. All down the Mall people were standing and looking up into the sky. (pp. 23–4).

Everyone's attention is distracted from the car which '(went in at the gates and nobody looked at it)'. The repeated word 'up' disengages the people from society. In their gazing the whole world becomes 'perfectly silent, and a flight of gulls crossed the sky ... and in this extraordinary silence and peace; bells struck eleven times, the sound fading up there among the gulls'. The contemplative erasure of meaning accompanies the wait for meaning. Instead of the expansion of the car's hum to cathedral size, the plane produces a modest insufficiency of meaning, and amalgamates with sky and gulls, its sound fading instead of resonating. It becomes an image of equalizing as opposed to hierarchy, of freedom and play, racing and swooping 'swiftly, freely, like a skater'. It includes death, 'dropping dead down', the baby 'lying stiff and white in her arms', but it does not impose it. Then, as in *Orlando*, 'the aeroplane rushed out of the clouds again'. Each person reads the plane's message differently. To Septimus 'the smoke words' offer 'inexhaustible charity and laughing goodness'. The communality is not in single meaning but in the free access to meaning. The ecstatic joke is about insufficiency of import: 'they were advertising toffee, a nurse-maid told Rezia'. The message does not matter; the communal act of sky-gazing does. For each person, their unacted part becomes alerted: Mrs Dempster 'always longed to see foreign parts' but goes on the sea at Margate, 'not out o' sight of land!'. The plane swoops and falls; Mrs Dempster pulls on the thought of 'the fine young feller aboard of it'. The eye of the writer now expands the aeroplane's height '*over the little island of grey churches*, St Paul's and the rest' until, with an easy and macabre shift of perspective, the plane reaches the 'fields spread out and dark brown wood' (we are still soaring visually), then the eye of the writing homes downwards in magnification to 'where adventurous thrushes, hopping boldly, glancing quickly, snatched the snail and tapped him on a stone, once, twice, thrice'. The aggression of the aeroplane is displaced on to the bird.

The liberated, egalitarian extreme of the aeroplane's height, and the distanced eye of the writing, dissolves bonds and flattens hierarchies. The passing plane raises half-fulfilled musings in the thoughts of another momentary figure. Mr Bentley, vigorously rolling his strip of turf at Greenwich thinks of it as

> a concentration; a symbol ... of man's soul; of his determination, thought Mr Bentley, sweeping round the cedar tree, to get out-side his body, beyond his house, by means of thought, Einstein, speculation, mathematics, the Mendelian theory – away the aero-plane shot. (p. 32)

The comic and disturbing discrepancies now are between the tight 'strip of turf' swept in Greenwich and the yearning towards the newly insubstantial 'real world' of post-Einsteinian theory. So the aeroplane becomes an image of 'free will' and ecstasy, silent, erotic, and absurd. It is last seen 'curving up and up, straight up, like something mount-ing in ecstasy, in pure delight, out from behind poured white smoke looping, writing a T, and O, and F' (p. 33). Toffs and toffee are lexically indistinguishable, farts in the wake of lark, of sexual rapture. Virginia Woolf's disaffection from the heavily bonded forms of Eng-lish society often expresses itself paradoxically thus as affection and play – and in this novel, as in *Orlando*, the aeroplane figures as the free spirit of the modern age returning the eye to the purity of a sky which has 'escaped registration'.[24]

The aeroplane in *Mrs Dalloway* is no war-machine. Its frivolity is part of postwar relief. It poignantly does *not* threaten those below. It is a light aircraft, perhaps a Moth. The D.H. Moth first flew in 1925 and, as Gibbs-Smith puts it, 'heralds the popularity of the light aero-plane movement'. At this period the aeroplane could serve as an image of extreme individualism and of heroism, as well as of international-ism. The hooded pilot becomes, in the 1930s, a trope in the work of W. H. Auden and it may be that Woolf's response to the work of Auden and his associates, sketched in 'The Leaning Tower', is more intense than has yet been charted. Certainly, the question of the individual artist's responsibility to produce revolutionary change in society becomes the matter of an impassioned argument between Woolf and Benedict Nicolson towards the end of her life. The argument is conducted in letters written with the drone of enemy aircraft overhead and in the period leading up to the evacuation of British troops from Dunkirk: that evacuation is a last island story, in which the little boats sailed by fishermen and amateurs from England impose a forlorn mythic victory upon a ghastly defeat. In the late 1920s and early 1930s, however, the aeroplane suggests escape and aspiration in her work.

Women were among the pioneers of early air travel and exploration. In the early 1930s came two individual exploits which drew immense acclaim: Amy Johnson flew solo from England to Australia in a Moth (4–5 May 1930), and in 1932 came the first solo Atlantic crossing by a woman (Earhart in a Vega).[25] The first woman to become a qualified pilot had been Baroness de Laroche as long ago as 1909. The figure of the aristocratic woman escaping ordinary confines is powerful symbolically for Woolf at the end of the 1920s, fuelled by her love affair with Vita Sackville-West, and permitting, as in dreams, an identification which brings impossible freedoms within the range of the everyday.

Woolf was fascinated, too, in a mood between the sardonic and the obsessional, with the failed dreams of escape, the Daedelean claims of women: we see it, at this period, in her story of Shakespeare's sister in *A Room of One's Own*. We see it also in the macabre comedy of her description of 'the flying princess', crossdressed in purple leather breeches, whose petrol gave out on a transatlantic flight in 1927 and who drowned with her companions:

> The Flying Princess, I forget her name, has been drowned in her purple leather breeches. I suppose so at least. Their petrol gave out about midnight on Thursday, when the aeroplane must have come gently down upon the long slow Atlantic waves. I suppose they burnt a light which showed streaky on the water for a time. There they rested a moment or two. The pilots, I think, looked back at the broad cheeked desperate eyed vulgar princess in her purple breeches & I suppose made some desperate dry statement – how the game was up: sorry; fortune against them; & she just glared; and then a wave broke over the wing; & the machine tipped. And she said something theatrical I daresay; nobody was sincere; all acted a part; nobody shrieked; Luck against us – something of that kind, they said, and then So long, and first one man was washed off & went under, & then a great wave came &

the Princess threw up her arms & went down; & the third man sat saved for a second looking at the rolling waves, so patient, so implacable & the moon gravely regarding; & then with a dry snorting sound he too was tumbled off & rolled over, & the aeroplane rocked & rolled – miles from anywhere, off Newfoundland, while I slept at Rodmell, & Leonard was dining with the Craniums in London.[26]

Woolf creates the incongruities of disaster: the clipped inhibited speeches 'nobody shrieked; Luck against us – something of that kind, they said, and then So long'; 'the rolling waves, so patient, so implacable & the moon gravely regarding'. The pernickety vengefulness of this description and the glamour of the seascape make of flight a foiled escape, equally from England and from the sea of death. Air and water alike place small social life out of its element. The flying princess seems like a haunting other imagination for her own fears of flying too high, as well as being a savage pastiche of aristocratic claims to dominance.

Even Woolf's initial working title for *The Waves*, 'The moths', may have had an additional resonance lost to our ears. Clearly it refers predominantly to those flying creatures, so like butterflies to amateur eyes, but so particularly phototropic that at night they cluster helplessly towards any light source, even if it burns them to death; but in 1925 the Moth aeroplane first flew. *Orlando*, published in 1928, recognizes the aeroplane as an emblem of modern life, along with the telephone and radio, the lifts. Going up in the lift in Marshall & Snelgrove, Orlando muses: 'In the eighteenth century we knew how everything was done; but here I rise through the air; I listen to voices in America; I see men flying – but how it's done, I can't even begin to wonder. So my belief in magic returns' (p. 270).

Accepting technology into everyday life renews the magical; explanation becomes unstable and unsought. On the book's last page Orlando's husband Shelmardine, returns from his rash voyage 'round Cape Horn in the teeth of a gale'. In an invocation of ecstasy which is both euphoric and comic the moment of midnight approaches:

As she spoke, the first stroke of midnight sounded. The cold breeze of the present brushed her face with its little breath of fear. She looked anxiously into the sky. It was dark with clouds now. The wind roared in her ears. But in the roar of the wind she heard the roar of an aeroplane coming nearer and nearer. "Here! Shel, here!' she cried, baring her breast to the moon (which now showed bright) so that her pearls glowed like the eggs of some

> vast moon-spider. The aeroplane rushed out of the clouds and
> stood over her head. It hovered above her. Her pearls burnt like a
> phosphorescent flare in the darkness. (p. 295)

The plane 'hovers' like a bird, mingling erotic and hunting imagery: 'it
stood over her head'. It hovers also like the spirit brooding creatively.
Pearls and landing lights are here confused: 'Her pearls burnt like a
phosphorescent flare' and there is no gap between sea and air, pilot
and captain, bird and plane and man: 'It is the goose!' Orlando cried.
'The wild goose'. Time coalesces: the time of the fiction and the time
of the hand concluding the writing of the fiction coincide: The book
ends: 'And the twelfth stroke of midnight sounded; the twelfth stroke
of midnight, Thursday, the eleventh of October, Nineteen Hundred
and Twenty Eight' (p. 295).

In this confluence the aeroplane is the central image, here conceived
as individualistic, erotic, and heroic. 'Ecstasy' is enacted as a brilliant
ricochet of ancient and immediate symbol, which lightly draws on
pentecostal signs; 'in the roar of the wind she heard the roar of an
aeroplane'. Sounds become tactile: 'breeze, brushed, breath'. The labials
and fricatives, 'br' repeated, lightly mimic the rumble of the approaching plane. The first stroke of midnight 'brushed' her face. 'The aeroplane *rushed* out of the clouds'. The man descends through the clouds
at the conclusion here, but then, Shelmardine is 'really a woman' and
Orlando 'a man', in their initial recognition of each other.[27]

The heady pleasures of air travel probably remained the more intense in Woolf's imagination just because she never flew. In her late
essay she describes flying over London with a convincing ease and élan
which mischievously resolves itself into fantasy at the end of the piece.
She had been in London under bombardment; she had looked up
anxiously after Vanessa vanishing by light plane to Switzerland. The
aeroplane gave a new intensity to the upward gaze and the downward
thump. Woolf saw the plane always from the point of view of the
island dweller, aware of the intimate abrasion of land and sea, that
intimacy now disturbed by the new pastoral of the aeroplane – pastoral
because so strongly intermingled with breezes and country sights,
lying so innocently 'among trees and cows', but sinister, too, ab-
rupting the familiar lie of the land, the ordinary clustering of objects:

> *Monday 26 January*
> Heaven be praised, I can truthfully say on this first day of
> being 49 that I have shaken off the obsession of Opening the
> Door, & have returned to Waves; & have this instant seen the

entire book whole, & how I can finish it – say in under 3 weeks. That takes me to Feb. 16th; then I propose, after doing Gosse, or an article perhaps, to dash off the rough sketch of Open Door, to be finished by April 1st (Easter [Friday] is April 3rd). We shall then, I hope, have an Italian journey; return say May 1st & finish Waves, so that the MS can go to be printed in June, & appear in September. These are possible dates anyhow.

Yesterday at Rodmell we saw a magpie & heard the first spring birds; sharp egotistical, like [illegible]. A hot sun; walked over Caburn; home by Horley & saw 3 men dash from a blue car & race, without hats across a field. We saw a silver & blue aeroplane in the middle of a field, apparently unhurt, among trees & cows. This morning the paper says three men were killed – the aeroplane dashing to the earth: But we went on, reminding me of that epitaph in Greek anthology: when I sank, the other ships sailed on.[28]

Woolf uses 'dash' three times in this diary entry. She will 'dash off the rough sketch of the Open Door'; she saw 'three men dash from a blue car' and, last, 'the aeroplane dashing to the earth'. Lateral, vertical, horizontal: all these are figured by the one word. The hand writes; the men run; the plane falls. Speed unites them – a speed allayed by the last allusion to the sea. Imaginatively sky and sea are akin; and pilots are still *aeronauts*; sky-sailors. Anne Olivier Bell's note reads:

> Mount Caburn is the bare down dominating the Ouse Valley on the far side of the river from Rodmell. The crashed aircraft was an Avro 40K from Gatwick aerodrome, where the three dead men were employed. 'I am the tomb of a shipwrecked man; but set sail, stranger: for when we were lost, the other ships voyaged on'. Theodoridas, no. 282 in book VII of *The Greek Anthology*, Loeb edition.

Woolf experiences a totalizing of experience: air, sea, land, death, and life. Suddenly she sees 'the entire book whole', not an island, yet a totality.

The island's identity depends on water. It is the sea which defines the land. Wave theory disturbed the land–sea antinomies: instead, over and under, inner and outer, stasis and flux, became generalized as motion. Thresholds and boundaries lose definition. Something of this can be read in *The Waves*, a book whose rhythmic life is the reader's only means of pursuit. Instead of the 'man clinging to a bare rock', which was Virginia Woolf's image for herself as writer in the summer she began to write it, this book engages with an imaginative scientific world in which substance is unreal, motion universal.

This does not render *The Waves* an apolitical novel, but its politics are in its refusal of the imposing categories of past narrative and past society, its dislimning of the boundaries of the self, the nation, the narrative. In *The Waves* Woolf pushes on to the periphery all that is habitually central to fiction: private love relationships, the business of government, family life, city finances, the empire. Each of these topics is, however, marked into the narrative so that we also *observe* how slight a regard she here has for them. Instead she concentrates, as she foresaw women writers must do, on 'the wider questions ... of our destiny and the meaning of life', instead of on the personal and the political. She does this by reappraising the world in the light of wave theory and the popular physics of Eddington and Jeans. Eddington writes in 1927: 'In the scientific world the concept of substance is wholly lacking. ... For this reason the scientific world often shocks us by its appearance of unreality'. He opens his argument by asserting that 'the most arresting change is not the rearrangement of space and time by Einstein but the dissolution of all that we regard as most solid into tiny specks floating in a void'.[29] Waves in motion are all the universe consists in: sound waves, sea waves, air waves – but as Jeans also observes in *The Mysterious Universe*: 'the ethers and their undulations, the waves which form the universe, are in all probability fictitious ... they exist in our minds'. Jeans is thereby led to privilege fiction or equalize it with the outer world: 'The motion of electrons and atoms does not resemble those of the parts of a locomotive so much as those of the dancers in a cotillion. And if the 'true essence of substances' is for ever unknowable, it does not matter whether the cotillion is danced at a ball in real life, or on a cinematograph screen, or in a story of Boccaccio'. He concludes that 'the universe is best pictured ... as consisting of pure thought'.[30]

Yet people drown and planes crash. The silver and blue aeroplane sits in a field intact, dead men invisibly inside it. The aircrash is a new form of death, and *thanatos* had great allure for Woolf. Septimus Smith and Percival both die falling from a height. However, 'when I sank the other ships sailed on', as Rhoda, in *The Waves,* recalls.

Motion is eternal, but the new forms of experience brought by flight also sharply focus social and national change. If, at one extreme, there is no island, only waves, at the other extreme the geographical ideal of England becomes more poignant in the Europe of the 1930s. Daedalus and Icarus – artificer, aeronaut, and unwilling sky-diver – were perhaps, I have suggested, imaginatively provoked into the writing of Joyce and Auden by the coming of the aeroplane. The conclusion of *Portrait of the Artist* foresees no aircrash. But Auden's poem, 'The Old Masters', combines the Bruegel image of Icarus falling through the air with attention to the unnoticeable disaster and its concurrence with the everyday. It is a poem which evades the allegorical and refuses to mark more than suffering and oblivion. Woolf's description of the crashed airmen in the field has the same blithe calm.

The Island and the Aeroplane

Woolf considered herself no patriot. On 29 August 1939 she wrote: 'Of course, I'm not in the least patriotic'. In January 1941, while she was revising *Between the Acts* she wrote in a letter to Ethel Smyth:

> How odd it is being a countrywoman after all these years of being a Cockney! … You never shared my passion for that great city. Yet it's what, in some odd corner of my dreaming mind, represents Chaucer, Shakespeare and Dickens. It's my only patriotism: save once in Warwickshire one Spring [May 1934] when we were driving back from Ireland, I saw a stallion being led, under the may and the beeches, along a grass ride; and I thought that is England.[31]

This passage occurs in a letter concerned with the repression of sexuality. We can gauge some of the counter-forces in Woolf's relations to the idea of England in the condensing of disparate elements within the remembered image: the invocation of Ireland as the necessary other island, the emphasis on maleness – the stallion – in the idea of England, and the sense of herself as exile. Only in London can she feel herself in kinship with the most 'English' writers, representing the phases of the literary canon (Chaucer, Shakespeare, Dickens).

The euphoric image of the aeroplane and the keen pleasure in its menace, which we have seen in her earlier responses, are set in a more difficult series of relations with the idea of island history in her novels of the later 1930s, *The Years* and *Between the Acts*. Virginia Woolf's insistence on her own 'unpatriotic' relation with England is nearly always formulated in relation to a concession. She resisted and deeply disliked the show of public mourning for the 'heroes' of the R101, lost in 1930 on an experimental flight from England to India – an attempt bound into imperialism and the wish to annex, beyond Wells's 'steamship empire'.[32] She disliked 'the heap of a ceremony on one's little coal of feeling': 'why should every one wear black dresses'. The sameness demanded by tight social forms always irritated her and roused her scepticism. Her use of plurals is a recurrent means of teasing island pomposity but it sometimes succumbs to a related social condescension: the opening of *The Years* employs the privilege of the narrative over-eye looking down on thousands of similar events. We begin with the sky: 'But in April such weather was to be expected. Thousands of shop assistants made that remark' ... 'Interminable processions of shoppers ... paraded the pavements'...

> In the basements of the long avenues of the residential quarters servant girls in cap and apron prepared tea. Deviously ascending from the basement the silver teapot was placed on the table, and virgins and spinsters with hands that had staunched the sores of Bermondsey and Hoxton carefully measured out one, two, three, four spoonfuls of tea.[33]

Something odd and uneasy occurs in this writing with its mixture of Dickensian super-eye and the autocracy of the air, gazing *de haut en bas*. The aerial view affords a dangerous narrative position, too liberating to the writer and demeaning to those observed here. The levity of this socially bantering view of London is corrected in the 1917 episode with the brief account of an air-raid, unseen from the cellar where the characters finish their dinner and wait for a bomb to fall. It does not fall on them; the silence, the 'greenish-grey stone', the oscillating spider's web are all seized into the writing with intense reserve (pp. 313–14). The remembered episode re-emerges in the 'Present day' section when Eleanor looks up to where she saw her first aeroplane and muses on the degree of change it has brought, thinking how it first seemed a black spot, then a bird. Next she recollects the 1917 raid, and then her eye falls on 'the usual evening paper's blurred picture of a fat man gesticulating'. Eleanor rips the paper violently, shocking her sceptical niece who has been feeling superior. 'You see', Eleanor interrupted, 'it means the end of everything we cared for'.

> 'Freedom?' said Peggy perfunctorily. 'Yes,' said Eleanor. 'Freedom and justice'. (p. 357)

Within the scan of two pages of memory the aeroplane has changed from bird to collusive war instrument, part of the oppression operated by dictators.

The writerly pleasure in the plane's fantastic powers, so prominent in *Mrs Dalloway* and *Orlando*, is now sardonically viewed. In *Between the Acts*, and in the diaries and letters which accompany its composition, Woolf works urgently on the problem of the artist's presence in society and in England's history. Outside the book she is in passionate controversy with her nephew on the artist's responsibility to bring about revolutionary change in society. In a caustic letter of 13 August 1940 she defends Roger Fry against Nicolson's charge of inaction.[34] As she writes *Between the Acts*, from May to August 1940, some of the worst of the war is going on directly over her head. On 9 June she writes: 'The searchlights are very lovely over the marsh, and the aeroplanes go over – one, a German, was shot over Caburn, and my windows rattled when they dropped bombs at Forest Row. But it's like a Shakespeare song today – so merry, innocent and very English.[35]

English literature and English weather form much of the material of *Between the Acts*. Despite her disclaimers and her sense of being the townie incomer, Woolf was clearly engaged and puzzled by English life in a quite new way at the beginning of the war. The Women's Institute asked her to produce a play for them; instead what she did was to write Miss La Trobe and *Between the Acts*.[36]

It proved harder to let go of the island story once it was under threat from invasion, and once it seemed that she and her friends might, through inertia, have contributed to its obliteration. In the excellent work that has been accomplished on the connections between *Three Guineas* and *Between the Acts*, critics such as Roger Poole and Sallie Sears have drawn attention to the connection Woolf makes between militarism bred in men through their education and the coming of the Second World War.[37] The novel itself offers a comedic threnody for an England which may be about to witness invasion, the final loss of 'freedom and justice', and the obliteration of its history. This sounds a solemn task, but that is not Woolf's way of either celebrating or disturbing. Within the work she alludes to and fragments the canon of English literature; she records a tight and antique village community in whose neighbourhood has recently been built 'a car factory and an aerodrome'; she places at the centre an ancient house, Pointz Hall; and she mimics the self-congratulatory forms of village pageants, then so often held on Empire Day:

> 'The Nineteenth Century'. Colonel Mayhew did not dispute the producer's right to skip two hundred years in less than fifteen minutes. But the choice of scenes baffled him. 'Why leave out the British Army? What's history without the army, eh?' he mused. Inclining her head, Mrs Mayhew protested after all one mustn't ask too much. Besides, very likely there would be a Grand Ensemble, round the Union Jack, to end with. Meanwhile, there was the view. They looked at the view. (p. 184)

THE ISLAND AND THE AEROPLANE: THE CASE OF VIRGINIA WOOLF

Woolf surrounds the people of the book with the contours of historical landscapes no longer perceptible to the naked eye. On the second page we move from the conversation about the village cesspool to the new forms of aerial observation. The bird, singing, dreaming of the 'succulence of the day, over worms, snails, grit' is, as in *Mrs Dalloway*, linked in sequence with the aeroplane. Mr Oliver 'said that the site they had chosen for the cesspool was, if he had heard aright, on the Roman road. From an aeroplane, he said, you could still see, plainly marked, the scars made by the Britons; by the Romans, by the Elizabethan manor house; and by the plough, when they ploughed the hill to grow wheat in the Napoleonic wars' (p. 8).

The aeroplane, in this opening of the book, allows history to surface in the landscape and be seen anew. The acceptance of change, new use, and continuity, of village inconvenience and incomings, allows the inconsequent of middle-class life a homely poetry which is as close as Woolf comes to affection. In this work the 'future is disturbing our present' (p. 100). Giles, returned from London, rages at the 'old fogies who sat and looked at views' when the whole of Europe was 'bristling with guns, poised with planes. At any moment guns would rake that land into furrows; planes splinter Bolney Minster into smithereens and blast the Folly. He, too, loved the view' (pp. 66–7). The swallows swoop as they have done since the world was a swamp, are caught into language as 'the temple-haunting martins' (instead of 'martlets' in the half-stirred allusion to *Macbeth* in the last serene evening before violence, just as this is the moment before war.) Their recurrence seems to offer assurance of continuity, perhaps as factitious in its way (there may soon *be* no temples) as *The Times* leader of yesterday:

> The swallows – or martins were they? – The temple-haunting martins who come, have always come. ... Yes, perched on the wall, they seemed to foretell what after all the *Times* was saying yesterday. Homes will be built. Each flat with its refrigerator, in the crannied wall. Each of us a free man; plates washed by machinery; not an aeroplane to vex us; all liberated; made whole. ... (p. 213)

But it is old Mrs Swithin who carries in her mind an awareness of the prehistory of England, of a voluptuous primal world even before England was an island; 'Once there was no sea', said Mrs Swithin. 'No sea at all between us and the continent' (p. 38). Now Giles reads in the morning paper of men shot and imprisoned 'just over there, across the gulf, in the flat land which divided them from the continent' (p. 58). So the lackadaisical conversations about how far it is to the sea from

Pointz Hall also become part of a general dislimning of securities.

The land shifts, the sea dries up, the impermeable island is a temporary form within the view of geological time. English life and language, on its shorter scale, is similarly impermanent, and here Woolf uses the parody sequences of the pageant to point the shifting markers of the island literary canon. Isa musing on the library 'ran her eyes along the books. "The mirror of the soul" books were, *The Faerie Queene* and Kinglake's *Crimea*; Keats and the *Kreutzer Sonata*. There they were, reflecting. What? What remedy was there for her at her age – the age of the century, thirty-nine – in books?' (p. 26). The pageant opens with a small girl who pipes:

> *This is a pageant, all may see*
> *Drawn from our island history.*
> *England am I* (p. 94)

The child sticks there, having forgotten her lines. The pageant scenes that follow include traditional elements (Queen Elizabeth played by the local shopkeeper) but these images are ruffled and undermined, sometimes by chance events – the wind, the cows lowing – sometimes by the plethora of language. Beneath this spume lie inalienable emotions: Love. Hate. To them, Isa, in this book, adds, Peace.

In *Mrs Dalloway* the dallying light aircraft represented the reassuring triviality of peace after the war, which is still melting and freezing the consciousness of Septimus Smith. Here the aircraft, still mingled in imagery with natural forms and with happiness, also presage the future: a future that may not exist.

Nothing holds its full form for long: that is one reason why rhyme, which fleetingly hitches unlike together, is so prevalent in the language of the book. Isa, dreaming of her tenuous secret love, looks out of her bedroom window at her little boy George with the two nursemaids in the garden.

> The drone of the trees was in their ears; the chirp of birds; other incidents of garden life, inaudible, invisible to her in the bedroom, absorbed them. Isolated on a green island, hedged about with snowdrops, laid with a counterpane of puckered silk, the innocent island floated under her window. (p. 20)

The fragile imagined island of security is succeeded by the image of arousal, here figured as aeroplane:

> the words he said, handing her a teacup, handing her a tennis racquet, could so attach themselves to a certain spot in her; and

thus lie between them like a wire, tingling, tangling, vibrating – she groped, in the depths of the looking-glass, for a word to fit the infinitely quick vibrations of the aeroplane propeller that she had seen once at dawn at Croydon. Faster, faster, faster, it whizzed, whirred, buzzed, till all the flails became one flail and up soared the plane away and away. ...

'Where we know not, where we go not, neither know nor care', she hummed. 'Flying, rushing through the ambient, incandescent, summer silent. ...'

The rhyme was 'air'. She put down her brush. She took up the telephone.

'Three, four, eight, Pyecombe', she said.

'Mrs Oliver speaking. ... What fish have you this morning? Cod? Halibut? Sole? Plaice?'

'There to lose what binds us here', she murmured. 'Soles. Filleted. In time for lunch please', she said aloud. (pp. 20–1)

Isa's habit of rhyming is skeined through the work without any satirical commentary and at times the same habit moves out into the communality of gossiping voices.

So abrupt. And corrupt. Such an outrage; such an insult; And not plain. Very up to date, all the same. What is her game? To disrupt? Jog and trot? Jerk and smirk? Put the finger to the nose? Squint and pry? Peak and spy? (p. 213)

The semantic cacophony of rhyme (auditory likeness without referential reason) suggests the reckless antiquity of the community. The forms of likeness are embedded in the sounds of the language, not in any reasoned relationships. The slippage between words and senses, and between separate units of speech, is constantly displayed in this work, where words collapse, reverse, become units of lexical play without sustained boundaries. In this passage, for example, the fish 'sole', effortlessly reverses in her next line of poetry into 'lose': '"There to lose what binds us here", she murmured. "Soles. Filleted"'. 'Filleted' takes up the sense of *binds* (a fillet is a ribbon which binds the hair); that sense flies loose, so to speak, beside the utilitarian boneless 'filleted' fish. The sole/soul fugue is elaborated a few pages later. The fugitive lightness of this linguistic play risks being lost in any act of analysis such as that I have just offered. But such inversions and smudging of semantic bounds are essential to the work's sense of smothered crisis. It has in itself contradictory functions: it signals collapse and fragmentation. Yet it also celebrates the insouciant resilience of the English language and of literary history: Woolf's one form of patriotism.

Poems do not survive intact in memory but single lines are absorbed and adapted. Past literature permeates the work, but as 'orts, scraps, fragments'. The canon of English literature is no tight island but a series of dispersed traces constantly rewritten in need, so that, for example, William Dodge misremembers Keats's 'Ode on a Nightingale' and is not corrected. Instead of the expected 'Grand Ensemble: Army; Navy; Union Jack; and behind them perhaps ... the church' (p. 209) the audience at the end of Miss La Trobe's pageant is offered mirrors and the present moment. That moment fills with rain – nature takes its part – but is followed by interrupting aeroplanes. Nothing remains intact, and, within the gossip another idea emerges: 'The very latest notion, so I'm told is, nothing's solid' (p. 232).

At the end of the pageant, composed as it also is of 'scraps, orts, and fragments' of past writing, Miss La Trobe holds the mirrors up to the audience 'reflecting. What?' 'Book-shy and gun-shy', all that is left to them is landscape and world gossip. Recurrence knits the island past together: the swallows fly in to the barn each year from Africa. 'As they had done, she supposed, when the Barn was a swamp' (p. 123). 'Before there was a channel ... they had come' (p. 130). The skeined-out interconnections of the work (Giles's youth in Africa, the flight of the swallows, '"Swallow, my sister, o sister swallow", he muttered, feeling for his cigar case', the scene of the reported rape even) call to mind *The Waste Land*, though the mood is closer to *Four Quartets*: 'History is now, and England'. In this work, however, 'the doom of sudden death' oppresses all the characters, because it threatens the whole history of England. No longer is the island a sufficient geometry, a sustaining autonomy. 'The future shadowed their present, like the sun coming through the many-veined transparent vine leaf; a criss-cross of lines making no pattern' (p. 136).

In the intervals of the pageant the talk is of coming war, and of old roses, of refugees, and the falling franc, of the royal family and Queen Mary's secret meetings with the Duke of Windsor, and of 'the Jews, people like ourselves, beginning life again' (p. 143). Mr Streatfield, the clergyman, tries to draw the pageant together into coherent message: we act different parts but are the same, a spirit pervades beyond our own lives, 'Surely, we unite?' These hopeful utterances lead to his announcement of the collection for 'the illumination of our dear old church'. Woolf's first readers would have felt the force of the irony here. This is mid-June; by mid-September 1939 all illumination will be doused and the blackout will be in place.[38] And, within the text, prompt on this cue, Mr Streatfield hears what he at first takes to be 'distant music'. His next words are severed. 'The word was cut in two. A zoom severed it. Twelve aeroplanes in perfect formation like a flight of wild duck came overhead. *That* was the music.'

Curiously, Woolf alludes irresistibly back here to the ending of *Orlando*: the wild duck or wild goose, the perfect formation, momentarily naturalize the aeroplanes. But in the ensuing pages, amidst the gossip, we realize that the audience has recognized that ominous zoom-drone music and what it portends: 'Also why leave out the Army, as my husband was saying, if it's history? *And if one spirit animates the whole, what about the aeroplanes?*' (pp. 230–1); 'What we need is a centre. Something to bring us all together. ... The Brookes have gone to Italy, in spite of everything. Rather rash? ... *If the worst should come – let's hope it won't – they'd hire an aeroplane, they said*' (p. 231); '*I agree – things look worse than ever on the continent. And what's the channel, come to think of it, if they mean to invade us? The aeroplanes, I didn't like to say it, made one think. ... No, I thought it much too scrappy*' (p. 232); 'Then when Mr Streatfield said: One spirit animates the whole – *the aeroplanes interrupted*. That's the worst of playing out of doors. ... Unless of course she meant that very thing' (p. 234).

Unless, of course, she meant that very thing! The section ends 'the gramophone gurgled *Unity – Dispersity*. It gurgled *Un ... dis ...* And ceased'.

The stare upward at the aeroplanes in *Between the Acts* is written in Woolf's diary in the same months as dread of invasion, and invasion by parachutists. The skittishness of the plane in *Mrs Dalloway* has vanished in *Between the Acts*. The twelve planes in perfect formation at the end of *Between the Acts* are machines, though the pattern of their flight mimics that of birds. The sombre untranslatability of the planes here is part of the new meaning of the aeroplanes after the Spanish Civil war. Even as she wrote, Leonard was on fire-watching duties and (15 May 1940) 'Behind that the strain: this morning we discussed suicide if Hitler lands. Jews beaten up. What point in waiting? Better shut the garage doors'. A month later, on almost precisely the first anniversary of that 'mid-June afternoon of 1939', in which *Between the Acts* sets its summoning of the island past, she records Harry West's account of Dunkirk: a survivor's tale in which the safe harbourage of the island still, amazingly, and perhaps only momentarily, holds.

175

It pours out – how he hadnt boots off for 3 days, the beach at Dunkirk – the bombers as low as trees – how no English aeroplanes fought. ... At Dunkirk many men shot themselves as the planes swooped. Harry swam off, a boat neared. Say Chum Can you row? Yes, he said, hauled in, rowed for 5 hours, saw England, landed – didnt know if it were day or night or what town – didnt ask – couldn't write to his mother – so was despatched to his regiment. (20 June 1940)[39]

The jarring within this account flings a further sardonic beam upon the refusal to accord, or to set in hierarchical order, or contain, that marks the writing of *Between the Acts*. Refusing to resolve is here not irresolution, but assertion. In the new world of flight and war the old axes are turned, the old geometries of the island giving way. Woolf writes always as a civilian from *within* the island, even as she records its dislimning. The 'we' of *Between the Acts* is that of the English language, of intertextual play, and mythologized English history, viewed with the sceptical yearning eye of Miss La Trobe. The slow flux of land-shifts described in the book repeatedly reminds the reader that islands are formed, not originary: Mrs Swithin, 'thinking of rhododendron forests in Piccadilly; when the entire continent, not then, she understood, divided by a channel, was all one' (p. 13). Overhead, rupturing the reiteration of island life, go the war planes. Woolf did not live through that war but she recorded a tonic and satiric elegy for the island.

Notes

1. For a thorough account of the history of flight see Charles Harvard Gibbs-Smith, *Aviation: An Historical Survey from its Origins to the End of World War II*, 2nd edn (London: HMSO, 1985).
2. Sigmund Freud, in 'On dreams', added a section on symbolism in the 2nd edn (1911): he there instances airships. *Standard Edition of the Complete Psychological Works of Sigmund Freud*, ed. James Strachey (London: Hogarth Press, 1953), vol. 5, p. 684; lecture 10 of *Introductory Lectures on Psycho-Analysis Standard Edition*, vol. 15, p. 155.
3. *The Diary of Virginia Woolf*, ed. Anne Olivier Bell (London: Hogarth Press, 1982), vol. 4, p. 113. In July 1932 the *Graf Zeppelin* 'took passengers for a circuit tour of Great Britain'.
4. Gertrude Stein, *Picasso* (London: Batsford, 1938), pp. 11, 50.
5. Virginia Woolf, *Between the Acts* (London: Hogarth Press, 1941), p. 231. All further references are to this edition.
6. H. G. Wells, *The War in the Air, Particularly how Mr Bert Smallways Fared* (London: Bell, 1908), pp. 243–4.
7. Naum Gabo, quoted in *St. Ives 1939–64: Twenty-Five Years of Painting, Sculpture and Pottery*, ed. David Brown (London: Tate Gallery, 1985).
8. Harald Penrose, *British Aviation: The Ominous Skies 1935–39* (London: HMSO, 1980), p. 290. Penrose gives no source for this remark. The emphasis on Chamberlain's *flight* to Munich to treat with Hitler in 1938 may seem curious to us, to whom such diplomacy is everyday. His flight, however, marked the entry of the aeroplane as a diplomatic instrument.
9. H. G. Wells. *Twelve Stories and A Dream* (London: Ernest Benn, 1927). p. 5. (First published 1903.)

10. 'The Argonauts of the Air' in *The Plattner Story and Others* (Leipzig: Tauchnitz, 1900). pp. 46–7.
11. *The Way the World is Going: Guesses and Forecasts of the Years Ahead* (London: Ernest Benn, 1928), p. 124.
12. Virginia Woolf, *Collected Essays* (London: Hogarth Press, 1966), vol. 4, pp. 167–72.
13. Gibbs-Smith, *Aviation*, p. 250.
14. James Joyce, *A Portrait of the Artist as a Young Man* (London: Jonathan Cape, 1916), p. 288.
15. W. H. Auden, *The English Auden: Poems, Essays and Dramatic Writings 1927–1939*, ed. Edward Mendelson (London: Faber, 1977), p. 237.
16. Ibid., p. 257; John Fuller, *A Reader's Guide to W. H. Auden* (London: Thames & Hudson, 1970), p. 127.
17. *Variorum Edition of the Poems of W. B. Yeats*, ed. Peter Allt and Russell K. Alspach (New York: Macmillan, 1957), pp. 328, 791.
18. *Collected Essays* (London: Hogarth Press, 1966), vol. 4, p. 173.
19. Since writing this essay I have been studying the ways in which the idea of the island has entered a number of scientific discourses, as well as political and literary ones, within the last 150 years. This section of the present essay overlaps briefly with a much longer paper, 'Discourses of the Island', in a collection of essays on literature and science, edited by Frederick Amrine (Amsterdam: D. Reidel Publishers, 1988).
20. For an excellent discussion of *The Tempest*, and of *Robinson Crusoe* in the context of Caribbean colonization see Peter Hulme, *Colonial Encounters: Europe and the Native Caribbean 1492–1797* (London: Methuen, 1986). *Robinson Crusoe* was one of Virginia Woolf's most admired works. See the discussion of its relation to the inception of *To the Lighthouse* in Juliet Dusinberre, *Alice to the Lighthouse: Children's Books and Radical Experiments in Art* (London: Macmillan, 1987), pp. 276–7, 323.
21. Compare 'Hume, Stephen, and Elegy in *To the Lighthouse*', chapter 2.
22. Stephen Kern, *The Culture of Time and Space, 1880–1918* (London: Weidenfeld & Nicolson, 1983), p. 242.
23. *Mrs Dalloway* (London: Hogarth, 1925), p. 90. All further references are to this edition. See, for an enlightening discussion of this passage, Makiko Minow Pinkney, *Virginia Woolf and the Problem of the Subject: Feminine Writing in the Major Novels* (Brighton: Harvester, 1987).
24. *Between the Acts*, p. 30: 'Beyond that was blue, pure blue, black blue, blue that had never filtered down; that had escaped registration'.
25. Gibbs-Smith, *Aviation*, p. 251.
26. *Diary*, vol. 3, pp. 154–5.
27. *Orlando* (London: Hogarth, 1928), p. 295. All further references are to this edition. Maud Bodkin, *Archetypal Patterns in Poetry: Psychological Studies of Imagination* (Oxford: Oxford University Press, 1934), p. 307, read Shel as a fantasy of masculinity in Orlando's mind: 'it is over his head – the aeroplane having now supplanted the ship – that there springs up the winged wild thing by which the woman finds herself haunted and lured'.
28. *Diary*, vol. 4, p. 7.
29. Arthur Eddington, *The Nature of the Physical World* (Cambridge: Cambridge University Press, 1928), p. 274.
30. James Jeans, *The Mysterious University* (Cambridge: Cambridge University Press, 1930), pp. 79, 136.
31. *The Letters of Virginia Woolf*, ed. Nigel Nicolson (London: Hogarth Press, 1980), vol. 6, pp. 354, 460.
32. *Diary*, vol. 3, pp. 322–3.
33. *The Years* (London: Hogarth, 1937), pp. 1–2. All further references are to this edition.
34. See for example *Letters*, vol. 6. pp. 413, 419, 421.
35. Ibid., p. 402. Caburn was part of the prospect from Rodmell and acted as something of an emotional barometer for her: see, for example, her complaining entry (*Diary*, vol. 3, p. 322) about Leonard Woolf's family which ends: 'It is the most miserable of days, cold and drizzling, the leaves falling; the apples fallen; the flowers sodden; mist hiding Caburn.' Compare also note 28 above.
36. *Letters*, vol. 6, p. 391.
37. See, for example, Roger Poole, *The Unknown Virginia Woolf* (Cambridge: Cambridge University Press, 1978), pp. 216–31; Sallie Sears, 'Theater of War: Virginia Woolf's *Between the Acts*' in Jane Marcus (ed.), *Virginia Woolf: A Feminist Slant* (Lincoln and London:

University of Nebraska Press, 1983), pp. 212–35.

38. 'At this very moment, half-past three on a June day in 1939' (p. 92); 'sitting here on a June day in 1939' (p. 208). Penrose, *British Aviation*, p. 276 points out that 'The thirtieth anniversary of Handley Page Ltd. was on 12th June (1939) – at that time the country was spending almost £2 million a week on aeroplanes'. Living as she did so close to what was then Gatwick aerodrome Woolf could not fail to be aware of the significance of the greatly increased air traffic in the later 1930s and its war menace. When she wrote the novel she was under the flight path of invasion – not now by sea, to be repelled from the island fortress, but by air, with the land below under threat from paratroops and bombs.

39. *Diary*, vol. 5, p. 297.

Index

INDEX

INDEX